International Trade
and Regional Economies

International Trade and Regional Economies

The Impacts of European Integration on the United States

David J. Hayward

WestviewPress

A Division of HarperCollins*Publishers*

Published in 1995 in the United States of America by Westview Press, Inc., 5500 Central Avenue, Boulder, Colorado 80301-2877, and in the United Kingdom by Westview Press, 12 Hid's Copse Road, Cumnor Hill, Oxford OX2 9JJ

Library of Congress Cataloging-in-Publication Data
Hayward, David J.
 International trade and regional economies : the impacts of
European integration on the United States / David J. Hayward.
   p. cm.
 Includes bibliographical references and index.
 ISBN 0-8133-8805-8
   1. European Economic Community countries—Commerce—United States.
2. United States—Commerce—European Economic Community countries.
3. Europe—Economic integration.   4. United States—Economic
conditions—1981–   I. Title.
HF3500.5.Z7U64   1994
382'.094073—dc20   93-49475
                                                                                  CIP

The paper used in this publication meets the requirements of the American National Standard for Permanence of Paper for Printed Library Materials Z39.48-1984.

10   9   8   7   6   5   4   3   2   1

To John and Christine

and the memory of Irene

Contents

vii

Tables and Figures

Figures

Preface

Perhaps the most prevalent feature of the contemporary space economy is the global-local dialectic. This is manifest in the global reach of production systems and in the terms under which local and regional economies are integrated into the global economy. Planners and policy makers at this level are increasingly aware of the international dimension and seek the tools with which to address it.

The project reported here considers this phenomenon. In doing so, it integrates three distinct topics of inquiry: regional economic analysis of the U.S. states; international trade and the impacts of economic integration; and the European Union's 1992 program. Thus, it is an ambitious attempt to explore the interconnectedness of supra-national and regional economies. Furthermore, it is an explicit attempt to chart new territory in the study of regional economies.

This project was undertaken as a doctoral thesis in Geography at the Pennsylvania State University. It is reproduced here in a rewritten form although substantively unchanged.

David J. Hayward

Acknowledgments

This project was undertaken in pursuit of my doctoral degree in Geography at the Pennsylvania State University. First and foremost, therefore, I wish to acknowledge the support and guidance of my adviser, Rodney A. Erickson.

The origin of this project can be traced back to a period spent as a research associate at the U.S. Bureau of the Census. This program operated jointly under the auspices of the American Statistical Association, the National Science Foundation, and the Bureau of the Census, and due acknowledgment is offered to these organizations. At a more personal level, a number of individuals were invaluable in navigating the labyrinth of the Bureau. I would like, therefore, to express my gratitude to: Arnold Reznek, formerly the Director of the ASA/NSF/Census research program; Michael Farrell, of the Bureau's Foreign Trade Division; and Philippe Morris, of the Bureau's Industry Division.

Others who contributed valuable advice and criticism on the dissertation version include Allan Rodgers, Anthony V. Williams, David N. Allen, and an anonymous referee. In addition, I would like to acknowledge the support of my peers and other members of the faculty at Penn State, my new colleagues at the University of Auckland and Anne De Caigney. Furthermore, for drawing the figures I would like to thank Jonette Surridge of the Department of Geography, Auckland.

Finally, I would like to express thanks to my editor, Alison Auch, and the publisher, Westview Press. Both have been patient and supportive with this novice. Nevertheless, neither they nor the good folks named above are in any way responsible for any errors that follow. As always, the buck stops with the author, me.

D. J. H.

International Trade
and Regional Economies

1

Introduction: International Trade and Regional Economies

Recent years have witnessed a growing concern among state policymakers and scholars of regional economic development with the external dimensions of regional economies. The increasing globalization of the U.S. economy and its constituent regional economies has caused state governments to "go international" in their industrial development promotion programs. These efforts have caught the attention of researchers concerned with external trade's implications for regional economies, particularly such aspects as the foreign trade component of state economies (Coughlin and Cartwright 1987a, 1987b, Fieleke 1986, Gillespie 1982, and Griffin 1989), states' relative export performance (Erickson and Hayward 1992), or the states' export promotion policies themselves (Archer and Maser 1989). The concern, however, has generally been for the exports side of the trade equation. These are seen as exogenous sources of demand for the states' products and, hence, unambiguous boosts to the states' economies. It is apparent from a review of the literature that exports dominate the regional economic development agenda, and that state-level policies for international trade are almost exclusively export-oriented. Concern for imports on the other hand, is most often exhibited at the federal level or in respect to their impact on particular industrial sectors. Nevertheless, both imports and exports have significant and direct implications for individual states.

The Globalization of the U.S. Economy

The increasing importance of international trade in the United States economy is indicated by the growth in the size of exports as a proportion of gross national product: from 4.2 percent in 1970 to 7.3

percent in 1990 (U.S. Bureau of Economic Analysis 1990, p. 804). During the same period, however, the U.S.'s external trade balance has worsened as the growth of imports has out-paced that of exports. This has heightened the concern for international trade in the political realm as well as the academic. The Omnibus Trade and Competitiveness Act of 1988 exemplified the twin thrusts of the policy response at the Federal level. The first has been to regain a balance in bilateral trade relationships through the greater use, in particular, of anti-dumping measures--these being one of the few protectionist options allowed under the General Agreement on Tariffs and Trade (GATT). The second has been to coordinate the resources of various Federal agencies in an effort to provide greater assistance to both current and potential exporters.[1] A notable feature of the persistent U.S. trade deficit--especially with Japan and other East Asian partners--is the dominance of trade issues in U.S. foreign relations, which is increasingly evident in the post-Cold War era as former East-West tensions subside.

Both academic and commercial concerns for the U.S. external trade imbalance have dwelt on its causes.[2] That foreign trade is an increasingly important factor in the U.S. economy is generally taken as axiomatic, and the primary issue has centered on whether the problem lies with an over-propensity to import (ie, demand) or a comparative inability to export (supply). In the political arena it is often claimed that the U.S. market is "too open", or that its partners--read "Japan"-- don't "play fair". Most research, however, tends to suggest that, in fact, the fault lies with the U.S.'s poor export performance. Hanink (1987) concludes that American firms in aggregate have failed to provide products that meet foreign demand patterns. By this assertion, the problem is effectively relocated from the realm of international diplomacy to one of domestic industrial policy, and hence into the domain of the individual states and regions.

The States as the Primary Actors in
Regional Development Policy

The involvement of state agencies in international trade concerns amounts to an additional dimension to regional development planning that has itself been largely transplanted in recent years from the federal to the state level. States have increasingly acted independently or in regional groupings to advance their own economic agendas. This has been partly a result of successive federal administrations having followed their ideological convictions that renounce interventionist regional and industrial policy. As the states have responded to the local dimensions of industrial restructuring, particularly in areas experiencing deindustrialization, they have employed a variety of development policies and have thereby been at the vanguard of development planning. Export promotion programs pursued by the states, therefore, should be viewed alongside other programs such as enterprise zones (Erickson and Friedman 1990), the promotion of entrepreneurship (Allen and Hayward 1990), or research parks (Goldstein and Luger 1990).

Exports and Economic Development

The relationship between exporting and state economic growth is rather ambiguous, although much of the general public and many state policymakers seem to regard it as axiomatic. (Erickson 1992)

The prevailing view holds that exports are an unambiguous positive contribution to regional economic growth, amounting to an increase in demand for domestically-produced (local) products. This largely unchallenged presumption of the regional economic value of exports owes much to the powerful concepts derived from export base theory. The topic was of great concern to regional economists and planners as long ago as the 1950s when it flourished as an offshoot of economic base theory with the seminal debate between North (1955, 1956) and Tiebout (1956a, 1956b). It is intuitively satisfying to conceive of exports as an exogenous impact on a regional economy, introducing external economic value into the regional system. Export base theory identifies industries that generate exports as being key to the regional development process, precisely because they produce "basic" goods that earn these exogenous revenues. North and Tiebout's dispute concerned the relative importance of these basic industries, but essentially centered on whether the remaining "non-basic" sectors could also generate economic development. They were, however, united in agreement on the positive economic benefit of the former.

Presently, the perceived importance of exports to regional economies persists although it is not usually invoked as part of an explicit export base strategy. Webster et al. (1990) evaluate the difference in the U.S. state employment multipliers for foreign and domestic--ie, intra-U.S.-- exports. They find that the foreign export employment multiplier was almost five times greater. Such findings lend support to export promotion as an increasingly important component of regional development policy. Here again, however, there is a leap of faith as it remains to be determined whether the additional economic benefits from increased *foreign* exports are sufficient to offset the additional costs of promotion activities overseas.

The alternative international trade theory founded upon the work of Linder (1961) and Krugman (1979; 1980) among others also supports state-level concern for international trade. This theory contradicts orthodox trade theory with its emphasis on comparative advantage and attention to the resource endowments of regions. Instead, the alternative theory contends that the driving force for trade is overlapping demand patterns in different regions. Similarity, rather than dissimilarity, is therefore the key, and so states have much to gain from trade even with other similarly-endowed regional entities. International trade is hence an extension of interregional trade, and, as such, takes place between regions of a larger economic entity; and that may be the United States economy, the Western industrial economy, or the global economy as a whole. Subnational political entities, therefore, are appropriately viewed as distinct economic units, and this is especially so with the increasing interdependence of the global economy.

A great deal of attention has been given to the contribution of international trade, and especially exports, to state and regional economies. McConnell (1987) identifies industrial sectors as the primary units for assessing the economic contributions of exports. However, given that states have unique industrial mixes, each will experience a different interrelationship with the global economy. Erickson and Hayward (1992) also showed that the differential export performance of industrial sectors produced a highly varied export contribution across the states. Coughlin and Cartwright (1987b) developed a time-series model that illustrates the relationship between exports and employment, suggesting it is both direct and substantial. Erickson (1989) also established a direct relationship between the states' industrial growth and their export performance, while Markusen et al. (1991) measured the contribution of exports in the industrial employment growth of nine U.S. regions using a shift-share analysis.

The contribution of exports to state and regional economies has often been reported for individual states and regions. In California (Griffen 1989), the Midwest (Gillespie 1982), and New England (Fieleke 1986) the export share of regional economies has been measured and inferences made about the dependence and, hence, prospects of these economies with respect to the global economy. The concern, as has been noted above, has almost exclusively been for exports, but both Fieleke (1986) and Gillespie (1982) introduce an import dimension. In particular, Gillespie (1982, p. 208) includes import-related employment in accounting for the regional economic dimensions of international trade.

State and Regional Factors Affecting
International Trade

A number of studies have addressed the factors underlying differential export performances among the states. Erickson and Hayward's (1991) analysis of the bilateral trade patterns of nine U.S. regions indicated the importance of location in the orientation of regions' exports and hence, indirectly, of their relative performance. Coughlin and Cartwright (1987a), Coughlin and Fabel (1988), and Erickson and Hayward (1992) all developed models which confirmed the importance of state endowments of physical and human capital in contributing to state export performance. Additionally, it has been shown that patterns of foreign direct investment (Erickson and Hayward 1991) as well as particularly active state export promotion programs also contribute to patterns of export performance.

Considerable attention has been devoted at the level of the individual firms, identifying both behavioral and environmental factors as instruments of exporting activity. Hirsch (1971) asserted that a key feature in a firm's propensity to export is its size such that there is a certain capacity threshold for exporting activity. McConnell (1979, p. 178) analyzed the characteristics of exporting firms and was able to develop a mean profile of a firm as having a risk-taking management, a competitive market strategy, and a medium level of sales. Namiki (1988) further identified successful exporting strategies from a survey of almost 400 computer manufacturers, identifying product differentiation strategies as being particularly important in successful export operations. The identification of corporate-behavioral factors itself suggests an opportunity for state-level action that could be directed towards encouraging appropriate business strategies. These may be complemented by other programs to address the environmental side as states attempt to create suitable export-oriented, local business climates through extensive export promotion programs.

Erickson (1992) asserts that state export promotion activities have "...become more formalized and, in many respects, came of age during the 1980s." State expenditures on international programs, of which export promotion is a major component, have grown well ahead of inflation in this period. Activities include information services, marketing support, establishing export trading companies, financial aid, or changes in regulations (Archer and Maser 1990). These programs have subsequently been analyzed for their effectiveness. Kudrle and

Kite (1989) discuss the problems of accountability and assessment in evaluating state programs; according to Erickson, "empirically-based research evaluating the effectiveness of state export promotion programs is practically nonexistent (1992). Coughlin and Cartwright (1987a) include the states' levels of export promotion activity in their model of trade performance, and show that it has a significant impact on levels of state exports.

The individual U.S. states, therefore, are more aware than ever of their place in the global economy, and of the power at their disposal to influence their own involvement in international trade. Consequently, states are increasingly sensitive to international trading events such as the GATT, the U.S.-Canada Free Trade Agreement, the forthcoming North American Free Trade Agreement, and even the European Union's EC-92 program. The international dimension to state level economies is more widely acknowledged and there is much need for detailed analyses of the states' exposure to such events.

The EC-92 Program

On December 31, 1992, the 12 nations of the European Community (EC) became a single, unified economic area; indeed, the largest single economy in the world with a population of approximately 320 million, mostly affluent consumers. The ramifications of this event--EC-92--are still being felt both within and outside the EC. One year later, with the passage of the Maastricht Treaty on European Union, the Community formally became the European Union (EU) and the level of integration deepened. These most recent changes largely affect political and macroeconomic structures as the former event effected a true common market in respect to trade.

The transformation of the separate western European economies into a monolithic market was not a climactic event--it is a process that has been under way since 1987 and continues as European industries restructure in its wake. Nevertheless, its progress by late 1992 has been impressive. Its epithet, the "largest single market," has subsequently been challenged by other international integration events: notably the North American Free Trade Area[3] (NAFTA) comprising the United States, Canada and Mexico, and more recently still, by the European Economic Area[4] (EEA) which merges the EU with the European Free Trade Association (EFTA). These factors have conspired to reduce some of its lustre but its importance is, nevertheless, undiminished and history may well regard it as the harbinger of a new global era of regional economic integration.

In the post-Cold War era, foreign relations, particularly among the industrialized countries, are concerned primarily with trade relations. The European Community's announcement of the 1992 (or, EC-92) program to remove the remaining non-tariff barriers to trade among its members in 1987, sent alarm bells ringing throughout its trading partners, and especially in North America. The fear of being excluded from a "Fortress Europe" neatly highlighted the ambiguous nature of America's position with respect to European unification. While supporting, indeed even nurturing, the goal of European integration in the post-war period, there remained the fear of creating a "Frankenstein's monster." European unity was a geopolitical imperative: to prohibit the possibility of another ruinous European war and to serve as a bulwark against Soviet imperialism. However, by the same token, an economically strong Europe necessarily threatens American post-war economic hegemony; particularly as it coincides with the ascension of America's other economic protege, Japan, to economic preeminence.

Although EC-92 is merely a stage in the process of European economic renewal, and will not be experienced as a climactic event-- indeed, at the time it passed largely unnoticed as the Maastricht Treaty debate was in full flow--it is nonetheless a defining moment in global economic relations. Not only does it underscore the re-emergence of a European economy with a global importance not seen since before First World War but it also probably marks the end of an era of U.S. global patronage which began informally following the First War and formally with the Marshall Plan (1947).

EC-92 is, therefore, one of several contemporary events that signify a shift not only in global economic power, but also in the U.S.'s place in the global system. Paradoxically, as the U.S. leads its western partners as "victors" in the Cold War, it is becoming increasingly evident that economic relations are moving to the forefront and with them, American hegemony is diminishing. In many arenas, such as the economic regeneration of the former Soviet bloc, the industrialization of East and Southeast Asia, and even the re-industrialization of parts of the U.S. itself, notably the Midwest, it is foreign rather than U.S. capital that is most prominent.

While such geopolitical and strategic issues fuel much debate at the Federal level, and in the editorial pages of influential national newspapers such as the New York Times or Washington Post, recent experience at the level of the individual states has engendered a reevaluation of the bounds of their legitimate economic interests. No longer does the purview of state-level economic planners extend only to the borders of the U.S., as individual states themselves, are giving attention to their own places in the global arena. Most have international trade programs. These may include export promotion seminars and overseas trade missions and, in many instances, foreign investors have been lured by state financial incentives not just to the U.S. but to particular states in preference to others. Some of these latter instances have been very high-profile, notably Tennessee's courtship of Toyota.

From their actions, it is evident that states are taking an independent interest in their foreign economic relations. In support of these developments, research has attended to both the nature of foreign investment in the U.S. and to the international trading activities of the states. With respect to the latter, in particular, the information available on individual states' exports and imports is fraught with weaknesses. Nonetheless, the demand for information is such that studies of state "trade balances" have proliferated, although many researchers disregard the problems inherent in the available data.

Although much of the debate over the external implications of EC-92 is limited to the geostrategic arena, the event is occurring in an era during which international economic relations have become a concern for even sub-national entities such as individual states. Indeed, these two dimensions are not unrelated. As this introduction has attempted to show, both the European Union's 1992 program and the states' concern for their role in the international economy are both symptoms and components of a new era of global capitalism.

This monograph addresses the topic of the role of European trade in the economies of the individual U.S. states and regions and of the potential impacts of EC-92 upon these economies. It represents an original contribution in three respects. First, the data used are unique estimates of state-level trade with the European Union. These are derived from published sources, but have undergone considerable manipulation to alleviate their inherent weaknesses. Second, the analysis includes an application of an extended international version of the popular shift-share model of regional economic growth. Third, an attempt is made to translate the external effects of the 1992 program to the economies of non-member trading partners--in this case, the individual U.S. states. The thesis, therefore, is a contribution to the study of regional economies and their international economic dimensions, and also to the study of international economic integration and its ramifications throughout the global economy.

The States and Trade with the European Union

The economic impacts of the EC-92 program on the individual states may occur through the formers' impacts on both trade and investment. Of these, the states' trade relations with the EC and the potential impacts of EC-92 on them will be the focus of this thesis since these are the more visible and will be the more directly affected by the formation of a true common market. For both exports to, and imports from, the EU, the state-level trade database described in Chapter 2 enables a detailed analysis of state-EU trade relations.

The impacts of EC-92 upon investment activities in U.S. states would be manifest through their impact upon global capital markets and upon the direct investment of European firms in the U.S. If EC-92 spurs a boom in the European economy, as is widely expected, then one may anticipate that the cost of capital will rise in the international market. Given the size of the EU as a single entity--the largest economy in the world--its ability to affect international financial markets will be increased. In such an indirect way, EC-92 may affect investment patterns throughout the world, including individual U.S. states. More specifically, the investment activities of EC-based firms may be affected by the single market. It is conceivable that investment may be redirected towards emerging domestic opportunities in preference to those in the U.S. Once again, the effects are indirect and there is little data with which to inform this question. In the present analysis, therefore, attention will be focussed upon trade effects alone.

For state economies, the impacts of EC-92 extend beyond considerations of their effects upon trade patterns. Indeed, trade itself needs to be considered as a component of the states' economies. In this way, trade is more appropriately viewed as a contribution to state GDPs, the personal and business incomes earned therein, and hence, local capital generation and tax revenues. Exports, in particular, may be regarded as a direct share of regional economic output. Imports, on the other hand, are an indirect and negative contribution to domestic economic output since they represent a substitute for domestic production. With the chosen method of calculating state imports in particular (described in Chapter 2 and Appendix 1), the competitive threat of imports to local economies is measured. Trade with the EU therefore is conceived of as an integral component of the states' economies, and so impacts upon this resulting from EC-92 necessarily also have domestic effects.

Although not a primary objective of this analysis, the state exports and imports may be compared to obtain state trade balances; however, these are by definition different from standard trade balances. With the data used here, a *production* trade balance is obtained as opposed to the standard *consumption* trade balance. Imports are calculated from total U.S. imports which are apportioned to the states according to their total production levels for different industries.[5] In this way, phoney apparent state imports (see Chapter 2) are avoided. State trade balances are informative in themselves but caution is required in using these as a basis for evaluations of states' trade performances. It is erroneous to infer that positive balances suggest "better" state international trade performances. While on the exports side, higher levels may be regarded as an indication of greater export performance, for imports they merely indicate the degree to which the states' industries are receiving competition from foreign producers. Higher import levels, therefore, do not indicate poor performance in the usual sense. The value of these state trade data lie in their indication of the relative importance of trade to individual state economies, and of the current direction--positive or negative--of that contribution.

Plan of the Book

The analysis proceeds in three stages and is reported in the following chapters. In Chapter 2, the pattern of trade with the European Union is examined. Trends in exports and imports over recent years are analyzed, and the leading industrial sectors for each, identified. The main purpose of this section, however, is to illustrate the state-by-state patterns and to do this, measures of relative *exposure* to trade with the EU are utilized. These exposure patterns provide a static representation of individual states' stake in the U.S.-European trade relationship. It offers a more reliable indication of trade patterns than that obtained from absolute trade flows.

In chapter 3, the analysis focuses upon the specific contribution of this trade to the recent economic growth of the individual states. Using the database of state exports and imports since 1983, an extended shift-share model is employed to evaluate the role of trade for each state. The widely different experiences of the states are highlighted by this approach.

Switching the focus of the shift-share model towards a forecasting role, the anticipated effects of the EC-92 program may also be evaluated. This analysis is reported in chapter 4. This exercise is highly sensitive to exogenous information which may itself be unreliable. Nevertheless, given the importance of trade for subnational economies established in the foregoing analyses, this technique demonstrates the opportunities for evaluating the potential impacts of international trade events.

In support of these analyses, two appendices are included. In the first, the methodology used to obtain the data set is documented. The source data are in the public domain but as they have undergone considerable manipulation prior to analysis, it is deemed vital that this procedure be described in detail. The process is outlined in chapter 2 but for specific details, the reader is advised to consult appendix 1.

Appendix 2 includes a comprehensive review of the European Union and the EC-92 program. This account is offered in support of the analysis in chapter 4 in which the potential impacts of EC-92 are estimated. In the first section, the progress of the EC up to the present is discussed with an emphasis upon the conditions leading to the Europe 1992 initiative. This is followed by a discussion of the program itself, identifying its specific goals: the elimination of the remaining physical, technical and fiscal barriers to trade among the member states. In particular, it is emphasized that EC-92 has specific and limited objectives and is not in itself intended to create a unified European state. The progress of the program and of the U.S. policy responses to it are also reviewed. The studies of the program's impact on the European economy are discussed as well as the limited information on its likely impacts upon external trade of the European Union.

Notes

1 The National Trade Data Bank was established under the auspices of the 1988 Omnibus Trade and Competitiveness Act [PL 100-418].

2 For example, *Business Week* (4-10-78); Hanink (1987).

3 The U.S., Canada and Mexico combined amount to a population in excess of 350 million (*New York Times* 1-30-91, p. D1).

4 The 19 states of the EU and EFTA would create a combined population of approximately 380 million people (*New York Times* 10-23-91, p. A1).

5 See chapter 2 and appendix 1 for descriptions of how state imports were calculated.

2

The States' Exposure to Trade with the European Union

State Trade Balances: A Problematic Endeavour

For the individual U.S. state and regional economies, the key impacts of any international trade event are those which affect their own production and employment levels, the two of which are, of course, intimately related. State and regional economic health is most directly determined by industrial (including the primary, manufacturing and service sectors') output and employment, and for the income and tax revenues they generate. The extent, therefore, to which trade impacts upon regional economies will be constrained by the proportion of a region's economy that is challenged in the international trade arena. In the case of exports, this may be measured as that portion of production that goes for exports, while for imports, it is equal to that portion of output facing a competitive threat from imports. In the case of the latter, a novel formulation is employed in this study.

Most previous attempts to apply the trade balance concept to the states are inherently flawed since they apply national accounting concepts to regions. This is not appropriate for regional economic analysis since states do not operate as separate economic entities and cannot be so narrowly defined. Economic units (including individuals) in the states pay taxes to federal authorities and transfer payments are returned, while undocumented cross-border commerce is considerably more substantial than is the case among nations. However, the recent availability of trade data at the level of individual states has sparked an interest in states' trade balances. Radspieler and Mehl (1991) delivered a scalding critique of the widespread use of simplistic trade balances by both scholars and journalists. In such cases, use is generally made of the unadjusted state by state origin and destination trade data reported by the Census Bureau, with balances calculated as imports subtracted from exports. As an example of the ill-conceived conclusions this exercise leads to they examine the case of New York which, being home to a major port, is often erroneously identified as both the origin of exports and, more often, the destination of many imports:

> Based on these numerical values, one is led to believe that the "surgical" removal of Manhattan Island would lead to an instantaneous improvement in the country's trade deficit. (p. 3)

An example of the kind of trade indexing that is being undertaken at the state level is the North Carolina World Trade Index described by Dutton and Erickson (1989). In this case, unadjusted data from the U.S. Bureau of the Census Foreign Trade Division's State by State Exports Series are employed to generate an international trade balance for North Carolina purporting to reveal the state's disproportionate positive contribution towards the nation's foreign trade balance. They note:

> If the U.S. as a whole had done as well as North Carolina, the deficit overall would have been cut by over 87 percent. (p. 22)

The problem with import data at the state level is that they are necessarily attributed to the states of importation--ie, where the major ports are located--rather than the home states of the final consumers.

A more appropriate definition of a state trade balance and one used here is a *production* balance wherein exports produced in a state are balanced against the value of imports competing with the state's industries. In this formula, the first destination of imports is irrelevant as national import totals are used and apportioned to states according to their corresponding sectors. This differs from a *consumption* balance in that states' trade balances would be represented by the balance of state exports and its share of competing imports. From a macroeconomic, national accounts perspective there would be no difference between the two approaches, but for regional economic analysts the production approach is the more relevant. Furthermore, the objective of such an exercise is not to determine which states are performing "best" with respect to trade--that is, "good citizens"--but to show which are more involved directly in trade and, therefore, the more vulnerable to external trade events.

Regional Trade Data in the United States

The structure of the data used in this study is intrinsic to the methodology being pursued and is itself determined by the quality and limitations of the available data. The objective is to compile a database of the contiguous forty-eight states' industrial output, exports and imports, identifying those destined for or originating from the European Union, respectively. Although compiled entirely from published U.S. Bureau of the Census sources, the database is original and unique owing to the considerable manipulation undertaken in its construction. The limitations and weaknesses of the existing state-level trade data have previously prevented any reliable state-level analysis of the kind being proposed here. The data have undergone substantial modifications and, in the interests of enabling critical evaluation and replication, the data compilation procedure is fully documented below.

The Original Data Sources

The most important data source for this project is the series of state-by-state exports produced by the Massachusetts Institute of Social and Economic Research (MISER). These were first available for 1987 and are released quarterly at only a few month's lag. This data series contains the values and volumes of export shipments summarized by state, industry (2-digit SIC) and foreign (country) destination. These data are themselves an adjusted form of those released by the U.S. Bureau of the Census' Foreign Trade Division (FT), which are compiled from the Shippers' Export Declarations filed with the U.S. Customs at the point of exportation. The original Census FT data contain a large number of exports for which no state of origin is known. MISER's contribution is to complete the Census data set by attributing these "missing" values to individual states.

The MISER data series has for the first time provided export values for states of origin as well destinations and with a very short time lag. As a result, these data have been enthusiastically used by academics and analysts alike with varied attention to the warnings from MISER and the Foreign Trade Division (Farrell and Radspieler 1989) of the inherent weaknesses in the data. In particular, the export values are known to be biased towards the states of exportation, such that there is a tendency for exports to be attributed to those states rather than to the true states of production. This is a very serious problem for regional analysis, rendering statements made on these patterns highly prone to error. For instance, Woodward (1990) acknowledges this problem and attempts to overcome it by aggregating states to the larger Census regions, that is, burying the problem through scale. The biases, however, are still evident in his tables and, in any case, one loses the major advantage of this data series, namely the ability to conduct state-level analyses.

A second weakness of this data series is that the export values are available only at the rather aggregated, two-digit level of the Standard Industrial Classification (SIC). This is because the original data derived from the Shippers Export Declarations are collected under the very detailed international Harmonized Tariff System. This is a *product*-based classification scheme--the SIC being *process*-based-- and an adequate correspondence with the latter can be made only at the fairly aggregated two-digit level. At this level, for instance, both the Transportation Equipment and Industrial Machinery sectors incorporate a large number of important and distinctly different sub-sectors.

Finally, a third weakness is that equivalent state-level data have not been available for imports. This, however, is not considered to be a significant problem for our objectives owing to the discussion above, where a *production* balance approach is advocated.[1] For regional economic analysis, the state of first destination of an import shipment is of little consequence since one may presume that once it enters the U.S. market it may be distributed to consumers throughout the country, thereby having a diffused economic impact. The competitive threat posed by an imported good, therefore, will not be confined to firms in a single state but rather will be felt throughout the national economy. A more appropriate way of attributing U.S. imports by states is to apportion imports according to production patterns.

Other necessary trade data including imports and pre-1987 exports were obtained from published, U.S. level data. Generally, Census foreign trade publications use product-based classifications schemes (eg., the Standard International Trade Classification, [SITC]) and so these SIC-based industry data were purchased from the U.S. Department of Commerce's COMPRO system, an internal database.

In order to alleviate the biases in the state-level exports data, additional information was sought from complementary data published by the U.S. Bureau of the Census' Industry Division. The Census of Manufactures (CM) is conducted every five years and the Annual Survey of Manufactures (ASM), in the intervening years. These surveys record the values of output and employment among a variety of specific production-related variables at the source, the actual business establishments. The value of exports, however, is reported for only manufacturing sectors in the CM and ASM series, and is not available for the corresponding agricultural, mining, wholesaling and other service sectors. For this reason, the analysis is necessarily limited to the 20 two-digit SIC manufacturing sectors (SICs 20-39). Another constraint imposed by these data series is the period of analysis. At the time this database is being compiled the most recently available year is 1987 because of the lag in the reporting of the export values which, in addition, have only been continuously reported since 1983. These constraints effectively limit the analysis to the period since 1983, although with the manipulation discussed in Appendix 1 it will be possible to extend the data to 1990.

One may presume, however, that these data are free from the biases of the MISER data since they are recorded at the point of production, the industrial establishment. However, the destinations of the export shipments are not reported and total export values by sector are likely to be less accurate overall than those reported from the Customs sources which measure actual shipments on a current basis rather than from a one-time annual survey. Two data items are of particular interest in the CM/ASM data series: (1) the exports of states' industries and (2) the value of their total output. A full account of the data manipulation procedure leading to the complete data set is given in Appendix 1.

Thus, a hybrid database of state exports and imports is created using a variety of off-the-shelf sources. However, owing to concerns about the accuracy of the original data for export and production values for some of the smaller states a number of them were grouped together. This was carried out in several instances for contiguous states to produce multi-state regions. Figure 2.1 illustrates the resulting 38 states and regions used in the following analysis.

International Trade Patterns
of the States and Regions

The values for the total manufacturing production, exports and imports for 1990 are reported in Table 2.1 below. The production data are estimates based upon the 1987 Census of Manufactures (as explained in Appendix 1) although by the time of publication more recent official data may be available. The exports measure is an estimate of the value of all manufactures originating from each state or region. The imports figures represent each state's share of the nation's imports as determined by the value of their industries production. While it is acknowledged that error has necessarily been introduced in their compilation, it is nevertheless believed that these estimates are probably the most reliable from a regional economic perspective yet to be produced.

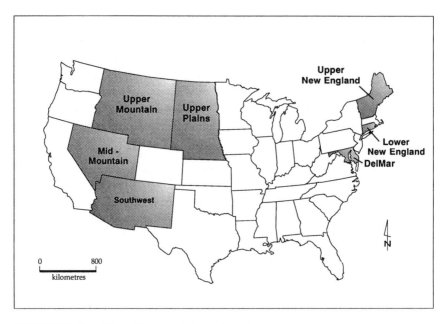

FIGURE 2.1 The 38 contiguous states and regions.

The states' levels of industrial production will be familiar to most observers. California records the greatest level of output by value, $302.9 billion, followed by Texas at $195.0 billion and a swath of north eastern and north Midwestern states. The export values, however, reveal some interesting patterns. While California and Texas register also the greatest levels of industrial exports, third place is claimed by Washington, one of the smaller states in respect to total production. In a less dramatic fashion other second-tier industrial areas such as the Lower and Upper New England regions also report comparatively large values of exports.

The relative sizes of the states' exports may be observed through the export production exposure measure reported in the third column. This is a simple measure expressing exports as a proportion of total production. The national average of 10.27 percent is bettered by fifteen states (although only marginally in the case of Kentucky). Washington's extraordinary export performance is revealed as amounting to 40.30 percent of its total manufacturing output. At the other end of the spectrum, New Jersey, the Upper Plains region and Arkansas have very low exposure levels (6.07, 6.36 and 6.47 percent, respectively). Evidently, the comparative importance of exports to regional economies is quite varied.

The pattern of export exposure across the 38 states and regions is displayed in Figure 2.2 and some distinct regional variations are revealed: above average levels are found throughout most of the west and south west, and in the north east. Below average levels are associated with the middle Atlantic, Southeast, Midwest and Plains regions, that is, much of the heartland. With the notable exception of the low exposure levels along the Mid and South Atlantic coast there appears to be a general tendency for the coastal and border areas to have relatively high exposures to exports, while the core of the nation has much lower levels.

As noted in the discussion of the data compilation, state and regional imports reflect to some extent the patterns of industrial output. Nevertheless, there remains some significant variations among the states' experiences with respect to imports and the competitive threat they pose to local industries. California ($55.8 billion), Michigan ($37.5 billion) and Ohio ($35.3 billion) have the largest import totals (Table 2.1). However, once again, the comparative importance of these is best illustrated by the import production exposure measure. As the U.S. as a whole experienced a substantial manufacturing trade deficit in 1990 the import exposure values are generally higher than the national average of 17.24 percent. The variation is due to the different sizes of the industries in each state. Michigan (21.38 percent) and Lower New England (21.32 percent) report the highest levels of exposure. On the other hand, several states appear to suffer a lower level of competition from imports: the Upper Mountain and Upper Plains regions, and Oregon (11.20, 12.46 and 12.76 percent, respectively).

A complementary pattern of import exposure values is shown in Figure 2.3. Once again, some notable regional clustering is revealed. Above average exposures are shared by all the states in the far north east, throughout the Midwest, and the far south west. Perhaps more notable, are the swaths of areas with low exposure values: the Middle Atlantic-Southeast-South, and the north west-northern Midwest regions. Clearly, the regional dimension to the competitive threat to imports is marked.

If we consider the two types of exposure simultaneously we can characterize the experiences of the individual states and regions as conforming to one of four types. For instance, states with high levels of both export and import exposure appear to have a balanced but nonetheless deep involvement in international trade. These include states in New England and the far west. Quite differently, the Middle Atlantic and south eastern states comprise the largest number of those with below average levels on both accounts. In these cases, while balanced, trade appears to be comparatively less important to their

TABLE 2.1 The States' Manufacturing Production, Trade and Exposure, 1990

	Production, 1990 ($ millions)	Exports, 1990 ($ millions)	Export Exposure, 1990 (%)	Imports 1990 ($ millions)	Import Exposure, 1990 (%)
Alabama	49,018.3	3,372.4	6.88	7,944.0	16.21
Arkansas	30,329.8	1,963.4	6.47	4,736.9	15.62
California	302,882.8	39,904.9	13.18	55,791.8	18.42
Colorado	27,847.1	2,734.7	9.82	5,576.0	20.02
Florida	67,847.5	7,573.5	11.16	11,136.0	16.41
Georgia	90,733.7	6,377.3	7.03	14,604.4	16.10
Illinois	158,440.2	15,604.4	9.85	25,303.3	15.97
Indiana	100,415.6	6,749.2	6.72	18,324.1	18.25
Iowa	42,435.4	3,638.2	8.57	6,010.7	14.16
Kansas	37,218.8	2,594.2	6.97	6,207.9	16.68
Kentucky	50,127.7	5,150.7	10.28	9,262.7	18.48
Louisiana	60,761.0	4,522.7	7.44	7,963.4	13.11
Massachusetts	75,255.1	8,074.2	10.73	15,455.4	20.54
Michigan	175,379.6	12,657.8	7.22	37,500.2	21.38
Minnesota	57,050.9	7,046.7	12.35	8,999.0	15.77
Mississippi	29,218.9	2,548.9	8.72	4,648.4	15.91
Missouri	71,774.3	5,907.5	8.23	14,083.4	19.62
New Jersey	98,813.4	5,997.9	6.07	15,979.6	16.17
New York	174,562.0	18,236.4	10.45	31,897.9	18.27

(continues)

Table 2.1 (*continued*)

North Carolina	114,233.0	9,764.7	8.55	16,936.9	14.83
Ohio	190,026.1	20,800.5	10.95	35,347.4	18.60
Oklahoma	28,851.4	2,603.0	9.02	5,261.8	18.24
Oregon	30,382.9	3,362.5	11.07	3,875.6	12.76
Pennsylvania	142,197.3	10,621.6	7.47	23,768.3	16.72
South Carolina	49,390.2	5,361.5	10.86	7,537.4	15.26
Tennessee	69,213.9	6,124.0	8.85	12,380.8	17.89
Texas	195,048.8	23,747.1	12.17	29,281.0	15.01
Virginia	62,202.1	5,083.4	8.17	8,643.3	13.90
Washington	55,766.0	22,475.6	40.30	9,478.5	17.00
West Virginia	13,855.0	1,176.3	8.49	2,075.1	14.98
Wisconsin	83,407.1	6,298.3	7.55	14,081.3	16.88
DelMar	46,426.9	3,892.5	8.38	7,452.8	16.05
Lower New England	55,807.8	7,855.0	14.08	11,900.7	21.32
Mid Mountain	15,220.6	1,349.5	8.87	2,540.3	16.69
Southwest	29,942.2	3,629.3	12.12	6,042.9	20.18
Upper Mountain	15,072.8	1,899.4	12.60	1,688.1	11.20
Upper New England	33,111.2	5,354.8	16.17	6,885.9	20.80
Upper Plains	26,975.8	1,715.2	6.36	3,360.0	12.46
U.S. (48 States)	2,957,242.8	303,769.2	10.27	509,963.5	17.24

Source: Data compiled from U.S. Bureau of the Census sources, see Appendix 1.

22

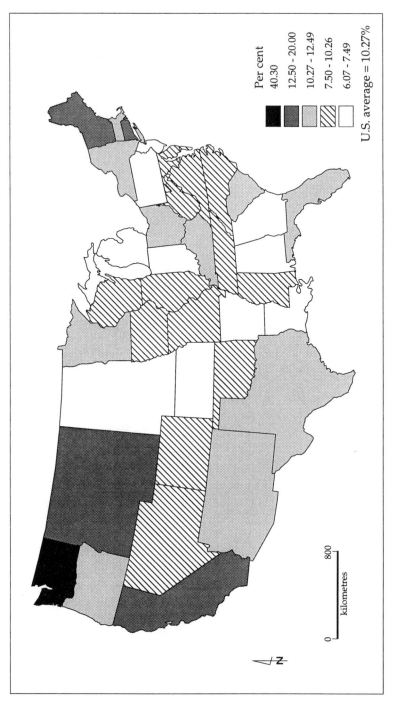

FIGURE 2.2 Export exposure, 1990: exports as a proportion of total production.

23

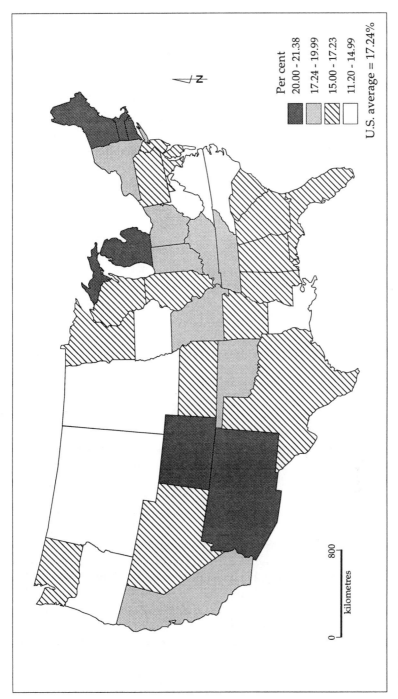

Per cent
20.00 - 21.38
17.24 - 19.99
15.00 - 17.23
11.20 - 14.99

U.S. average = 17.24%

0   800
kilometres

FIGURE 2.3 Import exposure, 1990: imports as a proportion of total production.

regional economies. The two other categories represent cases in which the trade experience is unbalanced. First, in a handful of cases, but including all of the north western states, above average export exposures are accompanied by below average import exposures suggesting that these states are gaining in their international trade experience. However, in the final category a number of states, all in the heartland, report below average export exposures along with above average import exposures. In these cases, the local industries are experiencing considerable foreign competition while themselves being predominantly oriented towards the domestic economy. These categories are revealed in Figure 2.4 and the regional pattern across the country is evident once again, with distinctly different trade experiences occurring to the north eastern and western states from those of the Middle Atlantic, south eastern and Mid western states.

Patterns of State and Regional Trade
with the European Union

We now turn our attention to the particular case of the states' exposure to trade with the European Union. As it is constructed, the database allows for trade with the EU to be separated from that with other nations. Table 2.2 reports the values of the states' exports and imports in 1990, and the balance between them. As noted earlier, owing to the method of compiling these data this balance is a *production* balance, purporting to indicate the trade balance between the states' industries not their consumers.

Once again, California registers the largest value of both exports and imports, and by a large margin, with a positive EU trade balance of $1,458.2 million. Towards the other end of the spectrum, Arkansas has the lowest level of exports to the EU ($374.8 million) and imports almost twice that value, yielding a large negative trade balance of -$333.1 million. West Virginia, on the other hand, exports little more to the EU ($381.6 million) but with only $403.2 million of imports has a trade balance of just -$21.5 million. Between these extremes, there is considerable variation in the state' trade with the EU. Of particular note are the cases of Washington and Michigan. The former is the second largest exporter to the EU ($6,848.0 million) and has a substantial positive trade balance of $5,339.0 million; in contrast, Michigan has comparatively few exports to the EU but experiences substantial competition from imports ($6,269.5 million) to yield a large negative trade balance of -$4,486.2 million. Clearly, these two states' situations in respect to trans-Atlantic trade are diametrically opposite.

25

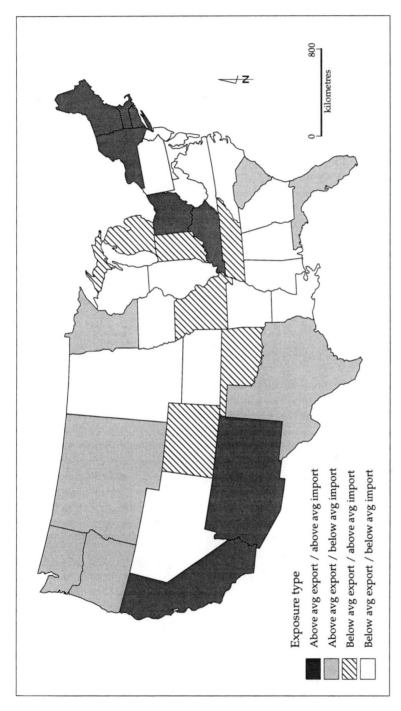

Exposure type

Above avg export / above avg import

Above avg export / below avg import

Below avg export / above avg import

Below avg export / below avg import

N

0   800

kilometres

FIGURE 2.4 Exposure types, 1990: categories defined by above and below average export and import exposure.

TABLE 2.2 The States' Trade with the European Union

	Exports to the EU, 1990 ($m)	Imports from the EU, 1990 ($m)	EU Trade Balance ($m)
Alabama	785.3	1,145.6	-360.4
Arkansas	374.8	707.8	-333.1
California	10,250.2	8,792.0	1,458.2
Colorado	910.2	908.1	2.1
Florida	1,279.8	1,817.4	-537.6
Georgia	1,575.9	2,209.2	-633.3
Illinois	3,512.8	4,289.3	-776.4
Indiana	1,330.4	2,942.6	-1,612.2
Iowa	845.1	1,061.9	-216.7
Kansas	497.9	1,079.9	-582.0
Kentucky	1,759.2	1,473.7	285.5
Louisiana	1,146.6	1,471.9	-325.3
Massachusetts	3,186.2	2,457.1	729.1
Michigan	1,783.3	6,269.5	-4,486.2
Minnesota	2,299.8	1,553.6	746.2
Mississippi	690.6	665.2	25.4
Missouri	1,520.9	2,320.0	-799.1
New Jersey	1,674.6	2,807.2	-1,132.6
New York	4,820.8	4,962.7	-141.9
North Carolina	2,924.7	2,622.1	302.6
Ohio	4,545.3	5,891.0	-1,345.7
Oklahoma	729.9	830.5	-100.6
Oregon	697.6	535.1	162.6
Pennsylvania	2,352.0	3,764.2	-1,412.1
South Carolina	1,594.3	1,236.5	357.8
Tennessee	1,450.1	1,955.4	-505.2
Texas	4,193.3	5,145.7	-952.4
Virginia	1,872.9	1,424.8	448.0
Washington	6,848.0	1,509.0	5,339.0
West Virginia	381.6	403.2	-21.5
Wisconsin	1,794.4	2,293.2	-498.8
Delmar	840.4	1,314.9	-474.5
Lower New England	2,656.4	1,976.1	680.3
Mid Mountain	381.4	424.5	-43.1
Southwest	1,095.7	939.9	155.7
Upper Mountain	455.8	271.6	184.2
Upper New England	1,022.9	1,027.0	-4.1
Upper Plains	391.4	583.6	-192.2
U.S.	76,472.7	83,083.1	-6,610.4

Source: see Appendix 1

The database, with trade and production values for the years 1983-90 affords a more detailed analysis of the changes in EU trade. To display the exports and imports levels for each state and region for each of eight years in tabular form is prohibitive; thus the EU trade experiences for some selected states are illustrated graphically in Figures 2.5, 2.6 and 2.7.

In Figure 2.5 the chosen states exhibit the variety of experiences in exports to the EU over this period. Implicit price deflators were used to obtain values in 1990 dollars and in each case, exports to the EU were greater in 1990 than in 1983. However, it is clear that very different growth patterns have been experienced. Texas (TX) and Pennsylvania (PA) typify average growth patterns which are substantial but less than a doubling of exports over the period. In most cases there was one or more year-to-year declines: Texas experienced a decline in 1984 whereas the other selected states experienced a later decline, in 1987-88. Washington (WA) and Kentucky (KY) are examples of regions experiencing the greatest growth in exports. Although on a different scale, they both more than doubled their exports since 1983. In contrast, New Jersey (NJ) and Louisiana (LA) represent the more sluggish growth paths. For the former, a modest growth has occurred recently after a

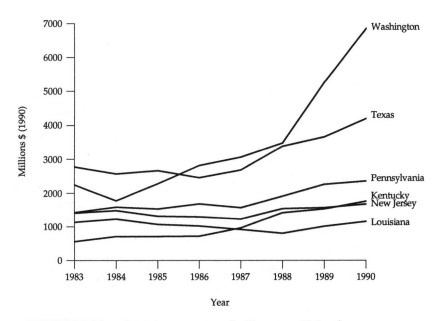

FIGURE 2.5 Manufacturing exports to the European Union for selected states, 1983-1990.

decline in the mid-1980s. For the latter, this period was one of almost complete decline in exports to the EU, returning to the 1983 levels only recently.

Imports from the EU over the same period are indicated in Figure 2.6. Again, states were selected to illustrate the range of import growth trajectories. As with exports, this period saw an increase for all regions but with less variation which is partly attributable to the method of calculating state imports. In each case, the earlier part of the period saw the most rapid increases which was succeeded by a period of more modest growth with relatively little change since 1988. This pattern probably reflects national trends in imports from the EU, but the earlier--and in some cases, rapid: Michigan (MI) and Florida (FL)--increase is notable and indicates the particular exposure of these states' industries to European competition at that time. Texas (TX) and Louisiana (LA) display a more erratic experience with EU imports; in both cases, a substantial dip occurred in 1986 followed by renewed increases.

The balance between exports and imports over this period presents the most interesting and varied pattern. Once again, six states were selected and included in Figure 2.7, each representing a different

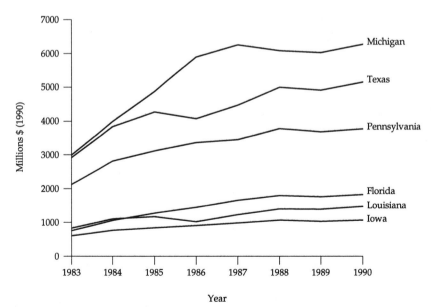

FIGURE 2.6 Manufacturing imports from the European Union
for selected states, 1983-1990.

experience. Minnesota (MN) and Pennsylvania (PA) had the most stable patterns, the former having a continuous and steady positive balance and the latter a complementary negative balance. In contrast, Washington (WA) and Michigan (MI) represent the other extremes, the former displaying a large and rapidly growing positive balance and the latter, a negative but similarly precipitous experience. In addition to these relatively continuous patterns, California (CA) and New York (NY) both began this period with positive balances that became negative in 1985, reached their lowest points in 1986-87, and then became less negative. By the end of the period, California had a positive balance and New York maintained a small negative balance. There are no instances of the reverse pattern.

Trade Exposure to the European Union

In place of absolute trade flows between U.S. states and regions and the European Union, their trade orientations may be better expressed as a proportion of their total international trade. Following the data contained in Table 2.2, these measures are shown in Table 2.3 and are referred to as *trade exposure*, and calculated for both exports and imports. The average export trade exposure for the U.S. as a whole is

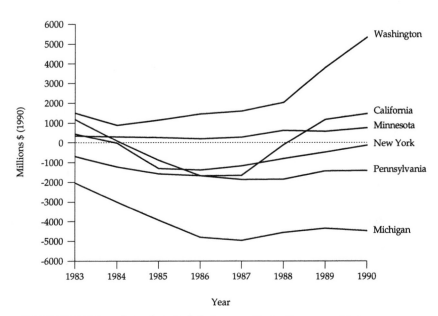

FIGURE 2.7 Manufacturing trade balance with the European Union for selected states, 1983-1990.

30

TABLE 2.3 Trade Exposure to the European Union, 1990

	Export Trade Exposure (%)	Import Trade Exposure (%)
Alabama	23.3	14.4
Arkansas	19.1	14.9
California	25.7	15.8
Colorado	33.3	16.3
Florida	16.9	16.3
Georgia	24.7	15.1
Illinois	22.5	17.0
Indiana	19.7	16.1
Iowa	23.2	17.7
Kansas	19.2	17.4
Kentucky	34.2	15.9
Louisiana	25.4	18.5
Massachusetts	39.5	15.9
Michigan	14.1	16.7
Minnesota	32.6	17.3
Mississippi	27.1	14.3
Missouri	25.8	16.5
New Jersey	27.9	17.6
New York	26.4	15.6
North Carolina	30.0	15.5
Ohio	21.9	16.7
Oklahoma	28.0	15.8
Oregon	20.8	13.8
Pennsylvania	22.1	15.8
South Carolina	29.7	16.4
Tennessee	23.7	15.8
Texas	17.7	17.6
Virginia	36.8	16.5
Washington	30.5	15.9
West Virginia	32.4	19.4
Wisconsin	28.5	16.3
Delmar	21.6	17.6
Lower New England	33.8	16.6
Mid Mountain	28.3	16.7
Southwest	30.2	15.6
Upper Mountain	24.0	16.1
Upper New England	19.1	14.9
Upper Plains	22.8	17.4
U.S.	25.2	16.3

Source: see Appendix 1.

25.2 percent; that is, manufacturing exports to the EU amount to 25.2 percent of the total U.S. manufactured exports. Evidently, there is considerable variation around this mean with Massachusetts and Virginia having levels of 39.5 and 36.8 percent, respectively, while Michigan and Florida have only 14.1 and 16.9 percent of their manufactured exports are destined for the European Union.

The state by state pattern of export trade exposures is illustrated in Figure 2.8 and indicates that the U.S. average of 25.2 percent in much of the north east, the South Atlantic, west and south west regions. In addition, two northern states, Minnesota and Wisconsin, as well as some South Central states, have relatively high export trade exposures. In contrast, the areas of low exposure exhibit an equally well-defined pattern: the Mid-Atlantic, Midwest, the Southeast, and most of the North and South Central states. Evidently, the trade orientations of U.S. states and regions to the EU may be easily described by broad geographic regions.

A detailed inspection of the changes in export trade exposure since 1983 allows further statements on the states' experiences to be ventured. The South Atlantic, some central states (such as Mississippi, Oklahoma and Missouri), Washington and Wisconsin, and the Southwest and Mid Mountain regions each have high export trade exposures that have grown consistently since 1983. In this respect, therefore, the recent growth in exposure of these areas may be distinguished from that of the more established EU-oriented trade patterns found for the north east, Minnesota, California, Louisiana and South Carolina, each of which are areas of high exposure in 1990, but little changed over the period. Of the areas of low exposure, the Middle Atlantic, Southeast, Texas and several Midwestern and northern regions have experienced little increase and hence show little inclination toward trade with the EU. In some other regions of low exposure, all located in the heartland, the levels have nevertheless increased since 1983. Finally, in one odd case, the Upper New England region went from being an area of above average exposure to being well below in 1990. One may speculate that this small region's proximity to Canada (ie, a non-EU country) may have affected its export patterns.

Import trade exposure values are also reported in Table 2.3. For the United States as a whole just 16.3 percent of its imports originate in the EU, and owing to the method of compiling the data there is comparatively little variation among the states. Nevertheless, import trade exposure values of as high as 19.5 percent are reported for West Virginia, and as low as 13.8 percent for Oregon. An interesting state-wide pattern is revealed in Figure 2.9.

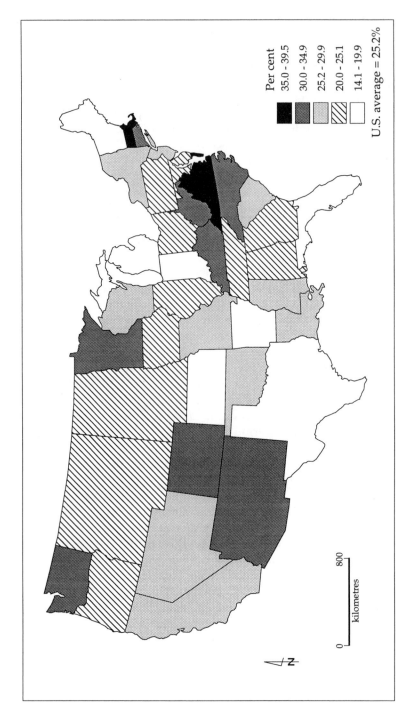

Per cent

35.0 - 39.5
30.0 - 34.9
25.2 - 29.9
20.0 - 25.1
14.1 - 19.9

U.S. average = 25.2%

0   800

kilometres

N

FIGURE 2.8 Export trade exposure to the European Union, 1990.

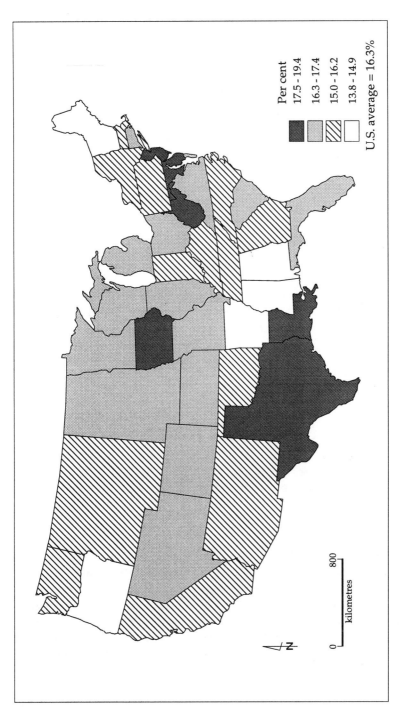

FIGURE 2.9 Import trade exposure to the European Union, 1990.

Above-average import trade exposures are found for most of the states west of the Mississippi and east of the Rockies. Evidently, given their industrial structures, these are particularly exposed to competition from the EU. In addition, on the east coast, much of the Middle and South Atlantic regions, and Florida have relatively high exposures. In the remaining eastern states and throughout the west, generally below-average import exposures are found including even the states of the north east, despite its location on the North Atlantic seaboard.

Once again, inspection of the import trade exposure values for the years 1983-1990 allows some refinement of these patterns. In the case of the comparatively high value Middle Atlantic and South Central states the high exposures are in fact recent, whereas in the North Central states the high values have been consistent throughout the period. Of those areas with low values they have been constantly so for the eastern states while in the west they have actually been increasing, although are still below average.

This consideration of trade exposures reveals the relative trade orientations of the individual states and regions towards the European Union. What is evident from these patterns is that there are distinct regional variations in trade patterns. For exports, the New England and South Atlantic states are comparatively-biased toward the EU while their east-coast neighbors in the Middle Atlantic and Southeast are not. Furthermore, it is interesting that several heartland states and most of those in the West are EU-oriented despite their geographical location away from the Atlantic seaboard. For imports, it is apparent that those states most exposed to EU competition are to be found in only a few eastern states but throughout the heartland. These exposure values represent shares of the states' trade being associated with the EU. To consider the importance of this trade in the regional economies of these states, the following section explores their *production* exposures to the European Union.

Production Exposure to the European Union

As in the earlier discussion of the states' foreign trade with all countries, *production exposure* represents the trade as a proportion of its total manufacturing output. This, therefore, indicates the relative dependence of regional industrial production (and hence, by extension, its employment, tax revenues and regional income due to these sectors) on the European market. It embodies not only trade orientations, but also the relative importance of these to the individual states and regions. Once again, this measure is specified for both exports and imports. These values are reported in Table 2.4 along with a third

TABLE 2.4 Production Exposure to the European Union

	EU Export Production Exposure (%)	EU Import Production Exposure (%)	Net Production Exposure (%)
Alabama	1.6	2.3	-0.7
Arkansas	1.2	2.3	-1.1
California	3.4	2.9	0.5
Colorado	3.3	3.3	0.0
Florida	1.9	2.7	-0.8
Georgia	1.7	2.4	-0.7
Illinois	2.2	2.7	-0.5
Indiana	1.3	2.9	-1.6
Iowa	2.0	2.5	-0.5
Kansas	1.3	2.9	-1.6
Kentucky	3.5	2.9	0.6
Louisiana	1.9	2.4	-0.5
Massachusetts	4.2	3.3	1.0
Michigan	1.0	3.6	-2.6
Minnesota	4.0	2.7	1.3
Mississippi	2.4	2.3	0.1
Missouri	2.1	3.2	-1.1
New Jersey	1.7	2.8	-1.1
New York	2.8	2.8	-0.1
North Carolina	2.6	2.3	0.3
Ohio	2.4	3.1	-0.7
Oklahoma	2.5	2.9	-0.3
Oregon	2.3	1.8	0.5
Pennsylvania	1.7	2.6	-1.0
South Carolina	3.2	2.5	0.7
Tennessee	2.1	2.8	-0.7
Texas	2.1	2.6	-0.5
Virginia	3.0	2.3	0.7
Washington	12.3	2.7	9.6
West Virginia	2.7	2.9	-0.2
Wisconsin	2.1	2.7	-0.6
Delmar	1.8	2.8	-1.0
Lower New England	4.8	3.5	1.2
Mid Mountains	2.5	2.8	-0.3
Southwest	3.7	3.1	0.5
Upper Mountain	3.0	1.8	1.2
Upper New England	3.1	3.1	0.0
Upper Plains	1.5	2.2	-0.7
U.S.	2.6	2.8	-0.2

Source: see Appendix 1.

measure, a balance of the export and import production exposure values. This latter measure may be termed *net production exposure*, as it summarizes the net dependence of the states' manufacturing economies on trade with the EU.

Export Production Exposure. For the U.S. as a whole, exports to the European Union represent 2.6 percent of the total manufacturing output. While at first glance this may appear a paltry amount, one should note that this is not an inconsequential chunk of the U.S. industrial output to be dependent upon European consumers. Furthermore, from Table 2.4 it is evident that there is considerable variation among the states. In particular, Washington is well above the average with an export production exposure value of 12.3 percent. More typical of the higher values are those found for Lower New England region and Massachusetts with 4.8 and 4.0 percent, respectively, while lower values of just 1.0 and 1.2 percent are reported for Michigan and Arkansas.

Figure 2.10 illustrates the regional pattern of export production measures for 1990 which is similar, but perhaps less ambiguous, to that found for export trade exposure in Figure 2.8 above. Distinct regions of high exposure are again found in the north east (except the Middle Atlantic states), the South Atlantic, Minnesota, and much of the Mountain and Western regions. Notable "drop-outs" from the ranks of the high exposure areas (in Figure 2.8) include New Jersey, several in the heartland (including Wisconsin, Missouri and Oklahoma), and Louisiana and Mississippi in the South. For these cases, it appears that while their trade may be oriented towards the EU, it nevertheless represents a relatively insignificant part of their total industrial output. Regions of production exposure below the U.S. average include the Middle Atlantic, the Southeast, the South Central, the Midwest and the Plains.

Import Production Exposure. As with the import trade exposure values reported in Figure 4.2, the variation across the states is less-marked owing to the manner in which state imports are calculated. Nevertheless, there are some notable deviations from the U.S. mean of 2.8 percent. For example, for Michigan and the Lower New England region, imports from the EU amount to 3.6 and 3.5 percent of the states' total manufacturing output. Unlike the export production exposure measure, this represents not an actual share of the regional industrial output being export-bound but is a measure of the competitive threat of imports (in this case, from the EU) expressed in terms of the regions' industrial output. Again, these figure are not-inconsequential, especially when it is noted that for some states, the import exposure values are half those of the two above. Oregon and the Upper

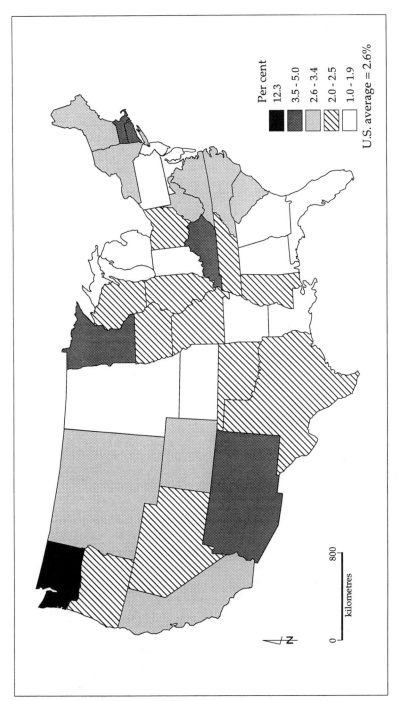

FIGURE 2.10 Export production exposure to the European Union, 1990.

Per cent

12.3
3.5 - 5.0
2.6 - 3.4
2.0 - 2.5
1.0 - 1.9

U.S. average = 2.6%

N

0   800
kilometres

Mountain region, for instance, have import production exposures of only 1.8 percent. Clearly, one may presume that, to a commensurate degree, these states' industries are less-threatened by EU competitors.

Figure 2.11 reveals the pronounced pattern of import production exposures across the 38 states and regions. A swath of states with above-average exposure is apparent from south west to north east, encompassing the south western states, some Central states, including Kansas, Oklahoma and Missouri, the eastern Great lakes states, and the north east, including New England but excluding Pennsylvania. Equally remarkable are those regions with below-average import exposures. These include the Southeast, South, and a broad northern tier from Washington to Wisconsin. Evidently, there is a distinct regional pattern in the degree to which states' industries are exposed to competition from the EU.

Net Production Exposure. The export and import production exposures indicate the degree by which trade with the European Union represents positive and negative contributions to the states' industrial economies, respectively. They can be summarized, therefore, by a simple balance--the *net production exposure* reported in Table 2.4. An interesting but potentially ambiguous measure of the regional economies' net exposure to trade with the EU is revealed. The net production exposure is offered not as a definitive statement of the states' trade performance with the EU but rather, in a purely comparative sense, to illustrate simultaneously their net trade orientations toward the EU as well as the importance of this trade to their regional economies.

The U.S. average net production exposure to the EU is -0.2 percent. This reflect the largely balanced US-EU industrial trade relationship although, in 1990, this was slightly negative. Around this mean, there is considerable variation among the states. Once again, the notable outlier is Washington with a net production exposure of 9.6 percent while other relatively high values are reported for Minnesota, Lower New England and the Upper Mountain region with 1.3, 1.2 and 1.2 percent, respectively. At the other extreme, Michigan and Indiana have exposures of -2.6 and -1.6 percent, respectively, indicating their relatively low trading orientation toward the European Union and their high exposure to imports from the EU.

Figure 2.12 reveals a distinct regional pattern of net production exposure to the EU. Regions of above-average exposure include New England (including New York) the South Atlantic (plus Kentucky), Minnesota, Mississippi, and most of the states west of the continental divide. Below-average economic exposure is found in the Middle Atlantic, Midwest, Plains, Southeast and South-Central regions. The

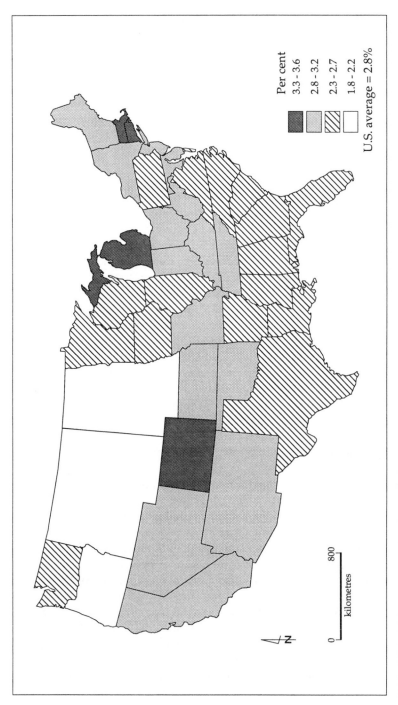

39

Per cent

3.3 - 3.6

2.8 - 3.2

2.3 - 2.7

1.8 - 2.2

U.S. average = 2.8%

0   800

kilometres

N

FIGURE 2.11 Import production exposure to the European Union, 1990.

regional experience of trade with the European Union has clearly very disproportionate effects.

Interpreting the State and Regional Exposure Patterns.. Some general conclusions can be drawn from the exposure patterns across the 38 states and regions. Specifically using these three production exposure measures, six categories of region can be identified. These are illustrated in Figure 2.12 and are defined by above- or below-average export and import production exposures and net production exposures. Also, the states are referred to as having "positive" net production exposures if their values are above average, but not necessarily above zero.

Those regions characterized by positive net production exposure, and both high export and import production exposure, include New England (plus New York), West Virginia, Kentucky, and California, the Southwest and Colorado. This group is distinctly different from the other states with positive net production exposure due to their high import exposure. For these states and regions, their trading relationship with the EU are not only important to their industrial production, but also of a bilateral nature such that it is a highly competitive relationship. The second and third classes both have positive net production exposures and low import exposures. For the second group, in particular, the trading relationship with the EU is one-sided: exports are a substantial proportion of their total output but imports pose comparatively little threat. This class includes the states of the South Atlantic and north west, and Minnesota. For the third group, a positive net production exposure is reported but both export and import exposures are below average. Trade with the EU therefore is generally less important to these states' economies, including just Mississippi and Oregon.

The fourth and fifth groups include states with negative net production exposures. For the fourth group, this grouping results from low export exposures and high import exposures. This class includes the Mid Mountain region, the Central states of Kansas, Oklahoma, Missouri and Tennessee, the eastern Great Lakes states, and Delmar and New Jersey in the Middle Atlantic region. For these, their trading relationship with the EU is comparatively one-sided with exports being relatively unimportant and imports posing a substantial competitive threat. For the final group, both export and import exposures to the EU are below average and a negative net production exposure results. Nevertheless, for these states--including much of the eastern Midwest, South and Southeast, and Pennsylvania--trade with the European Union is a relatively insignificant factor in their

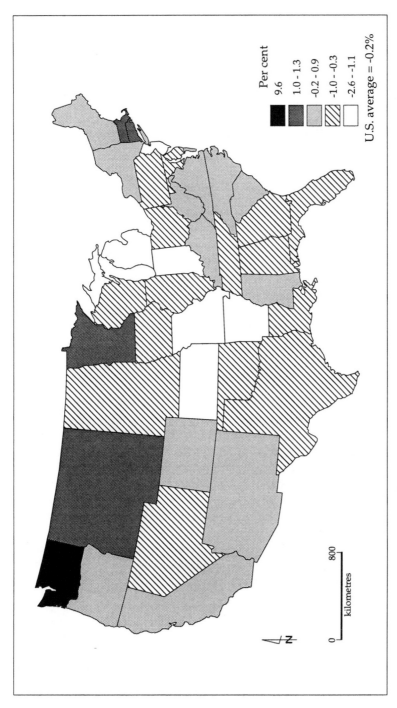

Per cent

9.6

1.0 - 1.3

-0.2 - 0.9

-1.0 - -0.3

-2.6 - -1.1

U.S. average = -0.2%

800

0

kilometres

N

FIGURE 2.12 Net production exposure to the European Union, 1990.

industrial economies.   In this respect, groups three and five are very
much alike.

These patterns of exposure, and particularly the summary
classification scheme presented in Figure 2.13, are interesting and
perhaps should also be quite sobering for policy makers and analysts
concerned with the international dimensions of regional economies.
Clearly, they highlight the considerable variation in the states' trade
relations with the European Union and hence, one must presume, their
exposure to European economic events.

Interpreting the potential impacts of European integration with
these patterns is, however, quite ambiguous.   The measures of exposure
do suggest that those states with a greater export production exposure
to the EU, and especially those with positive net production exposures,
may be in the most favorable position with respect to the EU.   They
are, however, also highly exposed and susceptible to any negative
impacts of the program.   Concomitantly, relatively low exposure
suggests a greater degree of insularity from European events, and given
the uncertainty of such developments, a low dependence on trade with
the EU may also result in less economic disruption.   In short, these
exposure patterns reveal a greater texture to the trading relationships
of states and regions with the EU than might be evident in simple trade
statistics.

Sectoral Variations as a Factor in State Exposures

As has been postulated above, the regional variations in exposure
patterns may be presumed to arise from two sources: either (a)
differences in the exposures of individual industry sectors and the
sectoral mixes of the regions, or (b) through some innate qualities of the
regions themselves, manifest as residual biases in trade orientations.
Owing to the method of calculation, the states' exposure to imports
from the EU are entirely due to the former factors of industry mix and
differential sectoral exposures.   For exports, on the other hand, it is
likely that both of these sources of variation are at play.   In the
following analysis, therefore, attention will be given to the sectoral
pattern of trade with, and exposures to, the European Union and an
analysis of variance will evaluate the importance of sectoral and
regional factors in exposure patterns.

Patterns of Industry Sectors' Trade with the European Union

Trade flows with the European Union by industry sector are reported
in Table 2.5.   With respect to both exports and imports, Industrial

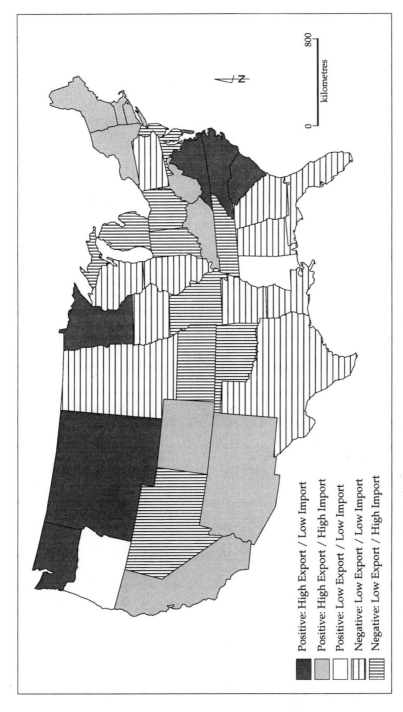

FIGURE 2.13 Types of production exposure to the European Union, 1990.

TABLE 2.5 Trade with the European Union by Industrial Sector, 1983-1990

Industry Sector	Exports to the EU, 1990 ($ millions)	Avg. Ann. Growth, 1983-90 (%)	Share of Total (%)	Imports from the EU, 1990 ($ millions)	Avg. Ann. Growth, 1983-90 (%)	Share of Total (%)	Balance ($ millions)
Food Products	2,503.9	-0.7	16.6	5,063.1	5.0	21.9	-2,559.2
Tobacco Products	1,450.8	23.2	37.9	23.9	-2.5	15.9	1,426.8
Textiles	792.2	13.9	21.6	1,565.0	13.3	18.1	-772.9
Apparel	417.4	19.9	14.6	1,716.5	18.3	6.3	-1,299.1
Lumber	1,035.4	10.5	19.4	245.5	15.1	4.3	789.9
Furniture	167.6	11.1	11.3	1,115.1	16.5	16.9	-947.5
Paper	2,076.7	8.3	26.3	896.8	22.7	6.8	1,179.9
Print/Publishing	602.1	12.8	20.0	696.9	12.4	26.7	-94.8
Chemicals	9,486.1	8.7	27.2	9,204.9	12.1	28.0	281.2
Petroleum/Coal Products	1,360.8	7.6	23.7	2,920.3	7.2	15.7	-1,559.5
Rubber	1,164.5	11.0	19.4	1,871.9	9.7	15.7	-707.4
Leather	323.1	25.2	21.8	2,001.3	7.7	15.1	-1,678.1
Stone/Glass/Clay Prods	609.2	9.6	18.5	2,262.4	11.8	26.8	-1,653.2
Primary Metals	2,116.1	13.1	17.1	4,236.0	1.7	14.3	-2,119.9
Fabric. Metals	1,889.6	15.8	17.7	2,741.1	13.8	17.8	-851.5
Industrial Machinery	17,687.7	8.2	29.5	14,389.2	14.0	19.9	3,298.4
Elect/Electronic Equip	8,042.9	13.1	20.5	5,139.7	15.9	8.2	2,903.2
Transportation Equip	16,664.1	18.2	26.5	18,086.9	13.3	16.6	-1,422.7
Instruments	6,873.8	9.0	36.6	5,019.9	15.1	21.5	1,854.0
Miscellaneous	1,208.8	7.4	22.9	3,886.8	9.7	15.8	-2,678.0
U.S. (48 states)	76,472.7	9.7	25.2	83,083.1	11.1	16.3	-6,610.4

Source: see Appendix 1.

Machinery and Transportation are the largest sectors by value, followed by Chemicals, Electrical and Electronic Equipment, Instruments, Food Products and Primary Metals. However, the trade patterns do vary as Transportation Equipment, Food Products and Primary Metals sectors experienced negative balances. For the former two, these amount to less than one percent of their total output but for the latter, it represents a more substantial amount. For Machinery, Electrical and Electronic Equipment and Instruments, the balances are positive and quite substantial. In contrast, however, Chemicals' positive balance of 0.12% represents an insignificant part of the sectors' total production. Some of the greatest net production exposures are found in the less important sectors. Leather goods, a rather minor trading sector, nevertheless posted a negative balance amounting to 17 percent of its output. In contrast, Tobacco Products, a sector with significant regional importance, experienced a positive balance of over six percent. Evidently, these sectoral variations contribute to the regional differences noted above. Furthermore, a consideration of these sectors' experiences over the period 1983-90 reaffirms this further.

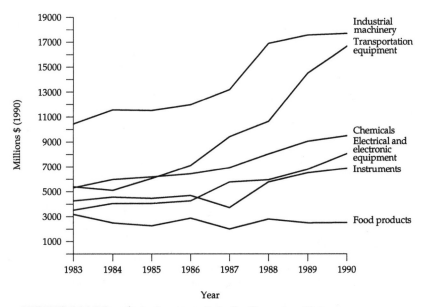

FIGURE 2.14 Manufacturing exports to the European Union for selected industry sectors, 1983-1990.

The changes in the largest EU-exporting sectors since 1983 are indicated in Figure 2.14 With the exception of Food Products only, this period saw considerable growth for all sectors. For Transportation Equipment, and Electrical and Electronic Equipment, in particular, exports in 1990 were more than double those of 1983. The Chemicals sector's experience represents a more typical and even growth pattern, whereas Industrial Machinery and Instruments had more erratic growth trajectories. In both cases, there was relatively little growth through 1986/87 respectively, followed by a sudden spurt and a recent levelling-off once again. Finally, Food Products was the only sector to post an actual decline in exports. This is possibly a reflection of European Union agricultural policies and partly explains the U.S. government's overriding concern for agricultural trade in trans-Atlantic diplomacy.

The equivalent pattern for imports is shown in Figure 2.15. The pattern is noticeably contrary to that for exports noted above. The first half of the period witnessed considerable growth for most sectors that was succeeded by several recent years of little change, or even decline. For most sectors, the period witnessed an absolute growth in imports to

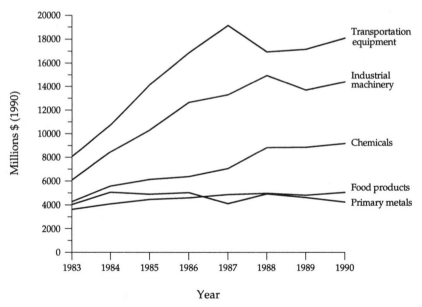

FIGURE 2.15 Manufacturing imports from the European Union
for selected industry sectors, 1983-1990.

levels double those of 1983. Alone among these more important sectors, Primary Metals and Food products experienced little or negative growth, respectively.

Finally, Figure 2.16 illustrates the export-import balances for the largest trading sectors since 1983. There is a distinct pattern of generally positive balances in 1983 declining to low positive or negative balances between 1986/87, and then improving subsequently. The variation across sectors, however, is still quite marked. Instruments maintained a positive balance throughout the 1983-1990 period while Food Products sustained a steadily increasing negative balance. In contrast, both Industrial Machinery and Electrical and Electroinc Equipment experienced precipitous declines into negative balances before resuming their original levels. For Chemicals, the balance remained close to zero throughout, while for Transportation Equipment, a substantial negative balance declined to an extraordinary deficit before improving to a level comparable to that of 1983.

The trading patterns of this particular period is, of course, merely a snapshot in time and so statements on the long-term trends in US-EU trade will be avoided. Of more immediate interest for the purposes of this project, however, are the great variations evident among and between sectors since these indicate the potential volatility of trading patterns for regions.

Sectoral Exposures to EU Trade. The production exposure values for individual sectors are reported in Table 2.6. There is considerable sectoral variation in exposure patterns. The U.S. average for export production exposure is 2.6 percent but the values for individual sectors varies from as much as 6.8 and 5.9 percent for Machinery and Tobacco Products, respectively, to as little as 0.4 and 0.6 percent for Printing and Apparel, respectively. For import production exposures, a similarly wide variation around the U.S. mean of 2.8 percent is found. Leather Goods and the Miscellaneous Manufactures category have values of 18.1 and 10.3 percent, respectively, while for Tobacco and Lumber, the values are just 0.1 and 0.3 percent, respectively. As might be anticipated, these values result in equally-dispersed net production exposure values (ie, balances). Apart from the extreme values for some of the relatively minor trading sectors such as Leather Goods (-15.1 percent), Miscellaneous Manufactures (-7.1 percent), and Tobacco (5.8 percent), the net production exposures are less dramatic for the more important sectors. Of the two largest trading sectors with respect to the EU, Industrial Machinery and Transportation Equipment have exposures of 1.3 and -0.4 percent, respectively. Similarly, for Food Products, the value is slightly negative, while for Chemicals it is

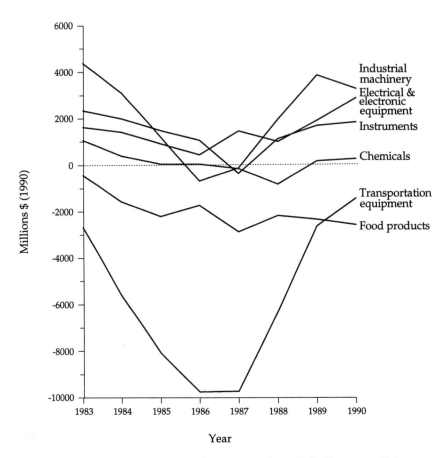

FIGURE 2.16 The balance of manufacturing trade with the European Union for selected industries, 1983-1990.

TABLE 2.6 Production Exposure to the European Union by Sector

	EU Export Production Exposure (%)	EU Import Production Exposure (%)	Net Production Exposure (%)
Food Products	0.6	1.3	-0.7
Tobacco Products	5.9	0.1	5.8
Textiles	1.1	2.1	-1.0
Apparel	0.6	2.2	-1.7
Lumber	1.2	0.3	1.0
Furniture	0.4	2.5	-2.1
Paper	1.6	0.7	0.9
Printing/Publishing	0.4	0.4	-0.1
Chemical Products	3.5	3.3	0.1
Petroleum/Coal Products	0.9	1.9	-1.0
Rubber Products	1.1	1.8	-0.7
Leather Goods	2.9	18.1	-15.1
Stone/Glass/Clay Products	0.8	3.0	-2.2
Primary Metal Products	1.5	3.0	-1.5
Fabricated Metal Products	1.1	1.6	-0.5
Industrial Machinery	6.8	5.5	1.3
Electrical and Electronic Equipment	3.9	2.5	1.4
Transportation Equip.	4.2	4.6	-0.4
Instruments	5.3	3.9	1.4
Miscellaneous	3.2	10.3	-7.1
U.S. Average	2.6	2.8	-0.2

Source: see Appendix 1.

marginally positive, and for both Electrical and Electronic Equipment and Instruments economic exposures are positive.

From these exposure values, one may presume that sectoral patterns of exposure themselves account for much of the variation among regions. It is of particular interest therefore to discern the relative importance of sectoral versus regional variations in accounting for the pattern of exposures across the entire regional and sectoral data matrix.

Evaluating Regional Versus Sectoral Factors in Exposure Patterns

The proposition concerning the relative importance of regional and sectoral factors in exposure patterns may be tested with the application of a two-way analysis of variance procedure. The full data set contains 760 observations--38 states and regions and 20 sectors--and each of the four exposure measures may be calculated for individual state/region-by-sector cells. It has been noted above that, given the method of estimating regional imports, the variation among regions is entirely attributable to sectoral variations filtered through the regions' industrial mix. That being the case, the analysis will consider just the export trade, export production and net production exposure measures.

Two-way analysis of variance is a common technique used for analyzing research data that have two classification variables, in this case, regions and sectors.[2] The analysis examines the variances of the values of the specified variable (exposure) within the categories defined by each classification variable. With this technique, it is possible to statistically test the significance of each classification variable in accounting for the variance in the research variable. In this case, we wish to test the significance of regions and sectors in accounting for the variations in exposure. At the outset the null hypothesis (H_0) is specified: that neither of the classification variables account for significant proportions of the variance in exposure. Correspondingly, two alternative hypotheses are specified:

> H_1 that there are significant variations in exposure among the sectors, taking the regions into account.

> H_2 that there are significant variations in exposure among the regions, taking the sectors into account.

The results of the analysis of variance are F statistics which may be compared to F distribution tables in order to accept or reject the hypotheses according to the critical values corresponding to a desired level of significance. The Statistical Analysis System (SAS)[3] procedure ANOVA was employed and the results are presented in Table 2.7. For each model specified, the exposure values were inspected for their conformity to normal distributions

Analyses were conducted for export trade exposure, export production exposure, and net production Exposure. For each, two analyses were conducted, the first using the 38 state/regions and the 20 industry sectors as the independent variables and, in the second, using the five exposure types identified above in Figure 2.13 and the 20 industry sectors. For each model tested (I through VI) the degrees of freedom, F statistic, and probability level for rejecting the null hypothesis, are given in Table 2.7. For this analysis, the 95 percent significance level for rejecting the null hypothesis is used which is equivalent to a

TABLE 2.7 Results of the Two-Way Analysis of Variance

A. 38 States/Regions and 20 Industrial Sectors

Model I: Export Trade Exposure, 1990

	Degrees of Freedom	F	Probability Level
SECTOR	19	6.12	0.0001
STATE	37	2.45	0.0001

Model II: Export Production Exposure, 1990

	Degrees of Freedom	F	Probability Level
SECTOR	19	1.74	0.0267
STATE	37	1.21	0.1864

Model III: Economic Exposure, 1990

	Degrees of Freedom	F	Probability Level
SECTOR	19	2.63	0.0002
STATE	37	1.21	0.1880

B. 5 Exposure Types (EXPOTYPE) and 20 Industrial Sectors

Model IV: Export Trade Exposure, 1990

	Degrees of Freedom	F	Probability Level
SECTOR	19	6.12	0.0001
EXPOTYPE	4	3.37	0.0095

Model V: Export Production Exposure, 1990

	Degrees of Freedom	F	Probability Level
SECTOR	19	1.74	0.0267
EXPOTYPE	4	2.91	0.0211

Model VI: Economic Exposure, 1990

	Degrees of Freedom	F	Probability Level
SECTOR	19	2.63	0.0002
EXPOTYPE	4	2.85	0.0233

critical probability level of 0.0500. For results below this level, the null hypothesis may be rejected.

In each of the six models, one is able to reject the null hypothesis and accept the first alternative hypothesis (H_1), that there is significant variation in exposure among the sectors, taking the regions into account. Thus, the SECTOR classification variable was proven to contribute significantly to the variation in exposure and one may conclude that sectoral variations in exposures is a significant factor in regional patterns.

However, it is also apparent from these results that the regions themselves account for much of the total variation even taking sectoral variation into account. Among the first three models, however, specifying the 38 states and regions as the regional classification variable, for only Model I is one able to reject the null hypothesis and accept H_2, that regional variation is significant. Thus in only the case of trade exposure can the states themselves be considered statistically significant in accounting for variations. This is understandable when using as a classification variable with 38 different values. For Models IV, V and VI, however, one is able to reject the null hypothesis in each case, and accept that the exposure type (EXPOTYPE) classification, wherein regions are classified according to the exposure patterns identified above, significantly accounts for some of the variation in exposure.

These results confirm the proposition made above, that regional variations in exposure are attributable to both the sectors and inherent biases among the regions themselves. While the individual states and regions appear to be significant factors for only the trade exposure case, distinct types of regions are a significant explanatory factor in every case. The implications of this result for the research is that, while sectoral patterns of exposure are key factors in the regional pattern of exposure to the European Union, one cannot overlook residual regional biases. The relative importance of sectoral and regional effects will be evaluated further when the international trade shift-share model is applied to these data in Chapter 3.

Summary: States, Trade and the European Union

The discussion above has attempted to reveal the texture of the trading relationship between U.S. states and the European Union. Attention has focussed on the comparative exposures of the states to this trade rather than on absolute trade values. It is evident that there is considerable variation in the overall trade experiences of the states, and also that in respect to the EU.

The data employed has been compiled carefully in order to overcome the well-recognised limitations with published trade data. Of particular interest is the treatment of imports wherein state-level imports are developed from total U.S. imports and the states' industrial production data. In addition to compensating for otherwise non-existent data this method also produces data upon which meaningful state trade balances can be based. In contrast to the use of such balances elsewhere the implication of negative trade balances using these data (in Table 2.2, for instance) is a comparatively poor performance of local industries with respect to exports and/or in competition with imports nationally. In other words, it is a *production* balance and has no relevance for the states' consumers. The trade balances with the EU are reported in Table 2.2 and some significant regional patterns emerge. In general, substantial negative balances are revealed in the states of the north east, Midwest and south central regions. In contrast, positive balances are reported by New England, the Southeast and western regions among other states.

In this chapter the relative importance of trade with all nations was first examined, followed by a specific attention to that with the EU. Various exposure measures revealed those states most heavily engaged in exports and those experiencing the greatest competition from imports. Through combining these measures the states can be classified according to their overall trade experiences. Distinct regional patterns are revealed in Figure 2.13 where states with positive net production exposures (and positive trade balances with the EU) are found almost exclusively in the New England, South Atlantic and western regions. In all cases a high export exposure is found although in the former and in the south west this is matched by a high exposure to imports. In these areas a fairly deep and bilateral trade relationship exists with the European Union. In the other areas with positive net production exposures a one-sided trade relationship is revealed.

In the Middle Atlantic and throughout the Midwest and south, negative net production exposure values are found. These areas perform comparatively poorly in trade with the EU while in some of the Mid western states this is compounded by a heavy exposure to European imports. Clearly the trade experiences of the states vary quite markedly, and this variation is regional in nature.

These findings add greater depth to the observations of Woodward (1990) who observed the comparatively strong EU trade orientations of the east and west coast regions. Likewise, the importance of industry sectors and their widely different trade performances was considered.

It is evident that much of the pattern is attributable to the differential competitiveness of industries, and when coupled with the differing industrial structures of the states this factor accounts for a great deal. However, the relative importance of these two factors--regions versus industry sectors--is not clear from these data. In the following chapter the growth in output and trade is modelled with the specific intention of identifying this.

The data reported in this chapter and the analysis undertaken offers a more refined description of the trade experience of the states than that which has formerly been used. This is not least because the data themselves have been adjusted to ameliorate the biases which are too often overlooked. In addition, however, the analysis has employed standardized measures throughout in order to highlight the *real* patterns which are too easily obscured by absolute, raw data.

Nevertheless, the measures used are relatively simple and can easily be replicated for subsequent years as newer data becomes available. It is felt that these measures are more appropriate than raw trade data and ought to be employed in the first instance to examine trade patterns, thereby better informing policy discussions concerning trade.

Notes

1 There are plans to produce data on the states of destination for U.S. imports but these would be of most value for the study of commodity flows and transportation.

2 For reference, see Norcliffe (1977).

3 Documented in SAS Institute Inc. (1988) pp. 125-154.

3

The Trade Component of Regional Economic Growth

Analyzing Regional Economic Growth through Shift-Share Analysis

The analysis in Chapter 2 revealed considerable variation among the individual states and regions with respect to their trading relations with the European Union. This illustrated the current orientation of states toward the EU, that is, a snap shot view of the varied importance of trade. Implicit in this was a belief that trade also represents a significant factor in regional economic growth. In this chapter this proposition will be examined and, specifically, an attempt will be made to quantify the contribution of trade to the recent economic growth of the thirty-eight states and regions. To do so, a well-understood technique--shift-share analysis--is employed in an extended form to identify the unique contribution of trade.

Shift-Share Analysis

Shift-share analysis is a well-established technique which attempts to decompose regional economic growth into its constituent parts. The operating premise is that a region's employment (or output) growth over time (*positive* or *negative*) may be apportioned between one of three components. In the first of these, the region is presumed to experience similar growth effects to the nation as a whole and so the *national* shift component reflects the share attributable to the underlying national growth. Second, the *industrial-mix* shift component reflects the separate growth rates of industrial sectors such that each region's unique industrial mix yields an equally unique pattern of aggregate growth rates. Finally, any residual growth (or decline)--that portion remaining after deducting the national and industrial shift components from the region's actual growth--is presumed to reflect the region's unique experience. This is referred to as either the *regional* or *competitive* shift component as it reflects the growth attributable to changes in the region's unique competitive position. The shift-share method of decomposing economic growth affords an explanation of growth patterns in an historical sense, as well as offering a method of forecasting future growth. The shift-share approach has been widely employed since its first appearance in the 1960s and has spurred lively debate among proponents and critics:

> Shift-share fits the expectation that, when a technique is simple and apparently useful, it will be both widely used and heavily criticised. (Fothergill and Gudgin 1979, p. 309)

The basis for most criticisms of the technique is that it is an empirical device having no real grounding in theory. Stilwell (1970) went so far as to claim that it had "little relevance to the theory of regional growth" (p. 451) although, nevertheless, he defended its application *ex post* and its usefulness in forecasting. Richardson (1978a), however, is less generous in his criticism, describing it as "a harmless pastime for small boys with pocket calculators" (p. 202). For him, the absence of theory is a chronic weakness and the results of decomposing regional economic growth are illusory; he pleads: "is it not time to abandon this primitive standardization technique in favor of more reliable methods of regional analysis with more content?" (1978b, p. 20) In the face of such vociferous opposition, Fothergill and Gudgin (1979) make the standard defense of the technique by citing its efficacy as a tool in the analysis of regional growth. In their research on the U.K. they find that in comparison to other techniques, such as analysis of variance, it is found to be "robust."

Nevertheless, care must be taken in its application and particularly in the level of aggregation of the industry sectors used. The technique is vulnerable to the type of industrial classification used such that the relative values of the three components vary with different levels of disaggregation . This is a frequent problem when applying shift-share analysis in practice, as the level of aggregation is usually dictated by the available data.

The Basic Shift-Share Model. The basic shift-share model has been successively revised and extended to counter its perceived weaknesses and to adapt to specific cases. The continued widespread use of the model is testimony to both its usefulness and its efficacy in highlighting the structure of regional economies. Typically, the subject of shift-share models is employment change although output growth may be used instead as an alternative measure of regional economic growth. Changes in employment and production are obviously closely linked; the former being largely dependent upon the latter as well as to changes in labor productivity. In the following analysis the database contains information on exports, imports and production values. To specify a model of employment change would require the inclusion of information on productivity changes as well--which was the case for Markusen et al. (1991). However, output change is an important factor in regional economies in its own right since it directly affects not only employment but tax receipts and local investment levels. It is, therefore, the object of analysis in this research.

A simple shift-share model for changes in output can be represented as follows:

$$Q_r = \sum_i Q_{ri0} + \sum_i Q_{rio}(q_i - q) + \sum_i Q_{rio}(q_{ri} - q_i) \qquad (2.1)$$

where Q_r is net output change in region r, i represents industry sectors, 0 represents the initial time period, and q is output growth over the period. Growth rates are calculated thus:

$$q = \frac{(Q_t - Q_0)}{Q_0} \qquad (2.2)$$

where t represents a later time period.

Net output change (Q_r) is the sum of three separate components. The first of these is the *national* shift component, calculated as a function of the region's output in the initial period and the national growth rate, summed across all industry sectors. This measures the regional economic growth that would have occurred had all the industries of the region grown at the national rate. It represents, therefore, that part of the *net output change* attributable to national growth effects. The second component is the *industrial-mix* shift, in which the growth rate is calculated as the difference between national growth rates and those of specific industry sectors. This figure represents that portion of actual growth attributable to the region's specific industrial mix. It may have positive or negative values as it represents a deviation from the national--ie, average--trend. Finally, the third component captures the remainder, the residual change in output, which is deemed to be due to the region's unique competitive position. This *regional* shift component is calculated as a function of the region's initial output and a growth rate measured as the difference between the (national) industrial sectors' and the region's own sectors' growth rates. Together, these three components account for the entire change in a region's output over the specified time period.

Extending the Model to Include the Effects of Trade. Over time a number of enhancements have been made to the basic model. Of particular interest for the present topic, is the incorporation of external trade into the model. Markusen, et al. (1991) achieved this by further decomposing the national and industrial-mix shift effects into separate export, import and domestic demand components. Domestic demand (*D*) is calculated according to the convention in national income accounts: total output (*Q*), *minus* exports (*X*--as these are attributable to foreign demand), *plus* imports (*M*--as these are a response to demand in the domestic market). The formula is simply:

$$D_t = Q_t - X_t + M_t \tag{2.3}$$

In Markusen et al.'s (1991) model, international trade effects on regional economies are estimated as distinct from those attributable to domestic economic growth. In this specification, both the national and industrial-mix shift components are each decomposed into a further four components: the (1) export, (2) import, and (3) domestic demand components, as well as (4) a labor productivity shift component. The latter adjusts for the latent employment shift accruing to changes in labor productivity. This was necessary as Markusen et al.'s analysis was concerned with employment change although it analysed production and trade data. As was noted above, if the focus is upon changes in output rather than employment these labor productivity considerations are unnecessary. Thus is the present case, and so using this same methodology would leave us with three national shift components, three industrial-mix shift components, and the regional (or competitive) shift component. Figure 3.1 describes the shift-share components for a Markusen-type specification for a change in output.

This methodology may be profitably applied to the present topic where it can be further decomposed to account for different foreign export destinations and import origins. Following Markusen et al.'s (1991) logic, the export and import components may be divided into those attributable to the European Union and the remainder, which are associated with all other destinations. In this way, the regional economic impacts of EU-related trade may be identified separately from those for other trading partners, and those attributable to domestic demand. With this innovation, our shift-share model is extended to 11 separate components: 5 national and 5 industrial-mix shift components, and the regional shift.

FIGURE 3.1 Incorporating International Trade Effects in the Shift-Share Model

---

National Export Shift

$$NX = \sum_i Q_{ri0}\left[\frac{X_0}{Q_0}x\right]$$

National Import Shift

$$NM = \sum_i Q_{ri0}\left[\frac{M_0}{Q_0}m\right]$$

National Domestic Demand
   Shift

$$ND = \sum_i Q_{ri0}\left[\frac{D_0}{Q_0}d\right]$$

Industrial-Mix Export Shift

$$IX = \sum_i Q_{ri0}\left[\left(\frac{X_{i0}}{Q_{i0}}x_i\right)-\left(\frac{X_0}{Q_0}x\right)\right]$$

Industrial-Mix Import Shift

$$IM = \sum_i Q_{ri0}\left[\left(\frac{M_{i0}}{Q_{i0}}m_i\right)-\left(\frac{M_0}{Q_0}m\right)\right]$$

Industrial-Mix Domestic
   Demand Shift

$$ID = \sum_i Q_{ri0}\left[\left(\frac{D_{i0}}{Q_{i0}}d_i\right)-\left(\frac{D_0}{Q_0}d\right)\right]$$

Regional/Competitive Shift

$$R = \sum_i Q_{ri0}\left[q_{ri}-q_i\right]$$

Where:

$Qi0$ is the total value of output in region r, and industry i, in period 0.
$X0$ is the total value of U.S. exports in the initial period.
$Q0$ is the total value of U.S. output in the initial period.
x is the national growth rate of exports.
$M0$ is the total value of U.S. imports in the initial period.
m is the national growth rate of imports.
$D0$ is the total value of U.S. domestic demand in the initial period.
d is the national growth rate of domestic demand.
$Xi0$ is the value of U.S. exports in industry i and period 0.
xi is the growth rate of exports by industry sector, i.
$Xri0$ is the value of exports in region r, industry i, and period 0.
xri is the growth rate of exports in region r and industry sector, i.

with other variables following a similar nomenclature.

Decomposing the Regional Shift. In most applications of the shift-share model, including Markusen et al. (1991) and Barff and Knight (1988), the regional or competitive shift component is usually found to be a substantial portion of the total shift. Interpretations of based upon these analyses usually conclude that for many regions their unique competitive shifts account for much of their growth experience. As a result, the regional shift component is of particular interest as it reflects the particular qualities of individual regions. Fothergill and Gudgin (1982, pp. 153-169) examined the regional shifts for individual regions of England as evidence of a spatial relocation of manufacturing activity from northern to southern regions, while in Markusen et al. (1991) the regional shift were viewed as evidence of a Sunbelt-Frostbelt dichotomy in the economic performances of U.S. regions. This component, however, embodies the regions' unique performances in respect to many dimensions.

With the present database, however, the actual export flows from the states are known, and so the regional shift component may be further decomposed, too. Specifically, the effects of exports can be removed from the component to produce three separate components: the EU export regional shift, the non-EU export regional shift, and the balance, the domestic demand regional shift component. The former two are calculated much as the industrial-mix shifts: as the product of *regional* growth rates and the initial state outputs, summed across all the sectors. The regional growth rates are measured as the deviation from the individual industry growth rates; ie, the difference between actual growth rates and the industry growth rates. The third shift is the residual after accounting for all others. Owing to the method of accounting for state imports it may be presumed that the effect of imports is absorbed by the national and industrial-mix shifts and that it would be misleading to specify separate import regional shift components. Nevertheless, with this further extension of the basic model a total of 13 separate components are specified and these are described in Figure 3.2.

A further improvement over the basic shift-share model is the use of a *dynamic* rather than a *comparative-static* method for calculating the shift components. In the latter, trade and output values are taken for only the initial and final years of the period under analysis, and growth rates are calculated from these for the period as a whole. However, in the dynamic model specified by Barff and Knight (1988), growth rates are recalculated for each incremental year over the period, thereby allowing growth rates and industry-mixes to vary over the period of analysis. It is argued that this dynamic method, while requiring considerably more computing, nevertheless obtains more meaningful components since they more accurately reflect the changing industrial structures of the regions. In the following analysis this method was employed.

The national shift components as described in Figure 3.2 illustrate the proportion of the regional change in the value of output attributable to national growth effects. Across all the regions under study, the national effects will be proportionally equal, varying in magnitude only as a result of the different sizes of regional output in the initial period. The two export shift components represent that share attributable to national export growth. These are calculated as a function of the national growth rates for each type of export, the proportion of total output accounted for by that type of export in the initial period, and the actual value of regional output. In a typical situation where national exports grew over a period under study, the export shift components would be positive values for all regions. The import shift components are calculated similarly but are given a negative value since imports detract from regional productive economies. The domestic demand shift components, too, are calculated by a similar method and represent that proportion of regional output growth attributable to the growth in national domestic demand.

The industrial-mix shift components illustrate the combined effects of regions' industrial mixes and differential industry-sector growth rates. The difference between industry sector and national growth rates are applied to the regions' sectoral output totals and summed for all sectors. The net shift, in each case, reflects not only the differential sectoral growth rates but also the magnitudes of each region's sectoral output values. In the formulas expressed in Figure 3.2, EU and non-EU import shifts are specified as negative values, however the net values of any of the five industrial shift components may be either positive or negative. It is important to note that these components do not themselves represent the sum of a region's export, import or domestic demand growth but instead, they indicate the deviation of the region's economic growth from the national mean that is attributable to the its industrial structure.

In a similar manner, the regional shift components represent that part of the regions' growth in output not attributable to national or industrial sector trends. The EU export shift component measures the extent to which regions' growth differs from that accounted for by sectoral growth. This calculation is an innovative feature of the present shift-share model and is made possible through the availability of actual regional export data. For instance, in Markusen et al. (1991), only aggregate national trade data were available and so the regional shift could not be decomposed into export shifts. The EU-

FIGURE 3.2 The Extended International Shift-Share Model

National Shifts

European Union
Export Shift

$$NXE = \sum_i Q_{ri0}\left[\frac{XE_0}{Q_0}\,xe\right]$$

Non-EU Export
Shift

$$NXN = \sum_i Q_{ri0}\left[\frac{XN_0}{Q_0}\,xn\right]$$

European Union
Import Shift

$$NME = \sum_i Q_{ri0}\left[\frac{ME_0}{Q_0}\,me\right]$$

Non-EU Import
Shift

$$NMN = \sum_i Q_{ri0}\left[\frac{MN_0}{Q_0}\,mn\right]$$

National Domestic
Demand Shift

$$ND = \sum_i Q_{ri0}\left[\frac{D_0}{Q_0}\,d\right]$$

Industrial-Mix Shifts

European Union
Export Shift

$$IXE = \sum_i Q_{ri0}\left[\left(\frac{XE_{i0}}{Q_{i0}}\,xe_i\right)-\left(\frac{XE_0}{Q_0}\,xe\right)\right]$$

Non-EU Export
Shift

$$IXN = \sum_i Q_{ri0}\left[\left(\frac{XN_{i0}}{Q_{i0}}\,xn_i\right)-\left(\frac{XN_0}{Q_0}\,xn\right)\right]$$

European Union
Import Shift

$$IME = \sum_i Q_{ri0}\left[\left(\frac{ME_{i0}}{Q_{i0}}\,me_i\right)-\left(\frac{ME_0}{Q_0}\,me\right)\right]$$

Non-EU Import
Shift

$$IMN = \sum_i Q_{ri0}\left[\left(\frac{MN_{i0}}{Q_{i0}}\,mn_i\right)-\left(\frac{MN_0}{Q_0}\,mn\right)\right]$$

Industrial Domestic
Demand Shift

$$ID = \sum_i Q_{ri0}\left[\left(\frac{D_{i0}}{Q_{i0}}\,d_i\right)-\left(\frac{D_0}{Q_0}\,d\right)\right]$$

(continues)

Figure 3.2 (*continued*)

Regional Shifts

European Union
    Export Shift

$$RXE = \sum_i Q_{ri0}\left[\left(\frac{XE_{ri0}}{Q_{ri0}} xe_{ri}\right) - \left(\frac{XE_{i0}}{Q_{i0}} xe_i\right)\right]$$

Non-EU Export
    Shift

$$RXN = \sum_i Q_{ri0}\left[\left(\frac{XN_{ri0}}{Q_{ri0}} xn_{ri}\right) - \left(\frac{XN_{i0}}{Q_{i0}} xn_i\right)\right]$$

Domestic Demand
    Shift

$$RD = \sum_i \left[Q_{ri0}(q_{ri} - q_i) - RXE - RNE\right]$$

Where:

Q_{ri0} is the total value of output in region r, and industry i, in period 0.

$XE0$ is the total value of U.S. exports to the EU in the initial period.

$Q0$ is the total value of U.S. output in the initial period.

xe is the national growth rate of exports to the EU.

$XN0$ is the total value of U.S. exports to non-EU countries in the initial period.

xn is the national growth rate of exports to non-EU countries.

$ME0$ is the total value of U.S. imports from the EU in the initial period.

me is the national growth rate of imports from the EU.

$MN0$ is the total value of U.S. imports from non-EU countries in the initial period.

mn is the national growth rate of imports from non-EU countries.

$D0$ is the total value of U.S. domestic demand in the initial period.

d is the national growth rate of domestic demand.

XE_{i0} is the value of U.S. exports to the EU in industry i and period 0.

xe_i is the growth rate of exports to the EU by industry sector, i.

XE_{ri0} is the value of exports to the EU in region r, industry i, and period 0.

xe_{ri} is the growth rate of exports to the EU in region r and industry sector, i.

with other variables following a similar nomenclature.

and non-EU regional shift components, therefore, illustrate that part of the total regional shift--ie, the regions' unique competitive position-- that is attributable specifically to the regions' export trade relations with the EU and other countries, respectively. The final, domestic demand regional shift component measures the regional economic growth not accounted for by national or industrial trends, and the two export regional shifts. This component therefore represents the shifts due to the regions' unique competitive position with respect to both imports and domestic demand, but is measured simply as the residual.

Taken together, these thirteen components account for the total growth in regional output over a specified period. Applying this model to the present data, the growth in value of manufacturing output between 1983 and 1990 can be modelled, and the relative importance of exports, imports and domestic demand, as well as that of national, sectoral and regional effects, may be revealed for each of the 38 states and regions.

Modelling the Contribution of Trade to Growth, 1983-1990

The application of the shift-share model is undertaken in two stages in order to pursue two specific goals. First, an eight-component model is specified which comprises export, import and domestic demand shift components of both *national* and *industrial-mix* types, plus export and domestic demand *regional* shift components. In this first model, the exports and imports components are not sub-divided into EU and non-EU related shifts and so it is a simpler version of the model specified in Figure 3.2. The purpose of this application is to demonstrate the value of the international trade form of the shift-share model in identifying the unique contributions of trade in regional economic growth.

In the second stage of this analysis, the extended, 13 component model is used. In this stage, the trade components are sub-divided into EU and non-EU related trade. With this analysis, the unique contributions of trade with the European Union are isolated as distinct from those attributable to other foreign trading partners. The two models are otherwise identical and so the three domestic demand shift components in each are equal, and the trade components in the former equal the sum of the respective EU and non-EU components in the latter.

The Role of International Trade in Regional Economic Growth

The reduced, eight-component shift-share model was applied to the state trade database for the years 1983 through 1990. The results of this application are reported in Tables 3.1a and 3.1b. In the former the shifts are expressed as actual dollar values (millions) while in the latter, these are expressed as percentages of the total economic shift of the states over this period. Each shift component represents that portion of the states' manufacturing growth (in 1990 dollars) attributable to each component of the regional economy. Together, these sum to the states' total growth over the period; in Table 3.1b, therefore, the shifts sum to 100 percent.

National Trends in Regional Economic Growth. The three national shift components are proportionally the same for each state with respect to their manufacturing output in 1983, the initial year. Owing to the differential growth experiences, these national shifts represent varying proportions of the states' total shift. This value represents the share of output growth attributable to the national growth in exports; ie, the growth in output each state might have expected had they grown at a rate equal to the U.S. as a whole. In every case, the national export shift component is a positive value, since exports represent a positive contribution to the states' manufacturing output and at the national level, U.S. exports experienced a positive growth during this period. The states' export shift components vary considerably, amounting to between 7.40 and 44.53 percent (Georgia and Louisiana, respectively). Without resort to the other components, interpreting these values is ambiguous at best but they nevertheless form part of the developing picture of state economic growth.

The national import shift components similarly represent the regional economic impact of the growth in imports if it were equally spread among the states. Since imports represent a negative impact on regional economies--competing as they do with local producers--and total U.S. imports grew over this period, they are measured as negative values. The magnitudes, however, are approximately three times those of the exports shift components indicating the respective growth rates of imports and exports. The import shift components vary from 21.81 to 140.20 percent of the states' total output shift. It should be noted that in the case of Louisiana, Oklahoma and Texas, each of the eight shift components are exceedingly large. These cases may be explained by the particularly low growths in manufacturing output experienced by these three states, such that each component is relatively large relative to the comparatively small net growth.

The national domestic demand component may be interpreted similarly; since total domestic demand grew during this period it, too, is a positive value in all cases. In magnitude, however, the domestic demand shift components are almost four times the national import shifts and eleven times those of exports. This, therefore, is

TABLE 3.1a The International Trade Shift-Share Model (all values in millions of dollars)

	National Shifts			Industry-Mix Shifts			Regional Shifts		Total
	Exports	Imports	Domestic Demand	Exports	Imports	Domestic Demand	Exports	Domestic Demand	
Alabama	1,366.9	-4,129.6	15,473.5	-135.0	426.4	-559.6	-737.9	1,976.8	13,806.7
Arkansas	856.3	-2,550.7	9,552.2	-137.9	336.2	-216.2	-1,269.8	1,755.5	8,523.7
California	8,476.3	-25,507.3	95,413.7	769.5	-1,751.7	-1,785.6	3,636.9	6,494.5	84,618.0
Colorado	798.2	-2,365.8	8,760.0	-65.5	-423.5	2,481.3	-451.7	-1,343.6	7,454.5
Florida	1,859.7	-5,504.6	20,871.2	3.2	-102.2	1,577.4	417.5	4,383.1	23,756.5
Georgia	2,441.6	-7,193.5	27,748.4	90.4	317.7	352.3	503.7	8,725.9	33,097.7
Illinois	4,402.4	-14,035.9	52,220.6	-463.8	1,094.2	-1,739.0	1,539.6	-6,435.6	36,712.1
Indiana	2,808.2	-8,614.7	32,111.2	442.7	131.4	-2,132.8	-2,781.7	4,491.5	27,106.5
Iowa	1,222.3	-3,736.4	13,753.9	-333.9	538.8	-203.1	-200.2	-2,236.3	8,788.2
Kansas	1,021.8	-3,400.6	12,554.7	-172.6	280.2	-960.4	-50.6	-1,216.6	8,226.3
Kentucky	1,395.5	-4,205.7	15,704.9	319.3	-128.2	-416.4	1,116.9	1,554.1	14,873.0
Louisiana	1,872.8	-5,896.6	20,639.8	-1,019.8	3,411.7	-13,379.5	-1,560.1	137.6	4,683.5
Massachusetts	2,019.0	-6,559.5	24,673.0	369.4	-2,672.6	6,428.5	-1,932.0	-636.9	21,829.6
Michigan	4,672.4	-14,907.3	56,763.3	2,128.4	-4,720.9	10,355.5	-9,607.6	8,254.0	55,374.5
Minnesota	1,580.5	-4,786.5	17,985.8	-220.4	246.2	871.9	1,613.0	125.8	16,801.0
Mississippi	826.2	-2,514.5	9,301.4	-168.7	414.5	-1,615.6	19.7	1,343.5	7,513.0
Missouri	1,880.8	-6,025.7	23,109.3	546.8	-1,095.7	2,640.9	-901.7	3,649.4	23,973.8
New Jersey	2,833.2	-8,675.2	31,968.8	-379.4	49.3	1,690.8	-2,754.6	-3,078.3	22,501.0
New York	4,802.0	-15,416.7	57,584.6	-450.8	-4,262.3	17,723.4	-687.8	-18,320.2	41,399.7

(continues)

Table 3.1a (*continued*)

North Carolina	3,121.1	-9,243.3	35,227.7	667.3	619.3	226.4	-492.8	8,179.2	38,144.0
Ohio	5,211.2	-16,048.1	60,341.6	1,041.8	-888.2	1,325.1	2,161.2	3,800.4	57,424.9
Oklahoma	836.5	-2,721.1	9,790.5	-13.8	107.3	-1,560.0	-201.0	-2,281.9	3,965.7
Oregon	847.1	-2,437.7	9,256.0	-141.2	813.1	1,165.7	207.0	335.1	10,109.6
Pennsylvania	4,012.1	-12,545.3	46,455.4	-548.5	694.1	-1,410.6	-1,473.8	-3,746.9	31,893.1
South Carolina	1,357.8	-3,964.7	15,170.8	-120.6	184.8	527.0	1,566.3	1,485.0	15,788.7
Tennessee	1,881.1	-5,715.9	21,751.4	-73.8	-336.1	1,003.8	43.8	3,527.7	22,214.3
Texas	5,802.5	-18,877.5	66,997.8	-2,075.3	6,512.4	-27,436.4	650.4	-12,693.7	19,345.3
Virginia	1,689.7	-5,127.4	19,518.4	248.7	952.7	-13.7	-271.2	2,982.2	19,842.9
Washington	1,530.2	-4,662.0	17,705.2	17.5	603.2	-614.5	9,416.2	-8,410.3	11,709.4
West Virginia	385.5	-1,218.3	4,549.8	-31.2	278.0	-225.3	-390.3	-237.8	3,102.0
Wisconsin	2,281.3	-7,047.1	26,595.6	-49.6	-284.5	1,889.4	-560.4	1,955.4	24,789.1
Delmar	1,300.5	-3,954.4	14,715.1	25.5	162.2	184.4	-187.7	83.8	12,541.8
Lower New England	1,526.4	-4,917.4	18,465.4	204.6	-2,025.4	5,158.8	255.6	-5,245.4	12,972.0
Mid Mountain	411.3	-1,380.5	5,137.3	-91.9	70.2	-496.3	-187.2	-1.8	3,435.2
Southwest	825.4	-2,361.3	9,017.8	229.2	-289.7	-337.3	169.9	3,421.6	10,491.7
Upper Mountain	447.0	-1,351.3	4,894.1	-249.7	782.1	-1,547.6	933.6	-1,259.0	2,442.2
Upper New England	920.1	-2,640.8	10,079.0	190.1	-736.7	1,345.5	2,165.5	-330.1	10,877.1
Upper Plains	744.7	-2,388.6	8,906.9	-351.2	691.9	-298.3	-394.5	-657.2	6,262.3
U.S.	82,267.6	-254,629.5	950,766.1	-0.2	0.2	-0.1	-677.8	530.5	778,390.6

TABLE 3.1b The Shift-Share Components Expressed as Percentages of Total Shift

	National Shifts			Industry-Mix Shifts			Regional Shifts	
	Exports	Imports	Domestic Demand	Exports	Imports	Domestic Demand	Exports	Domestic Demand
Alabama	9.99	-30.18	113.10	-0.99	3.11	-4.09	-5.40	14.45
Arkansas	10.28	-30.64	114.73	-1.65	4.04	-2.60	-15.25	21.09
California	9.89	-29.75	111.27	0.90	-2.04	-2.08	4.25	7.57
Colorado	10.81	-32.02	118.55	-0.89	-5.73	33.58	-6.11	-18.18
Florida	7.91	-23.42	88.79	0.01	-0.44	6.71	1.77	18.65
Georgia	7.40	-21.81	84.12	0.28	0.96	1.07	1.52	26.45
Illinois	12.03	-38.37	142.75	-1.27	3.00	-4.75	4.21	-17.59
Indiana	10.61	-32.56	121.38	1.68	0.49	-8.06	-10.51	16.98
Iowa	13.89	-42.43	156.21	-3.79	6.12	-2.31	-2.28	-25.40
Kansas	12.68	-42.21	155.84	-2.14	3.48	-11.92	-0.63	-15.10
Kentucky	9.09	-27.42	102.38	2.08	-0.84	-2.71	7.28	10.13
Louisiana	44.53	-140.20	490.73	-24.25	81.11	-318.11	-37.10	3.27
Massachusetts	9.31	-30.24	113.76	1.70	-12.33	29.64	-8.91	-2.94
Michigan	8.83	-28.16	107.23	4.02	-8.92	19.56	-18.15	15.59
Minnesota	9.08	-27.48	103.27	-1.26	1.41	5.01	9.26	0.72
Mississippi	10.86	-33.06	122.28	-2.22	5.45	-21.24	0.26	17.66
Missouri	7.90	-25.32	97.08	2.30	-4.60	11.09	-3.78	15.33
New Jersey	13.08	-40.06	147.63	-1.76	0.23	7.81	-12.72	-14.22
New York	11.72	-37.63	140.55	-1.10	-10.40	43.26	-1.68	-44.71

(*continues*)

69

Table 3.1b (*continued*)

North Carolina	8.15	-24.13	91.97	1.74	1.61	0.59	-1.29	21.35
Ohio	9.15	-28.18	105.96	1.83	-1.56	2.33	3.80	6.67
Oklahoma	21.14	-68.78	247.45	-0.35	2.71	-39.43	-5.08	-57.67
Oregon	8.44	-24.27	92.14	-1.41	8.09	11.60	2.06	3.34
Pennsylvania	12.76	-39.91	147.78	-1.75	2.21	-4.49	-4.69	-11.92
South Carolina	8.38	-24.47	93.61	-0.74	1.14	3.25	9.67	9.16
Tennessee	8.52	-25.89	98.50	-0.33	-1.53	4.55	0.20	15.98
Texas	30.74	-99.98	354.86	-10.99	34.50	-145.32	3.45	-67.23
Virginia	8.46	-25.67	97.69	1.24	4.77	-0.07	-1.36	14.93
Washington	9.82	-29.92	113.60	0.11	3.87	-3.94	60.42	-53.96
West Virginia	12.39	-39.16	146.27	-1.00	8.94	-7.24	-12.55	-7.65
Wisconsin	9.20	-28.44	107.33	-0.20	-1.15	7.62	-2.27	7.89
Delmar	10.55	-32.08	119.35	0.21	1.32	1.50	-1.52	0.68
Lower New England	11.38	-36.63	137.57	1.52	-15.09	38.43	1.91	-39.08
Mid Mountain	11.88	-39.89	148.43	-2.65	2.03	-14.34	-5.41	-0.05
Southwest	7.73	-22.12	84.47	2.15	-2.71	-3.16	1.59	32.05
Upper Mountain	16.87	-51.01	184.75	-9.43	29.52	-58.42	35.24	-47.53
Upper New England	8.37	-24.02	91.69	1.73	-6.71	12.24	19.70	-3.00
Upper Plains	11.91	-38.19	142.42	-5.62	11.06	-4.77	-6.31	-10.51
U.S.	10.57	-32.71	122.15	0.00	0.00	0.00	0.00	0.00

confirmation of Markusen et al.'s (1991) observation (and, indeed, that of Erickson 1989) that while the focus may be on international trade in regional economic growth, one should not lose sight of the fact that domestic demand accounts for by far the largest proportion of regional economic growth.

The Effects of Differential Sectoral Growth. The industrial-mix shift components offer far greater detail, illustrating the particular effects of the states' unique industrial structures on their patterns of growth. For each of the three industrial-mix components, either positive or negative values may be revealed since these indicate the deviation of each state's growth experience from national trends attributable to the twin effects of industrial-mix and differential sectoral growth rates. In the case of exports, the industrial-mix shift components range from large positive values in the cases of California, Ohio, Kentucky, North Carolina and Michigan, among others. In these instances, the industrial structures of these states are skewed towards those sectors which experienced comparatively large export growth rates. In contrast, Illinois, Louisiana, Pennsylvania and Texas (among others) have industrial structures skewed toward sectors with relatively little export growth. These components may also be interpreted as modifications to the national export shift components after accounting for industrial patterns. Figure 3.3 illustrates the pattern of these industrial-mix export shifts across the 38 states and regions. The U.S. means for all industry-mix and regional shift components are necessarily zero, a fact evident from an inspection of the formula. Apparently, states with industrial structures favoring exports growth exhibit a fairly distinct pattern, including those of New England, the South Atlantic, the eastern Great Lakes and Missouri, and California, Washington and the Southwest region in the west. States with negative shift components comprise the Middle Atlantic, southern, western Great Lakes, Plains and Mountain states.

The industrial-mix import shift components similarly indicate the effects of the states' individual industrial structures on their particular exposure to imports. Again, these may be interpreted as modifications to the national import shift components. In some cases, the values are positive, indicating that the state's industrial structure is comprised of sectors experiencing relatively little import competition. Such is the case for Alabama, Illinois, Kansas, Louisiana, Oregon and Texas among others. On the other hand, many states and regions reveal a greater-than-average exposure to imports. These include California, Massachusetts, Michigan and New York. The state and regional pattern of industrial-mix imports shifts is illustrated in Figure 3.4. Once again, there is a very clear pattern with negative

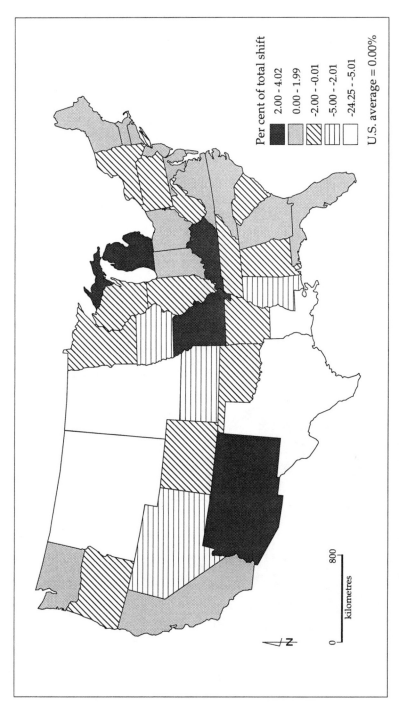

FIGURE 3.3 The industrial-mix export shift.

72

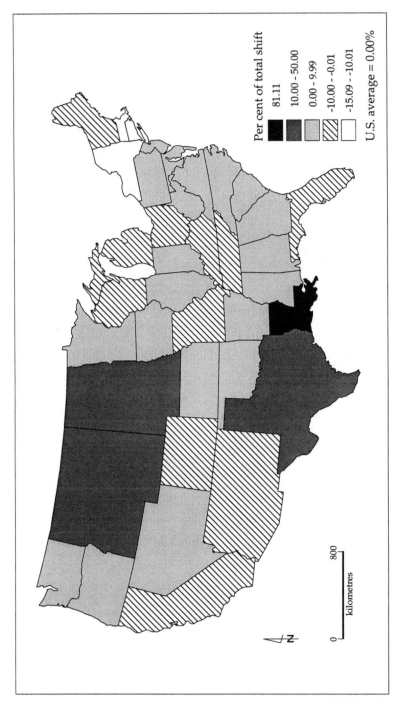

FIGURE 3.4 The industrial-mix import shift.

values reported in New York and New England, much of the Great Lakes, Florida, and some south western states. Throughout the Middle and South Atlantic, South, Plains and north west, states experience positive import shifts implying that these regional economies are comparatively immune from the competitive threat of imports.

The states' respective fortunes with respect to domestic demand and their industrial-mixes is evident in the domestic demand shift component. Here, too, there are wide variations, indicating the individuality of states' industrial structures and the vagaries of sectoral growth rates. Figure 3.5 illustrates the state by state pattern. It is evident that domestic demand growth was so skewed towards certain sectors that relatively few states have positive shift components. These are concentrated in the north east, Southeast and around the Great Lakes.

The industrial-mix shift components are interesting since they isolate the portion of state economic growth attributable to differential growth rates among sectors. Together with national growth trends, these components indicate the patterns of growth that *should* have taken place if regional variations had not existed. Having accounted for these and the foregoing national shift components, the remainder must necessarily be attributable to peculiarities of the regions themselves.

Regional Effects in the Patterns of Regional Economic Growth. The regional shift components indicate those portions of the states' output growth not attributable to national or sectoral trends and, hence, necessarily resulting from peculiar regional experiences. Thus, these shifts are usually of the greatest interest to the regional analyst. In previous versions of the shift-share model, these components are usually specified as a single, competitive shift component amounting to a catch-all measure, containing the residual, non-attributable growth. In the present specification, however, it is possible to isolate that part of the state's peculiar growth attributable to exports. The regional shift component can now be analyzed in further detail and the states can be explored for their trade orientations. The regional shift components may be interpreted similarly to the industrial-mix shifts. They illustrate the value of output growth not attributable to national or sectoral effects and are also a modification to the national components. As explained above the regional shift can be subdivided into only those attributable to exports and domestic demand components, with the latter effectively being a "catch-all," residual measure. These two regional shift components indicate the comparative advantage of individual states in their regional growth patterns. They indicate the relative performance of the states having

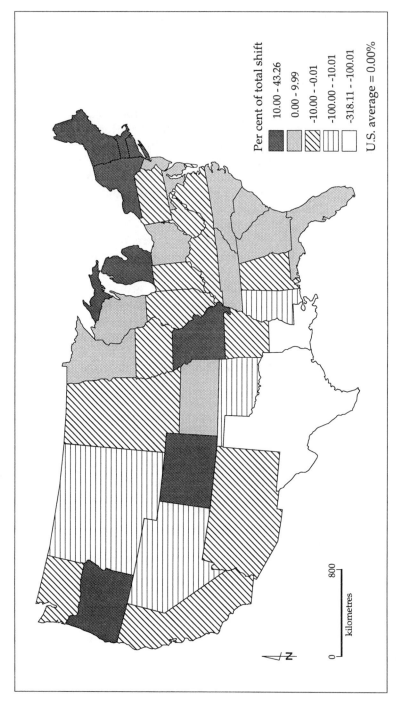

FIGURE 3.5 The industrial-mix domestic demand shift.

accounted for other factors. Furthermore, the regional export shift specifically indicates the contribution of exports in this comparative (dis)advantage.

The regional export shift component indicates the states' residual trade orientations. The components vary dramatically from 60.42 to -37.10 percent (Washington and Louisiana, respectively) of total shift. It is notable that some states, including California, Minnesota, South Carolina, Upper New England and the Upper Mountain regions, appear to be particularly export-oriented such that their actual export growth over this period greatly exceeded that which would be expected from their industrial bases. In contrast, other states including Arkansas, Indiana, Michigan, New Jersey, Pennsylvania and West Virginia report negative regional export shifts indicating negative orientations to export trade.

An interesting state by state pattern is depicted in Figure 3.6 States with greater export biases--evident as positive shifts--are found throughout the West, Southwest, much of the Southeast, and parts of the Midwest and New England regions. Equally notable are those regions with low export orientations: the Middle and South Atlantic, South Central and Plains, and parts of the Midwest. It is apparent from these results that there is a clear pattern of regional orientation to exports. For states with positive regional export shifts, exports played a disproportionate part of their manufacturing growth experiences in the 1980s.

The regional domestic demand shift components similarly reveal a wide variation across the 38 states and regions. From inspection of the two regional shift components in Tables 3.1a and 3.1b, it may be observed that there is little relationship between the two. In some cases, the regional export shift may be positive while the regional domestic demand shift is negative, or vice versa, or they may be of the same sign. Furthermore, their magnitudes vary such that although the latter is generally larger for most states, this is not always the case. For instance, in Minnesota, Louisiana and Upper New England--each with very different regional shifts--the regional export shift is considerably larger than that for domestic demand. In a simpler version of the shift-share model with only a single regional shift component, the significant role of exports in these regions' comparative (dis)advantage would go undetected.

Nevertheless, for many states the domestic demand (or, at least residual growth not otherwise attributable) accounts for a major portion of the manufacturing growth since 1983. Once again, a clear pattern is revealed when these shifts are mapped (Figure 3.7). There is a distinct cluster of states with large positive regional domestic demand shifts in

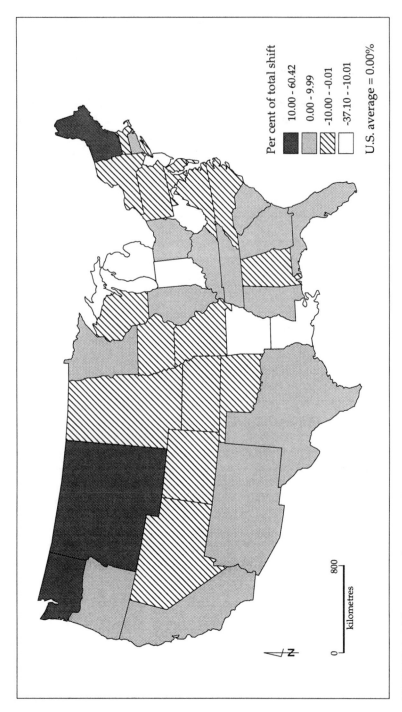

FIGURE 3.6 The regional export shift.

77

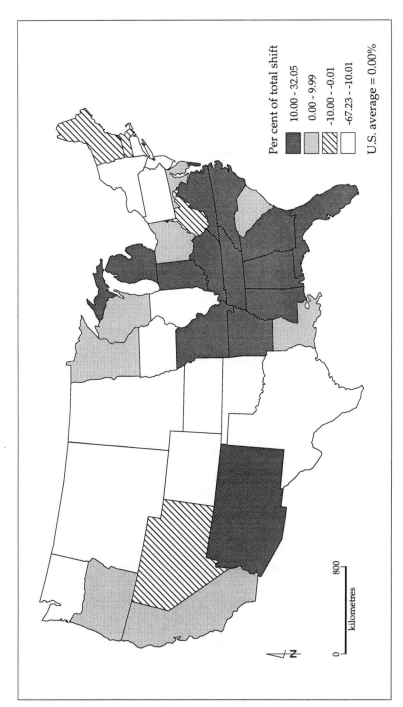

FIGURE 3.7 The regional domestic demand shift.

the south eastern quadrant of the U.S. In the north east, Plains and Mountain states, however, substantial negative shifts are reported.

Through isolating particular cases, one is able to make detailed descriptions of the trade and output growth experiences of individual states, typically through comparing the regional shift and national and industrial-mix components. In the case of Washington, for instance, its industrial-mix suggests only a negligible export shift (0.11 percent of total shift). However, its actual export activities (presumably, mostly accounted for by aircraft) yield a substantial exports shift of fully 60.42 percent. In contrast, Michigan has industry-mix and regional export shifts of 4.02 and -18.15 percent, respectively. The former measure is undoubtedly skewed by the level of sectoral aggregation wherein Transportation Equipment (SIC 37) includes both automobiles (which are a relatively insignificant U.S. export) as well as aircraft which are an important export. The former are a significant product of Michigan whereas the latter are not. Furthermore, noting Michigan's regional domestic demand shift component of 15.59 percent, it is apparent that the state's industrial production is oriented more toward domestic production than to exports. In the same manner, other state's growth experiences may be similarly dissected and detailed explanations of their growth experiences posited.

A Summary of the Simple Shift-Share Components. The overall value of the shift-share model's decompositional approach may be summarized with reference to the total national, industrial-mix and regional shift components. These are presented in Table 3.2, and are effectively equivalent to the shift components developed in simple shift-share models. For the U.S. as a whole, by definition, the national shift accounts for the total. For individual states and regions, however, the industrial-mix and regional shift components may amount to substantial portions of their total shifts. Broadly speaking, states and regions with national shifts exceeding 100 percent of the total shift experienced a growth rate below that of the U.S. as a whole and the reasons may be sought through reference to the other two components, one or both of which will be negative. For states with national components below 100 percent, their actual output growth exceeded that of the U.S. as a whole and, again, explanation may be found in the other components. In most cases, the national shift components fit the pattern of deviations around the U.S. average of 100 percent. In four cases, however, the peculiar industrial structures and regional experiences of states such as Louisiana, Oklahoma, Texas and Upper New England have led to little growth in manufactures over the period, with the result that proportionately very large negative industrial-mix and regional shifts are offset by large positive national

TABLE 3.2 The Simple Shift-Share Components

	National ($ m)	Share of Total (%)	Ind.-Mix ($ m)	Share of Total (%)	Regional ($ m)	Share of Total (%)
Alabama	12,710.8	92.91	-268.2	-1.97	1,238.9	9.05
Arkansas	7,857.8	94.37	-17.9	-0.21	485.7	5.84
California	78,382.7	91.41	-2,767.8	-3.22	10,131.4	11.82
Colorado	7,192.4	97.34	1,992.3	26.96	-1,795.3	-24.29
Florida	17,226.3	73.28	1,478.4	6.28	4,800.6	20.42
Georgia	22,996.5	69.71	760.4	2.31	9,229.6	27.97
Illinois	42,587.1	116.41	-1,108.6	-3.02	-4,896.0	-13.38
Indiana	26,304.7	99.43	-1,558.7	-5.89	1,709.8	6.47
Iowa	11,239.8	127.67	1.8	0.02	-2,436.5	-27.68
Kansas	10,175.9	126.31	-852.8	-10.58	-1,267.2	-15.73
Kentucky	12,894.7	84.05	-225.3	-1.47	2,671.0	17.41
Louisiana	16,616.0	395.06	-10,987.6	-261.25	-1,422.5	-33.83
Massachusetts	20,132.5	92.83	4,125.3	19.01	-2,568.9	-11.85
Michigan	46,528.4	87.90	7,763.0	14.66	-1,353.6	-2.56
Minnesota	14,779.8	84.87	897.7	5.16	1,738.8	9.98
Mississippi	7,613.1	100.08	-1,369.8	-18.01	1,363.2	17.92
Missouri	18,964.4	79.66	2,092.0	8.79	2,747.7	11.55
New Jersey	26,126.8	120.65	1,360.7	6.28	-5,832.9	-26.94
New York	46,969.9	114.64	13,010.3	31.76	-19,008.0	-46.39
North Carolina	29,105.5	75.99	1,513.0	3.94	7,686.4	20.06
Ohio	49,504.7	86.93	1,478.7	2.60	5,961.6	10.47
Oklahoma	7,905.9	199.81	-1,466.5	-37.07	-2,482.9	-62.75
Oregon	7,665.4	76.31	1,837.6	18.28	542.1	5.40
Pennsylvania	37,922.2	120.63	-1,265.0	-4.03	-5,220.7	-16.61
South Carolina	12,563.9	77.52	591.2	3.65	3,051.3	18.83
Tennessee	17,916.6	81.13	593.9	2.69	3,571.5	16.18
Texas	53,922.8	285.62	-22,999.3	-121.81	-12,043.3	-63.78
Virginia	16,080.7	80.48	1,187.7	5.94	2,711.0	13.57
Washington	14,573.4	93.50	6.2	0.04	1,005.9	6.46
West Virginia	3,717.0	119.50	21.5	0.70	-628.1	-20.20
Wisconsin	21,829.8	88.09	1,555.3	6.27	1,395.0	5.62
Delmar	12,061.2	97.82	372.1	3.03	-103.9	-0.84
Lower New England	15,074.4	112.32	3,338.0	24.86	-4,989.8	-37.17
Mid Mountain	4,168.1	120.42	-518.0	-14.96	-189.0	-5.46
Southwest	7,481.9	70.08	-397.8	-3.72	3,591.5	33.64
Upper Mountain	3,989.8	150.61	-1,015.2	-38.33	-325.4	-12.29
Upper New England	8,358.3	76.04	798.9	7.26	1,835.4	16.70
Upper Plains	7,263.0	116.14	42.4	0.67	-1,051.7	-16.82
U.S.	778,404.2	100.00	0.00	0.00	-147.3	0.00

shifts. These should be seen as outliers in the regional distribution around the mean national experience.

The industrial-mix and regional shift components account for the deviations from national trends in the states' growth patterns. Of particular interest are the instances where industrial-mix and regional shifts offset one another. Colorado, for example, has comparatively large shifts of both kinds, 26.96 and -24.29 percent, respectively, roughly equalling each other in magnitude: apparently, the growth potential of Colorado's industrial structure is negated by its competitive disadvantage. Similar experiences are evident for Massachusetts, New York and Lower New England. The opposite case is found for California, Mississippi and Indiana, for whom negative industrial-mix shifts are either compensated for or exceeded by regional shifts. Finally, in other cases, either the industrial-mix shift accounts for almost all the variation (eg, Michigan, Oregon and Delmar) or the regional shift is dominant (eg, Arkansas, Iowa, North Carolina and Washington).

The Contributions of the Trade Components. The purpose of this first stage of the analysis of the growth experiences of the states between 1983 and 1990, was to establish both the relevance of the shift-share model--decomposing growth into that attributable to national, sectoral or regional factors--as well as to isolate the specific contributions of international trade in the growth process. The eight-component model captured the individual export and import components for national, industrial-mix, and regional shifts, but the total contribution of trade to the states' manufacturing growth may be better analyzed through a summary of the total export, import and domestic demand shifts; these are presented in Table 3.3.

For the U.S. as a whole, exports accounted for a total of 10.48 percent of the net growth in manufactures. The states, however, exhibit considerable variation around this figure. For some, including Louisiana, Arkansas and Michigan, exports growth from 1983-90 was negative. For other states, the export contribution was considerably greater than the U.S. average, and these included Washington, Upper Mountain, and Upper New England which had total export shifts of 70.35, 42.68 and 29.80 percent, respectively. Evidently, for these and several other states, exports were a major component of their overall regional growth. It should be noted that for Texas and Oklahoma, the relatively high total export shifts resulted, in part, from rather low actual output growth as noted above.

The pattern of total export shifts across the 38 states and regions is illustrated in Figure 3.8. In addition to those cases of negative export shifts noted above, much of the Plains, South, Southeast and north east

TABLE 3.3 Total Export, Import and Domestic Demand Shift Components

	Exports ($)	Share of Total (%)	Imports ($)	Share of Total (%)	Domestic Demand ($)	Share of Total (%)
Alabama	494.0	3.60	-3,703.2	-27.07	16,890.7	123.46
Arkansas	-551.4	-6.62	-2,214.5	-26.60	11,091.5	133.22
California	12,882.7	15.04	-27,259.0	-31.79	100,122.6	116.76
Colorado	281.0	3.81	-2,789.3	-37.75	9,897.7	133.95
Florida	2,280.4	9.69	-5,606.8	-23.86	26,831.7	114.15
Georgia	3,035.7	9.20	-6,875.8	-20.85	36,826.6	111.64
Illinois	5,478.2	14.97	-12,941.7	-35.37	44,046.0	120.41
Indiana	469.2	1.78	-8,483.3	-32.07	34,469.9	130.30
Iowa	688.2	7.82	-3,197.6	-36.31	11,314.5	128.50
Kansas	798.6	9.91	-3,120.4	-38.73	10,377.7	128.82
Kentucky	2,831.7	18.45	-4,333.9	-28.26	16,842.6	109.80
Louisiana	-707.1	-16.82	-2,484.9	-59.09	7,397.9	175.89
Massachusetts	456.4	2.10	-9,232.1	-42.57	30,464.6	140.46
Michigan	-2,806.8	-5.30	-19,628.2	-37.08	75,372.8	142.38
Minnesota	2,973.1	17.08	-4,540.3	-26.07	18,983.5	109.00
Mississippi	677.2	8.90	-2,100.0	-27.61	9,029.3	118.70
Missouri	1,525.9	6.42	-7,121.4	-29.92	29,399.6	123.50
New Jersey	-300.8	-1.40	-8,625.9	-39.83	30,581.3	141.22
New York	3,663.4	8.94	-19,679.0	-48.03	56,987.8	139.10
North Carolina	3,295.6	8.60	-8,624.0	-22.52	43,633.3	113.91
Ohio	8,414.2	14.78	-16,936.3	-29.74	65,467.1	114.96
Oklahoma	621.7	15.71	-2,613.8	-66.07	5,948.6	150.35
Oregon	912.9	9.09	-1,624.6	-16.18	10,756.8	107.08
Pennsylvania	1,989.8	6.32	-11,851.2	-37.70	41,297.9	131.37
South Carolina	2,803.5	17.31	-3,779.9	-23.33	17,182.8	106.02
Tennessee	1,851.1	8.39	-6,052.0	-27.42	26,282.9	119.03
Texas	4,377.6	23.20	-12,365.1	-65.48	26,867.7	142.31
Virginia	1,667.2	8.34	-4,174.7	-20.90	22,486.9	112.55
Washington	10,963.9	70.35	-4,058.8	-26.05	8,680.4	55.70
West Virginia	-36.0	-1.16	-940.3	-30.22	4,086.7	131.38
Wisconsin	1,671.3	6.73	-7,331.6	-29.59	30,440.4	122.84
Delmar	1,138.3	9.24	-3,792.2	-30.76	14,983.3	121.53
Lower New England	1,986.6	14.81	-6,942.8	-51.72	18,378.8	136.92
Mid Mountain	132.2	3.82	-1,310.3	-37.86	4,639.2	134.04
Southwest	1,224.5	11.47	-2,651.0	-24.83	12,102.1	113.36
Upper Mountain	1,130.9	42.68	-569.2	-21.49	2,087.5	78.80
Upper New England	3,275.7	29.80	-3,377.5	-30.73	11,094.4	100.93
Upper Plains	-1.0	-0.02	-1,696.7	-27.13	7,951.4	127.14
U.S.	81,589.6	10.48	-254,629.3	-32.71	951,296.5	122.21

82

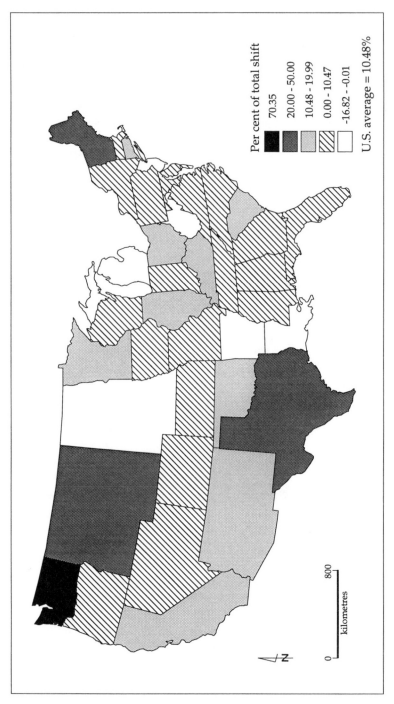

Per cent of total shift

70.35

20.00 - 50.00

10.48 - 19.99

0.00 - 10.47

-16.82 - -0.01

U.S. average = 10.48%

0   800

kilometres

N

FIGURE 3.8 The total export shift.

regions report below-average values, indicating that for these states exports were a comparatively less important factor in manufacturing growth since 1983. In contrast, for Upper and Lower New England, isolated parts of the Midwest, and much of the West and Southwest, exports accounted for a much greater share of regional economic growth.

The total imports shift for the U.S. as a whole amounted to -32.71 percent of net growth and again there are variations around this mean on the part of the individual states. In all cases, however, the total import shift is negative although Oregon, Georgia and Virginia have particularly low shifts: -16.18, -20.85 and -20.90 percent, respectively. In contrast, states with large total import shifts exhibit particularly high exposures to import competition; these include Louisiana and Lower New England with -59.09 and -51.72 percent, respectively. Once again, the large negative values for Oklahoma and Texas are due in part to comparatively low total growth in this period.

The state by state pattern of total import shifts is illustrated in Figure 3.9. Since the total imports shifts include, by definition, only national and industrial-mix components, there is no specifically regional variation and so the pattern is necessarily less-varied than that for exports, above. Those states with the greatest import shift components are clustered in the north east and South Central regions. In contrast, the Southeast, Western and Northern regions have generally lower import shifts indicating lower exposure to imports during the study period.

The total domestic demand shifts are also reported in Table 3.3. These deviate about the U.S. mean of 122.21 percent of total growth, although to a lesser extent than the export and import shift components. It is notable that domestic demand appears to be relatively less important in the growth experienced by Washington, the Upper Mountain region, Georgia, Virginia and the Southwest region in particular (55.70, 78.80, 111.64, 112.55 and 113.36 percent of total shifts, respectively). Indeed, one may infer that those states and regions with below-average total domestic demand shifts are, by default, those states more oriented toward international trade in general.

It is evident from the foregoing application of the shift-share model that international trade--both exports and imports--is an important component of regional economic growth. This analysis, however, addresses only the direct impacts of trade while one presumes that further *multiplier* effects occur as well. In effect, therefore, the model may be *under*-estimating the real importance of trade. This extended version of the shift-share model enables a detailed examination of the role of trade through identifying the source of trade's effects as being

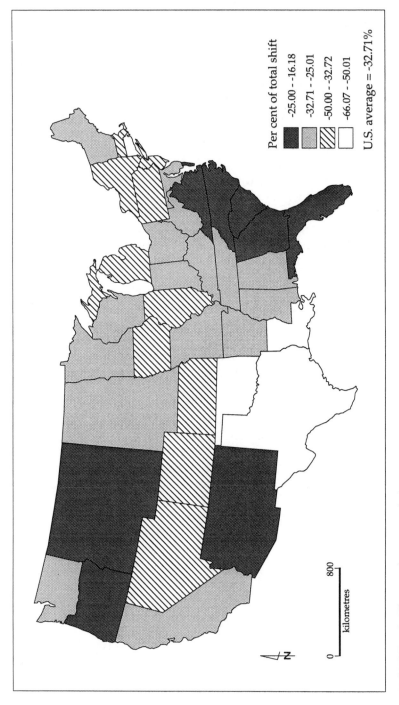

FIGURE 3.9 The total import shift.

due to national trends, sectoral-specific conditions, or unique, regional factors.

Modelling Trade with the European Union

The application of the full 13 component shift-share model specified in Figure 3.2, enables an examination of the particular contribution of trade with the European Union in the regional economic growth experiences of the 38 states and regions. In this way the model can be extended to investigate the effects of a particular trade relationship. This is a potentially powerful tool as it highlights trade with particular nations, offering a valuable indicator for the consideration of contemporary developments in trade policy.

In the full model, the trade components reported above are further decomposed into EU and non-EU shifts. In essence, therefore, the two models are identical; each identifying components of the same total regional (state) shifts. The values of the trade components alone are contained in Table 3.4, where the components are expressed as percentages of the total shift.

Once again, the national export and import shifts reflect the trade experience of the U.S. as a whole and divide simply into EU and non-EU components. In the case of exports, it is apparent that the shifts due to the European Union are little less than that for the rest of the world as a whole--amounting to around 80 percent of the latter. The comparative importance of exports to the EU is therefore revealed in these figures. For imports, however, the national EU shifts are much less than those attributable to the rest of the world (approximately 20 percent of the latter). Evidently, in comparison to other sources, EU imports have posed comparatively less of a challenge to industrial growth in the U.S.

Industrial Structure and Trade with the European Union. As before, the industry-mix and regional shifts are of more interest. The EU industry-mix export shift indicates that the economic effects of positive changes in exports to the EU are disproportionately felt among the states. In many cases, there is marked separation between the values of EU and non-EU export shifts. For Alabama, Colorado and Florida, for instance, the industry-mix EU export shift is negative while that for non-EU exports is positive, indicating a significant difference in the effects of EU and non-EU exports such that these states' industries are geared toward the latter rather than the former. On the other hand, for Massachusetts, Michigan and Lower New England, among others, the EU export shifts exceed those of non-EU exports. In these cases, one may infer that the states' respective

TABLE 3.4 EU and Non-EU Shift-Share Components (expressed as percentages of total shift)

	National Shifts				Industry-Mix Shifts				Regional Shifts	
	EU Exports	Non-EU Exports	EU Imports	Non-EU Imports	EU Exports	Non-EU Exports	EU Imports	Non-EU Imports	EU Exports	Non-EU Exports
Alabama	4.35	5.64	-4.98	-25.20	-1.11	0.12	1.10	2.01	-0.92	-4.48
Arkansas	4.40	5.88	-5.06	-25.58	-1.28	-0.37	1.20	2.84	-2.38	-12.87
California	4.29	5.60	-4.91	-24.84	0.33	0.57	-0.26	-1.78	1.32	2.93
Colorado	4.57	6.24	-5.30	-26.72	-0.46	-0.43	-0.83	-4.90	-0.88	-5.23
Florida	3.48	4.43	-3.85	-19.57	-0.13	0.14	-0.02	-0.42	-1.07	2.84
Georgia	3.29	4.11	-3.57	-18.24	-0.18	0.46	0.42	0.54	-0.34	1.86
Illinois	5.34	6.69	-6.37	-32.00	-0.63	-0.64	0.41	2.59	-0.35	4.56
Indiana	4.63	5.98	-5.39	-27.17	0.13	1.55	0.43	0.06	-2.46	-8.05
Iowa	5.90	7.99	-7.04	-35.39	-1.60	-2.19	0.95	5.17	0.19	-2.47
Kansas	5.78	6.90	-7.03	-35.18	-0.66	-1.48	0.15	3.33	-2.12	1.49
Kentucky	3.97	5.12	-4.53	-22.89	0.82	1.26	-0.07	-0.77	3.05	4.23
Louisiana	18.12	26.41	-23.59	-116.61	-6.34	-17.91	7.13	73.98	-11.36	-25.74
Massachusetts	4.29	5.02	-5.01	-25.23	0.90	0.80	-1.67	-10.66	-0.65	-8.26
Michigan	4.06	4.77	-4.64	-23.52	2.10	1.92	-1.72	-7.20	-4.60	-13.55
Minnesota	3.98	5.10	-4.54	-22.94	-0.46	-0.80	0.01	1.40	3.53	5.73
Mississippi	4.69	6.17	-5.48	-27.58	-1.33	-0.89	1.09	4.36	1.23	-0.97
Missouri	3.69	4.21	-4.17	-21.15	1.05	1.25	-0.85	-3.75	-0.71	-3.07
New Jersey	5.58	7.50	-6.65	-33.41	-0.53	-1.23	-0.24	0.47	-3.91	-8.81
New York	5.26	6.46	-6.23	-31.40	-0.20	-0.90	-1.10	-9.30	-1.04	-0.64

(continues)

Table 3.4 (*continued*)

North Carolina	3.59	4.56	-3.96	-20.17	0.44	1.30	0.50	1.11	0.42	-1.71
Ohio	4.07	5.08	-4.65	-23.53	0.73	1.10	-0.31	-1.25	-0.84	4.64
Oklahoma	9.15	11.99	-11.50	-57.28	0.25	-0.60	-0.19	2.90	-0.23	-4.85
Oregon	3.62	4.82	-3.98	-20.29	-1.09	-0.32	1.42	6.67	-0.64	2.70
Pennsylvania	5.56	7.20	-6.62	-33.29	-1.18	-0.57	0.75	1.46	-1.45	-3.24
South Carolina	3.65	4.73	-4.01	-20.46	-0.60	-0.14	0.26	0.88	2.58	7.09
Tennessee	3.80	4.72	-4.26	-21.63	-0.31	-0.02	0.07	-1.60	-0.60	0.80
Texas	13.02	17.72	-16.80	-83.18	-3.08	-7.91	3.02	31.48	-2.46	5.91
Virginia	3.77	4.69	-4.22	-21.45	0.53	0.71	0.80	3.97	0.68	-2.04
Washington	4.34	5.48	-4.91	-25.01	0.31	-0.20	0.37	3.50	24.87	35.55
West Virginia	5.47	6.92	-6.48	-32.68	-0.65	-0.35	0.70	8.24	0.27	-12.82
Wisconsin	4.10	5.10	-4.69	-23.75	-0.20	0.00	0.03	-1.18	-0.04	-2.23
Delmar	4.60	5.95	-5.29	-26.79	0.22	-0.01	0.13	1.19	-1.72	0.20
Lower New England	5.13	6.25	-6.06	-30.57	1.21	0.31	-2.15	-12.94	3.36	-1.45
Mid Mountain	5.50	6.38	-6.62	-33.27	-0.45	-2.20	0.14	1.89	0.75	-6.16
Southwest	3.35	4.38	-3.62	-18.50	0.72	1.43	-0.24	-2.47	1.72	-0.13
Upper Mountain	6.97	9.90	-8.50	-42.51	-3.80	-5.63	3.94	25.58	7.81	27.43
Upper New England	3.59	4.78	-3.93	-20.09	0.21	1.52	-0.40	-6.31	1.05	18.65
Upper Plains	5.33	6.58	-6.33	-31.86	-2.80	-2.82	1.82	9.24	-0.14	-6.17
U.S.	4.65	5.92	-5.41	-27.31	0.00	0.00	0.00	0.00	-0.02	-0.07

industrial structures are oriented more toward EU than non-EU trade. In every instance, there are subtle deviations from the national export patterns to render each state's trade relationship with the EU and, hence, its EU export shifts, unique. The pattern of industry-mix export shift components is displayed in Figure 3.10. The state by state pattern is, of course, very similar to that exhibited in Figure 3.3 for the industry-mix trade shifts; states with positive shifts include those in the New England, South Atlantic, eastern Great Lakes and Southwest regions as well as some outliers such as Washington, Missouri and Oklahoma. Negative EU industry-mix export shifts are found for states throughout the South, Plains and Mountain regions, and the Middle Atlantic. Florida and Georgia, in particular, are noteworthy for having negative EU industry-mix export shifts although positive total export shifts. Their industrial structures are geared more toward demands of foreign partners other than the EU.

The EU and non-EU industry-mix import shift components also illustrate subtle deviations from the total import shifts. Generally, however, these two do not radically differ from each other, with only a few cases having of a different sign. The state by state pattern is shown in Figure 3.11, and is very similar to that of the total industry-mix import shifts, shown in Figure 3.4. It appears, therefore, that the state-by-state pattern of EU industry-mix import shifts is not radically different from those for all imports.

The Regional Factor in Trade with the European Union. The regional export shift components are particularly interesting since they indicate the particular trade-orientations of the individual states and regions with respect to the European Union. For many, the shifts are similar for both EU and non-EU exports, but in several cases, there appears to be a significant difference between the two, indicating important biases in trade orientations. In some cases, a substantial negative shift for non-EU exports is paired with a much lower or perhaps even a positive shift for EU exports. For instance, this is the case with Colorado, Iowa, North Carolina and Wisconsin. Furthermore, in more extreme cases, positive EU export shifts exceed the negative non-EU shifts in absolute magnitude. This is the case for Mississippi, Lower New England and the Southwest, for which the total regional export shift component (ie, from the simpler eight-component model above--Table 3.1b) would be a lesser, positive value giving no indication that in fact, the degree to which exports to the EU had contributed positively to the regions' economic growth. In contrast, however, there are the alternative instances of negative EU shifts and positive non-EU shifts. This is the case for Kansas, Oregon and Texas. These observations confirm the proposition that the regional economic

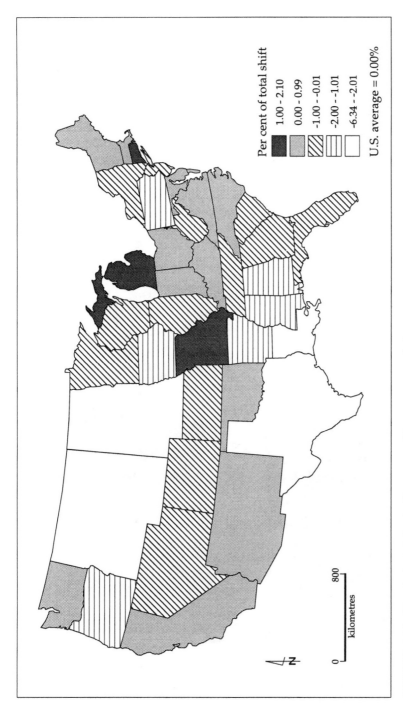

FIGURE 3.10 The industrial-mix European Union export shift.

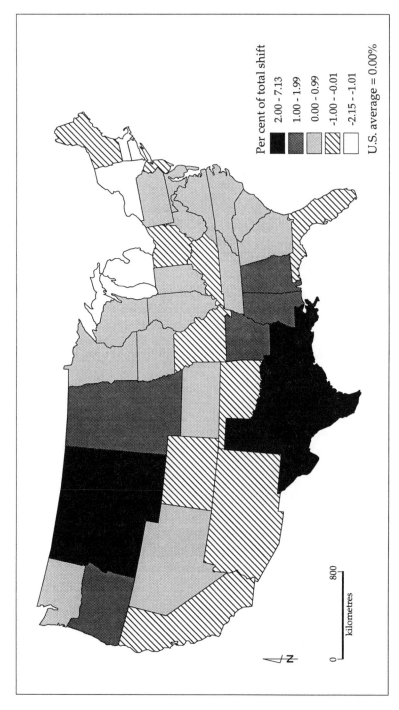

FIGURE 3.11 The industrial-mix European Union import shift.

impact of trade with the European Union is relatively complex and illustrates the value of this highly disaggregated analysis.

The state by state pattern of regional EU export shifts is displayed in Figure 3.12; this pattern may be compared with that for total regional exports shifts in Figure 3.6. A number of states which exhibit positive regional export shifts (from Figure 3.6) nevertheless report negative values in respect to the EU alone, and vice versa. In the west, a solid block of states with positive EU regional export shifts is evident, with the exception only of Oregon, which apparently does not share its neighbors' orientation to the EU. In the north, Minnesota is joined by Iowa in revealing an EU-export orientation while the previously-noted positive export shifts of Ohio and Illinois do not, apparently, include trade with the EU. Two other concentrations of EU-oriented regional economies appear in New England (except Massachusetts) and the South Atlantic states (Kentucky, West Virginia, Virginia, and the Carolinas). Negative regional EU export shifts are found throughout the Plains, South Central, eastern Great Lakes, and Middle Atlantic regions.

A Summary of EU-Related Trade in Regional Economic Growth. The industrial-mix and regional EU trade shifts discussed above are measured as deviations from the national shifts. Individually, each component illustrates a distinct dimension of the states' trade with the European Union: the industrial-mix identifies the states' potential competitiveness with respect to EU trade, exports and imports; the regional export shift identifies the particular trade orientations of the states, indicating greater or lesser bias in trade relations with the EU. As a final dimension in this analysis, the sum of the national, industrial-mix and regional EU shifts reveals the net contribution of EU trade to the regional economies' growth over the study period. The summarized EU export and import shifts are reported in Table 3.5. The total EU export shift component is the sum of the national, industrial-mix and regional shifts; for imports, it is the sum of the national and industrial-mix shifts. As before, these are expressed as both absolute shift values and as percentages of total shifts, the latter being more useful for comparative purposes. In addition, a simple balance of the two is reported as a third measure (in both dollars and as a percentage of the total shift) and the states are sorted according to this balance with the values for the U.S. as a whole marking the mean among them.

The total EU export shift for the U.S. as a whole was $36,040.6 million, amounting to 4.63 percent of the total. For all states, the component is a positive proportion of the total shift but there is considerable variation around the U.S. average. Washington, Upper Mountain, Lower New England and Oklahoma in particular reveal

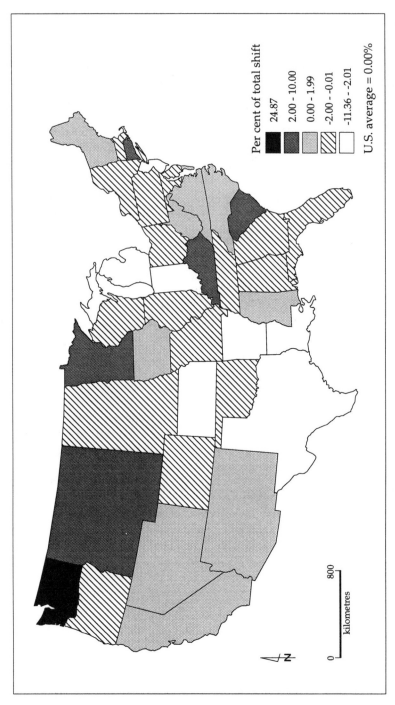

Per cent of total shift

24.87

2.00 - 10.00

0.00 - 1.99

-2.00 - -0.01

-11.36 - -2.01

U.S. average = 0.00%

800

kilometres

0

N

FIGURE 3.12 The regional European Union export shift.

TABLE 3.5. The Balance of EU Export and Import Shifts

	EU Exports ($m)	Share of Total (%)	EU Imports ($m)	Share of Total (%)	Balance ($m)	Share of Total (%)
Washington	4,601.0	29.52	-707.4	-4.54	3,893.6	24.98
Upper Mountain	291.1	10.98	-120.7	-4.56	170.4	6.42
Kentucky	1,203.1	7.84	-705.4	-4.60	497.7	3.24
Minnesota	1,227.6	7.05	-788.1	-4.53	439.5	2.52
Southwest	617.7	5.79	-411.4	-3.86	206.3	1.93
South Carolina	911.0	5.63	-607.2	-3.75	303.8	1.88
Virginia	995.7	4.98	-682.6	-3.42	313.1	1.56
Lower New England	1,301.1	9.70	-1,103.0	-8.21	198.1	1.49
North Carolina	1,704.7	4.45	-1,322.9	-3.46	381.8	0.99
California	5,089.8	5.94	-4,429.0	-5.17	660.8	0.77
Upper New England	533.9	4.85	-475.8	-4.33	58.1	0.52
Mississippi	349.4	4.59	-333.9	-4.39	15.5	0.20
Georgia	914.6	2.77	-1,037.7	-3.15	-123.1	-0.38
Oregon	189.3	1.89	-256.9	-2.56	-67.6	-0.67
Mid Mountain	200.7	5.80	-224.3	-6.48	-23.6	-0.68
West Virginia	158.3	5.09	-179.9	-5.78	-21.6	-0.69
U.S.	36,040.6	4.63	-42,111.3	-5.41	-6,070.7	-0.78
Wisconsin	957.1	3.86	-1,155.8	-4.66	-198.7	-0.80
Missouri	957.6	4.03	-1,195.4	-5.02	-237.8	-0.99
Ohio	2,255.6	3.96	-2,825.7	-4.96	-570.1	-1.00
Tennessee	636.9	2.89	-923.1	-4.19	-286.2	-1.30
Alabama	318.8	2.32	-530.4	-3.88	-211.6	-1.56
Florida	535.9	2.28	-908.6	-3.87	-372.7	-1.59
Illinois	1,593.8	4.36	-2,180.4	-5.96	-586.6	-1.60
Iowa	395.2	4.49	-536.4	-6.09	-141.2	-1.60
Delmar	381.3	3.10	-636.0	-5.16	-254.7	-2.06
Upper Plains	149.4	2.39	-281.8	-4.51	-132.4	-2.12
Massachusetts	984.3	4.54	-1,447.7	-6.68	-463.4	-2.14
Oklahoma	362.7	9.17	-462.5	-11.69	-99.8	-2.52
Indiana	609.0	2.30	-1,311.3	-4.96	-702.3	-2.66
Colorado	238.3	3.23	-452.9	-6.13	-214.6	-2.90
Pennsylvania	920.2	2.93	-1,846.6	-5.87	-926.4	-2.94
Arkansas	61.6	0.74	-321.8	-3.86	-260.2	-3.12
New York	1,648.3	4.02	-3,002.3	-7.33	-1,354.0	-3.31
Kansas	242.0	3.00	-554.0	-6.88	-312.0	-3.88
Michigan	825.6	1.56	-3,365.5	-6.36	-2,539.9	-4.80
New Jersey	249.0	1.14	-1,491.8	-6.89	-1,242.8	-5.75
Texas	1,411.2	7.48	-2,602.9	-13.78	-1,191.7	-6.30
Louisiana	17.8	0.42	-692.2	-16.46	-674.4	-16.04

substantial proportions of their total shifts being accounted for by exports to the EU (29.52, 10.98, 9.70 and 9.17 percent, respectively). In contrast, for Louisiana, Arkansas and New Jersey, among others, relatively little of their manufacturing growth is accounted for by exports to the EU (0.42, 0.74 and 1.14 percent, respectively). In Figure 3.13, the pattern across the states and regions is quite clear: large total EU export shifts throughout the western and south western states, the South Atlantic region and New England (except Massachusetts). In the remainder, the Middle Atlantic, Southeast and Midwest, exports to the EU accounted for relatively little of the regions' manufacturing growth.

In comparison to the pattern of total shifts for exports to all destinations (shown in Figure 3.8), this pattern differs only slightly: most notably, the South Atlantic states of Virginia and West Virginia exhibit a greater export orientation to the EU. On the other hand, for Ohio and Illinois, there is a lower export orientation to the EU. In general, the pattern is one of greater EU export orientation in the West, Southwest, New England and South Atlantic, plus Minnesota.

For the U.S. as a whole, imports from the EU accounted for -$42,111.3 million of the total shift, amounting to -5.41 percent. Again, the variation around this national average is quite substantial with several states reporting much larger shifts. For Louisiana, Texas and Oklahoma, -16.46, -13.78 and -11.69 percent of their total shifts respectively, are accounted for by imports from the EU. In Oregon, Georgia and North Carolina, on the other hand, the import shift amounts to merely -2.56, - 3.15 and -3.46 percent, respectively. The pattern across the states is presented in Figure 3.14, and may be compared with that for all imports, shown in Figure 3.9. The pattern is, of course, quite similar with greater import shifts being found in the north east, South Central and parts of the Midwest, and lower shifts in the Southeast, North and West states. Evidently, the competitive challenge of EU producers is focused upon the former group of states.

A crude balance between the export and import shifts is also reported in Table 3.5. This balance measures the net contribution of the regions' trade with the EU on their total manufacturing growth (shift) over the study period. For the U.S. as a whole, a slight negative balance is revealed, but for individual states, wide variations are found. At one extreme, Washington reports a positive balance of 24.98 percent while at the other, EU trade accounts for -16.04 percent of Louisiana's output growth. There are four states with negative balances which are nonetheless greater than the U.S. average and so should be considered as having a positive balance in relative terms.

The pattern of EU shift balances is illustrated in Figure 3.15. Distinct regional clusters are evident. States with positive overall

95

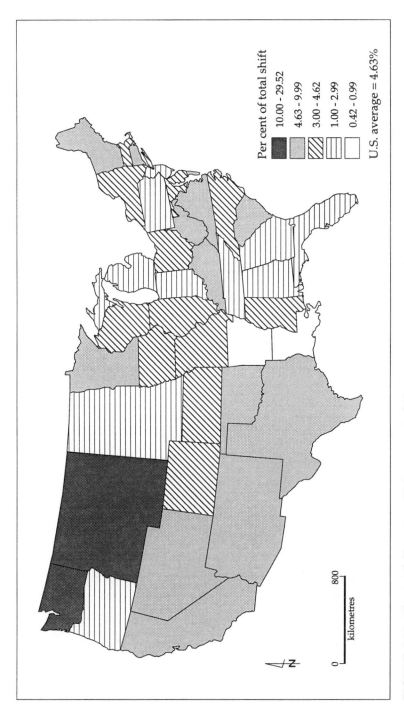

Per cent of total shift

10.00 - 29.52

4.63 - 9.99

3.00 - 4.62

1.00 - 2.99

0.42 - 0.99

U.S. average = 4.63%

0   800

kilometres

FIGURE 3.13 The total European Union export shifts.

96

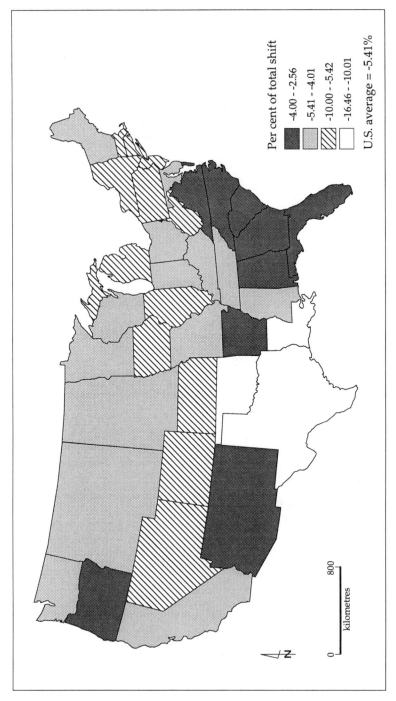

FIGURE 3.14 The total European Union import shifts.

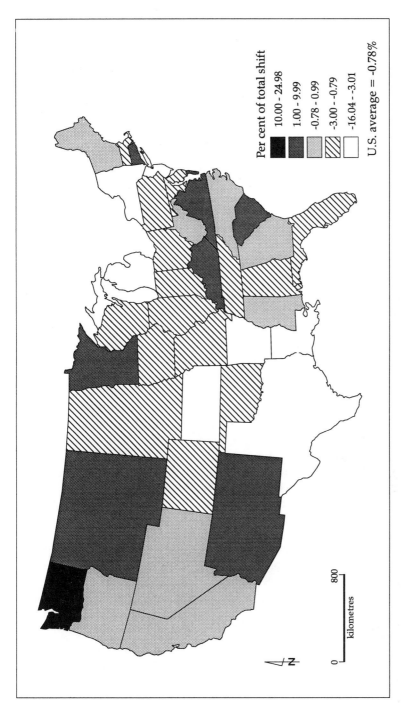

Per cent of total shift

- 10.00 - 24.98
- 1.00 - 9.99
- -0.78 - 0.99
- -3.00 - -0.79
- -16.04 - -3.01

U.S. average = -0.78%

N

0   800

kilometres

FIGURE 3.15 The balance of European Union shifts.

shifts due to trade with the EU include those in the West, South Atlantic and New England regions, plus Minnesota and Mississippi. Equally evident are those with negative overall experiences with respect to the EU including the Middle Atlantic, Midwest, Plains and South Central regions.

Regional Growth and Trade with the European Union. The application of the shift-share model to the manufacturing growth of these states and regions since 1983 has established and evaluated the role of international trade in regional economies. While domestic demand remains by far the largest contributor to total growth, both exports and imports are shown also to be substantial components. Moreover, the differential growth rates across the 38 states and regions is explained as a function of industrial structures and regional comparative advantage with respect to exports, imports and domestic demand. For individual states, therefore, their manufacturing growth experience can be dissected by the shift-share model and accounted for by several components.

The extended version of the international trade shift-share model further enables the evaluation of the specific contribution of trade with the European Union. While crude trade figures give some indication of the states' trading relationship with the EU, and the analysis in Chapter 4 indicates their relative exposures to EU trade, the shift-share model enables the relationship to be measured for its contribution to regional economic growth. Furthermore, the isolation of separate national, industry-mix and regional (except imports) shift components, enables a greater understanding of the nature of the states' trading relations. National and sectoral shift components account for all of the variation in imports from the EU and most of that for exports. The regional shift component accounts for the residual growth due to exports to the EU and so indicates the states' positive or negative orientations toward the European Union. Figure 3.12 therefore, is interesting for it reveals the states' residual export-biases toward the EU after having accounted for national and sectoral factors.

The shift-share model decomposes regional economic growth into its constituent components including international trade. The model, thus, may be applied with hindsight to historical data to evaluate the effects of differential sectoral growth rates, industrial structures, and regional comparative advantage. The model may also, be viewed from the opposite perspective, to reveal how economic growth is translated into net regional growth experiences. In this manner, the model may also be applied as a forecasting tool by introducing an exogenous growth stimulus, modelling its effects upon individual components, and aggregating them to obtain net state shifts.

Summary: The Trade Factor in Regional Economic Growth

The shift-share model is a simple but effective tool for disaggregating the components of regional growth. Additionally, when applied in the present context where the quality of the available data is of concern it is also an appropriate tool. The model affords multiple views on the growth experience and enables national and industry-specific trends to be separated from those pertaining to individual regions. The simple model can be easily extended and employed not only to identify the relative contributions of exports and imports, but also the importance of particular trade relationships. In the foregoing analysis, the model successfully highlighted the contribution of the states' trade with the European Union.

In the first instance, the model indicates the relative importance of trade in respect to domestic demand. Clearly, the latter is the major contributor to the growth of the states' manufacturing economies. The relative importance, however, varies quite markedly and in one case, the state of Washington, the growth due to exports even exceeds that due to domestic demand. While the contributions of exports and imports relate some interesting state-level experiences, the contribution of domestic demand remains in the background and must be borne in mind.

The European Union is a major trade partner for the United States as a whole but its importance varies greatly between regions. Evidently, there are comparative winners and losers in the contribution of EU trade to the states' economic growth.

The findings of the shift-share analysis above provide much of the illumination that is so lacking in our knowledge of states' trade relations. The current attention to state and regional-level trade promotion is undertaken with little understanding of the actual contribution of trade to growth over time. An interesting finding in these data are that many states, such as Pennsylvania, and even whole regions, are oriented primarily toward domestic demand. Armed with this information, state-level policy may need to be re-evaluated, especially if it is currently based upon erroneous estimates of the magnitude of local exports.

The particular attention to trade with the European Union also reveals findings that may surprise many state-level analysts. The relative importance or unimportance of EU trade in their state's recent growth may well prompt a reassessment of the targeting of trade promotion programs.

A final point relates to the interpretation of these findings. The analysis has been conducted solely at the macro scale, with no attention to the characteristics of firms or industries in the states. The shifts attributable to particular types of trade, domestic demand and to national or regional factors, merely highlight features of the aggregated data which in themselves cry-out for follow-up, micro level study. They are therefore an entré for a fuller understanding of trade linkages to regional economies, and should be complemented with analyses of local industries and firms.

4

The Regional Economic Impact of European Integration

Although the European Union has for much of its existence been popularly referred to as the "Common Market" it was in fact never one in the true meaning of the term. In fact, prior to 1993 it had achieved only the status of a customs union; in the latter case member countries agree only to remove all tariffs on trade between and among them, while in the former, a truly integrated market is created in which all barriers to trade--tariff and non-tariff--are eliminated. It is only with the Single Europe Act (1986) and the EC-92 program that the European Union finally begun to live up to its popular name. Appendix 2 contains a review of the history of post-war European economic integration and the scope and content of the EC-92 program.

Common Markets and Customs Unions

In parallel with the process of European economic integration since 1957 has been the development of a field of study--customs union theory--which specifically addresses such phenomena (Krauss 1972, p. 413). The key concepts of *trade creation* and *trade diversion* as the two main outcomes of integration were identified by Viner (1950). Trade creation results when an integration event such as a free trade area or customs union is seen to increase trade between countries--either members or non-members of the trading bloc. This is usually evident as a greater proportion of output going to trade at the expense of domestic consumption, hence trade is effectively *created*. Trade diversion, however, occurs when trade increases between partners in the trade bloc at the expense of third, or non-partner countries. That is to say, trade is effectively *diverted* away from non-partners to other members of the free trade area. These two processes are useful for summarising the effects of integration as they enable the impacts to be separated and the net effect on global trade to be accounted for:

> From a global viewpoint the net welfare impact of a customs union or free trade area...depends on the amount of trade created as compared with trade diverted or eroded. (Truman 1975, p. 19)

Thus, the net effect is measured as a balance of the two, and from a Pareto welfare perspective a positive impact results if trade creation exceeds trade diversion. However, as Nevin (1990) notes, economic integration cannot be said a priori as leading to either an increase or decrease in welfare. While generalizable features may result the balance of these means that each case is unique.

Studies of the impacts of earlier European initiatives, such as the initial formation of the European Economic Community (1957) or the recent EC-92 program, fall into one of two categories. Verdoorn and Van Bochove (1972) distinguish between *ex ante* and *ex post* approaches. In the former, the effects of integration are forecast through surveys of businesses involved prior to the actual process. In the latter, a more definitive statement may be made through time-series analysis of key variables before and after the event, and econometric analysis may be employed also to quantify the impact. Similarly, Mayes (1978) distinguished between *analytic* and *residual* approaches, respectively, which broadly corresponded to earlier descriptions.

Earlier expansions of the European Union have prompted ex ante as well as ex post analyses. Truman (1975) studied the trade impacts of the EEC and European Free Trade Association (EFTA) integrations in the 1960s. He identified six separate trade scenarios for each country's industrial sectors using the notions of trade creation and trade diversion. These are reported in Table 4.1. In general, Case 3--internal trade creation and external trade diversion--would be the expected scenario from an event such as EC-92 in which the economies of the members are further integrated in relation to non-partners. However, Cases 1 and 2 might occur also if the integration process included a net lowering of external tariffs. Truman used two methods to analyze the effects of the EEC and EFTA integrations. In one, he looked at members' industrial sectors and measured the changes in the consumption of goods from three different sources: other domestic sectors, imports from partners, and imports from third countries. In the second, he used a regression model to generate estimated trade patterns based upon pre-integration data and compared its deviations from the actual patterns post-integration. Both of these are examples of the ex post approach

TABLE 4.1 Possible Scenarios from International Economic Integration

Case	Description	Domestic Sector	Partners	Non-Members
		Effect on Share of Trade of:		
1	Double Trade Creation (Internal and External)	−	+	+
2	External Trade Creation and Internal Trade Diversion	−	−	+
3	Internal Trade Creation and External Trade Diversion	−	+	−
4	External Trade Diversion and External Trade Erosion	+	+	−
5	Double Trade Erosion (Internal and External)	+	−	−
6	Internal Trade Diversion and Internal Trade Erosion	+	−	+

Source: Truman (1975) p. 5. Reprinted by permission.

and he found that "there was net trade created from the formation of the two trade blocs" (1975, p. 38).

Balassa (1975) employed an alternative method to measure the trade creation and diversion effects of the European Union as it was formed in the 1960s. He reasoned that by measuring the income elasticities of demand for imports one would expect marked changes for those of partner countries (and also, too, for non-partners) after an integration process. A rise in elasticity would be an indication of an increase in intra-area trade and hence, gross trade creation. Alternatively, a decline in elasticity would indicate trade diversion. Several commodity groups were considered for the EU countries and he found that "trade creation has been substantial in absolute terms and has exceeded trade diversion several times" (Balassa 1975, p. 116).

Kreinin also found that the effect of the initial formation of the European Union was a net trade creation: "clearly trade creation was far in excess of trade diversion" (1972, p. 916). More recent evidence is presented by Jacquemin and Sapir (1988) who studied the changes in the respective shares of the three components of trade for the four larger EU countries--Germany, France, Italy and the United Kingdom--over the period 1975-82, and for each of up to 92 separate industrial sectors.

TABLE 4.2   The Experiences of Individual Industrial Sectors in Four EU
Members

Result upon International Trade of Economic Integration Event	Number of Industrial Sectors Experiencing Each Case			
	Germany	France	Italy	United Kingdom
1 Double Trade Creation (Internal and External)	51	72	57	54
2 External Trade Creation and Internal Trade Diversion	11	7	8	2
3 Internal Trade Creation and External Trade Diversion	3	3	6	7
4 External Trade Diversion and External Trade Erosion	0	1	1	6
5 Double Trade Erosion (Internal and External)	8	7	8	13
6 Internal Trade Diversion and Internal Trade Erosion	5	2	5	2

Source: Jacquemin and Sapir (1988), p. 131. Reprinted by permission.

The experiences of these countries and sectors are summarized according
to Truman's scheme in Table 4.2.   It is apparent that for the
overwhelming majority trade creation rather than trade diversion was
the result: case 1 (Double Trade Creation) was the most common
suggesting that trade increased among both the EU members and
between these and non-member countries.   In approximately equal
numbers of cases--but far fewer--there were instances where trade
increased with non-members and decreased with members (case 2), and
where double trade erosion (case 5) took place.   Neither of these would
have been the predicted outcomes of integration.   Indeed, the
anticipated outcome of trade creation among members and trade
diversion from non-members (case 3) occurred in few cases at all.   Past
experience, therefore, suggests that further economic integration
through the EC-92 program may have little negative impact on EU
trade with third countries such as the United States.

Quantitative Estimates of EC-92's Impacts

In support of the objectives of the Single Europe Act, the European Commission sponsored a series of research programs enquiring into the economic impacts of the proposed integrated market. The most important early report has been dubbed the "Cecchini Report"[1] after its committee chairman and bore a substantial responsibility for supporting and sustaining the momentum begun by the SEA. This provided detailed estimates of the expected gains in European Union income or gross domestic product (GDP) as well as its effects on prices, public finances and employment. Subsequently, these findings have been disputed and further research, mostly under EU-sponsorship, has addressed particular aspects of the program. The results of these third-party analyses have a significant, albeit indirect, bearing upon the project pursued here.

Impacts upon the Economy of the European Union

The Cecchini Report resulted from an exhaustive research program which employed a variety of methodologies and many sources of data. Estimates of the impacts for EC-92 were made using studies of the first nine members of the European Union (EUR 9).[2] Owing to the recent accession of Greece, Portugal and Spain these were not included. Quantitative analyses were undertaken by a microeconomic approach the results of which are displayed in Table 4.3 and a macroeconomic approach, with its results reported in Table 4.4.

As indicated in Table 4.3, impacts are divided into those stemming from the removal of the existing barriers to trade and those accruing from the integration of the much larger, unified market. The gains from the removal of the barriers consist of those which directly affect trade (Stage 1) and those which affect overall production (Stage 2). The former include those costs incurred at the internal frontiers such as customs duties and the administrative costs associated with cross-border trade.   The latter include the gains from the removal of technical barriers within each of the separate countries and it can be seen that these are estimated to be significantly larger than the mere costs of traversing borders.

The second set of estimates concerns those gains that may be achieved through the larger, integrated market. These include the effects of market size itself (Stage 3) such that post-1992 firms will be able to achieve better economies of scale through operating in a larger market. These calculations involved detailed surveys and, for each of many separate industrial sectors, estimates of minimum efficient technical scale (METS, Emerson et al. 1988, p. 126) were made. These

TABLE 4.3 Estimates of the Total Economic Gains from the Completion
of the Internal Market: the Microeconomic Approach

	$ billion	As a share of European Union GDP (%)
Stage 1. Gains from the removal of barriers affecting trade only	10--11	0.2--0.3
Stage 2. Gains from the removal of barriers affecting overall production	71--89	2.0--2.4
Subtotal, Stages 1 and 2:	81--100	2.2--2.7
Stage 3. Gains from exploiting economies of scale more fully	75	2.1
Stage 4. Gains from intensified competition reducing business ineffectiveness and monopoly profits	58	1.6
Subtotal, Stages 3 and 4:	75--133	2.1--3.7
Total Gains:		
for 7 members, 1985 prices	159--234	4.3--6.5
for 12 members, 1988 prices	213--313	4.3--6.5

Note: Dollar ($) values are in 1985 prices and are converted from European
Currency Units at a rate of 1 ECU = US$1.25.

Source: Emerson (1988) p. 203. Reprinted by permission of Oxford University
Press.

estimates indicate the minimum firm size to achieve the maximum
economies of scale and a cost gradient for firms operating below this
level. The METS were found to be particularly large in the
transportation, chemicals and machinery sectors and much smaller in
foods, textiles and clothing, for instance. Using these METS, the sizes
of the existing national economies, and the size of the proposed single
market, estimates were derived for the gains to be had if firms are able
to reach their METS.

In addition to economies of scale, it is presumed that gains may
accrue from the increased competition to be experienced by all sectors
through the creation of the single market (Stage 4). A number of
competition effects were identified as firms are compelled to compete
more aggressively on price as they lose their protected, local markets.

TABLE 4.4 Macroeconomic Consequences of the Completion of the Internal Market

	Percent of GDP	Consumer Prices (%)	Employment (1,000s)	Government Deficit (% GDP)	External Balance (% GDP)
Internal Market Measures					
Frontier Controls	0.4	-1.0	200	0.2	0.2
Public Procurement	0.5	-1.4	350	0.3	0.1
Financial Services	1.5	-1.4	400	1.1	0.3
Supply Effects	2.1	-2.3	850	0.6	0.4
Total					
Average	4.5	-6.1	1,800	2.2	1.0
Range	3.2 to 5.7	-4.5 to -7.7	1,300 to 2,300	1.5 to 3.0	0.7 to 1.3
Average with Accompanying Economic Policy Measures					
Policy I	7.5	-4.3	5,700	0.0	-0.5
Policy II	6.5	-4.6	4,400	0.7	0.0
Policy III	7.0	-4.5	5,000	0.4	-0.2

Source: Emerson (1988) p. 208 and p. 216. Reprinted by permission of Oxford University Press.

As markets are thrown open, it is anticipated that prices across the European Union will converge towards the lowest found in any of the members. Furthermore, within firms, the increased competitive environment will lead them to reduce some of their internal costs, referred to as X-inefficiency or "corporate slack" (Peck 1989, p. 279). Reduced prices will be welfare gains to all EU consumers, including both individual and commercial consumers.

Non-price gains are also hypothesized to occur in the restructuring of the EU business community to make better use of each regions' resources and the increase in consumers' welfare (utility) that arises with the availability of a greater number of products in the market. These, however, are not quantifiable and although discussed and promised as benefits of the single market, are not included in the estimates in Table 4.3.

The macroeconomic approach arrives at similar results but apportions the gains from EC-92 by the separate effects of the removal of frontier controls (the physical barriers), the opening up of public procurement, the liberalization of financial services, and the resultant supply-side effects (Emerson et al. 1988, pp. 205, 206 and 209). These latter three include the price reductions and the better allocation of resources resulting from a more optimal matching of industry with comparative advantage and the attainment of economies of scale (Emerson et al. 1988, p. 211). Table 4.4 displays the estimated consequences derived from this approach, measuring the relative changes in GDP and consumer prices and the absolute effects on employment, public borrowing and the EU's trade balance.

It was noted, however, that in the short-term, unemployment may actually increase as European industry is restructured and may be accentuated through localized effects. As a result and also to increase the benefits of the single market, macroeconomic policies should be used in support of EC-92. Examples of such policies include reducing public debt which would result in the gains reported as Policy I in Table 4.4. However, since it is estimated that this may result in a deterioration of the European Union's external trade balance, amending the policy to hold this in balance would result in the estimates given as Policy II. Finally, a compromise (Policy III) would still result in significant economic gains for the EU.

The estimates vary considerably but to many observers the percentage gains may seem rather small; as Baldwin (1989, p. 247) quipped, "If the effect is so small, why is everyone so excited ?" However, when one considers the scale involved the Cecchini Report clearly demonstrated that significant, one-time economic gains would result from the EC-92 program. The promise of a boost in GDP of "some

$270 billion....the creation of millions of new jobs, the reduction of inflation, and the harvest of large budgetary gains" (Hufbauer 1990, p. 7) was sufficient to whet the European Union's appetite for the project.

The Cecchini Report's estimates have not gone unchallenged, however, although the sheer scale and diligence of its undertaking has probably deterred many would-be dissenters. Peck (1989) levels his criticism at perhaps the weakest part of the report--its assumptions that EC-92 will indeed result in a single, fully-integrated market as advertised. He argues that the economic gains spelled out in the report are contingent upon the political realm and that here there are likely to be many obstacles. In particular, much of the anticipated gains are from the competitive effects--achieving economies of scale and reducing X-inefficiency--but the reality of this is that many firms will disappear. For example, he contends that Britain would lose 46 of its 65 existing footwear firms, 31 of 52 carpet firms, and 1 of its 3 automobile makers. Similar outcomes are anticipated for other members and, since the closure of firms is necessarily a localized affair, the political pressures that would result may compel governments to intervene thereby thwarting the creation of a truly-unified market. Similarly, political issues arise for members as they try to eliminate national technical standards, particularly the "purity laws" and others that are culturally-tied while for public procurement, it will be difficult to overcome "national nepotism" (Peck 1989, p. 291). Also, the uneven pattern of labor costs across the European Union may lead to industrial relocation akin to the U.S.'s post-war drift to the Sunbelt,[3] and this too may prompt national governments to act, especially when one recognizes that in parliamentary democracies their concern for their own electorate and tax-base may override pan-European fraternal sentiments.

Peck (1989) concludes that Cecchini's estimates should be halved, suggesting that EC-92 will boost European Union GDP by only about 2 percent, although his estimates are strikingly arbitrary in comparison to Cecchini's exactitude. Also, it should be noted that in the United States--which is often cited as a *model* fully-integrated economy-- individual state governments pursue industrial policies with relatively little negative effects on the functioning of the market. Similarly, in a thoughtful review of the EC-92 rhetoric, Wise and Gibb (1993) conclude that the Cecchini estimates are inflated and that the main achievements of the program will be to promote trade among members and to advance the cause of European unity.

In contrast, Baldwin (1989) argues that the Cecchini Report's estimates fall well short of the mark. He asserts that the acknowledged restriction to only static effects of EC-92 ignores the greater potential of dynamic effects. These are not well understood and so cannot easily be included in such a study. For Baldwin, the static effects represent only one-time gains, that is they have only a single impact on GDP, prices and employment. Dynamic effects, on the other hand, may permanently raise the European economy's growth rates by 0.2-0.9 percent resulting in a recurring impact. Considering the dynamic effects, Baldwin suggests that whereas the Cecchini Report estimated GDP growth of 2.5-6.5 percent, including dynamic effects these should be 11-35 percent! (1989, p. 263)   At the lower end of the estimate, few dynamic effects are evident and the effects are mostly static, while the higher end assumes that substantial industrial restructuring takes place. These effects, it should be noted, are spread over time with perhaps only half evident in the medium term (up to 10 years).

Estimates of Sectoral and National Impacts

The Cecchini Report necessarily considered separate industry sectors and individual member states in the process of generating its estimates. However, only the results of the microeconomic analysis were reported by sector (Emerson et al. 1988, pp. 223-250). These are contained in Table 4.5 with the largest gains being forecast for Electrical Goods, Motor Vehicles, Chemicals, Mechanical Engineering, and Credit and Insurance, respectively. With respect to the members, at least part of their individual impacts are perhaps foreseen by the tables indicating the price dispersions by sector (Emerson et al. 1988, pp. 277-285).

The Cecchini Report was drawn from a program of research under the title "Research on the Cost of Non-Europe." This consisted of a series of independent studies conducted by either independent researchers under EC sponsorship or staff of the Directorate-Generals of the Commission itself. These analyses evaluated the current welfare costs to the European Community of the present, non-unified market-- that is, "Non-Europe". Non-Europe became the straw man against which to compare the ideal, fully-integrated market envisioned in EC-92. The sixteen volumes and Annexes (European Commission 1988) consider nine key industrial and service sectors, the costs of frontier formalities and technical barriers, restricted public procurement, and a comparison with the North American experience.

A subsequent report continued an analysis of the sectors most affected by the completion of the internal market, focussing particularly on the removal of public procurement restrictions (Buiges et al. 1990). The analysis divided the sectors into four subgroups: (1) high-technology public procurement markets; traditional public procurement markets, including two sub-groups (2) sectors with national champions; and (3) private sectors dominated by public procurement; and (4) sectors with

TABLE 4.5 Welfare Gains from the Effects of Barrier Removal and Integration

	Barrier Removal Effects ($ billion)	Market Integration Effects ($ billion)	Total
Agriculture	0.9--3.8	0.0--1.4	0.9--5.2
Solid Fuels	0.0--0.1	0.0--0.3	0.0--0.4
Coke	0.0	0.0	0.0
Oil, gas, petrol	1.5--2.0	0.0--2.5	1.5--4.5
Electricity, gas, water	4.1	0.0--0.8	4.1--4.9
Nuclear fuels	0.0	0.0	0.0
Ores, metals	0.6--2.1	0.0--3.5	0.6--5.6
Non-metallic minerals	0.4	0.9--2.9	1.3--3.3
Chemicals	3.5--3.6	8.0--15.4	11.5--19.0
Metal articles	1.0--1.8	1.5--4.8	2.5--6.4
Mechanical engineering	3.3--4.0	10.9--13.5	14.2--17.5
Office machinery	2.0--2.1	6.3--6.5	8.3--8.6
Electrical goods	3.3--4.1	16.4--20.5	19.7--24.6
Motor vehicles	2.6--3.9	15.0--18.4	17.6--22.3
Other transport	2.1--2.4	2.5--5.1	4.6--7.5
Meats, preserves	0.6--2.3	0.6--1.4	1.2--3.7
Dairy products	0.6--2.5	1.4--2.4	2.0--4.9
Other food products	1.5--3.4	3.0--6.1	4.5--9.5
Beverages	0.5--0.6	1.1--1.9	1.6--2.1
Tobacco products	0.3--0.4	1.3--1.9	1.6--2.3
Textiles, clothing	2.0--2.1	1.8--2.0	3.8--4.1
Leather	0.9	0.8	1.7
Timber, furniture	0.9--1.1	0.9	1.8--2.0
Paper and products	0.8	2.6--5.5	3.4--6.3
Rubber, plastics	0.4	1.0--2.6	1.4--3.6
Other manufactures	0.9--1.1	0.8--0.9	1.7--2.0
Building, civil engineering	5.4--6.1	0.0--2.9	5.4--9.0
Wholesale, retail trade	4.4--4.8	0.0--1.9	4.4--6.7
Lodging, catering	1.4--2.3	0.0--1.1	1.4--3.3
Inland transport	1.9	0.0--0.5	1.9--2.4
Sea and air transport	1.8	0.0--0.4	1.8--2.2
Auxiliary transport	0.1	0.0--0.1	0.1--0.2
Communications	2.1	0.0--0.3	2.1--2.4
Credit and insurance	13.1--13.3	0.0--1.4	13.1--14.7
Rent	1.9--2.0	0.0--0.3	1.9--2.3
Other market services	7.4--7.5	0.0--0.6	7.4--8.1
Non-market services	7.3--8.0	0.0--3.3	7.3--11.3
Total	81--99.8	76.9--134.0	157.9--233.8

Source: Emerson (1988) pp. 246-247. Reprinted by permission of Oxford University Press.

moderate non-tariff barriers, including many consumer and capital goods industries. Subsequently, the member countries are described according to their relative performances in research and development (R&D), capital-intensive and labor-intensive sectors, and the implications of EC-92 are evaluated for each.

An earlier study commissioned by the EC was conducted by the Economists Advisory Group and considered the impacts of deregulation of the presently-regulated markets in the European Community (Economists Advisory Group 1987). This analysis was based upon the experiences of the deregulation of the civil aviation, telecommunications and road haulage industries in the U.S.A. and compared them to the situations in the U.K. and the rest of Europe. This study differed from Buiges et al. (1990) in that it was less empirical but focused instead on the actual experiences of selected industries and the restructuring they underwent.

Impacts on the International Trade of the European Union

Little attention was given to the European Union's external trade position in the aftermath of EC-92. The Cecchini Report (1988) estimated gains in the external trade balance (Table 4.4) and the net effect on the EU's trade balance is ambiguous: the estimated effects depending upon different macroeconomic polices. Furthermore, there was no detailed analysis of the impacts of the program on the foreign trade of specific sectors or on the European Union's trading partners. The external implications, however, have been of primary concern to non-member countries but the potential implications can be gleaned only from analyses of the EU's trade patterns prior to EC-92 and of the contemporary issues in trade policy. Table 4.6 indicates the Community's external trade links in 1992. According to these data, the EU's largest trading partner is EFTA most of whose members border directly on those of the European Union. The U.S., however, is the largest single trading partner by a large margin and, unlike Japan, its trade is approximately balanced between exports and imports. Evidently, the external implications of EC-92 are likely to be greater for the U.S. than for many of the European Union's other trade partners.

Implications for U.S. Trade. The combined European Union is America's largest trading partner and although no detailed analysis exists of the implications of EC-92 for U.S.-EU trade, the single market may have significant implications for the U.S. economy. It is expected that resultant growth in the European economy will be to the benefit of American exporters as much as European (domestic) producers. However, the key issue, as Hufbauer (1990, p. 22) notes, is whether this

TABLE 4.6. European Union Trade with Non-Member Countries, 1990

	Imports (percentage of total)	Exports (percentage of total)
European Free Trade Association	23.5	26.5
United States	18.4	18.2
Japan	10.0	5.4
Other Industrialized Countries	7.8	9.7
Eastern Europe	3.1	3.5
Soviet Union	3.6	3.2
OPEC	9.7	8.4
East and Southeast Asian Newly -industrializing Economies[1]	7.6	7.2
China	2.3	1.3
North Africa/Middle East	2.8	4.5
Latin America	5.0	3.1

[1] Hong Kong, Taiwan, South Korea, Philippines, Singapore, Malaysia and Thailand.

Source: Eurostat (1992) p. 233.

trade creation is (a) greater than, (b) balanced by, or (c) surpassed by *trade diversion*, in which U.S. exports are replaced by those from other EU countries. Previous experience of such events offers little guidance. Estimates of the impacts of the initial formation of the EEC, and of the two subsequent expansions of the EC indicate that, in general, trade creation far outstripped trade diversion. However, for the last expansion in 1986 (the accession of Portugal and Spain) resulted in a small loss of trade (Hufbauer 1990, p. 23; Yannopoulos 1988, p. 128). Nevertheless, the prevailing optimism is expressed by Calingaert (1988b):

...the completion of the internal market will, by all counts, result in an expanding market and thus greater opportunities for products exported to the European Union. (p. 19)

A more political concern but one that forms a major item on the agenda of U.S. Congressional Hearings[4] is the threat to the U.S.'s dominant position in the post-WWII world economy from a resurgent Europe. This topic is primarily the preserve of politicians and political commentators but is essentially an economic issue. Nevertheless, it is probably too ethereal to be quantified easily.

Another issue of concern for the U.S., although causing much less alarm, is the potential impacts for American firms operating in Europe. The 1988 sales of U.S.-owned affiliates operating in the European Union amounted to some $620 billion, a sum considerably greater than the $76 billion of U.S. goods actually exported to the EU. Hufbauer noted that:

> Whatever EC-1992 may hold for U.S. exports, it basically holds great promise for General Motors, International Business Machines, Merck, American Telephone and Telegraph, and a long list of other U.S. firms with a strong presence in Europe. (p. 25)

These firms are well placed to benefit from EC-92. Unlike many of their nationally-bound domestic competitors they typically have pan-European organizational structures already in place. Peck (1988, p. 244) observed that in food processing, for example, eight of the ten largest firms worldwide are American, the other two being European of which, only one (Unilever) is based in the European Union. Since, at present, most EU firms operate exclusively in national markets American firms operating within the EU are already in an advantageous position. The primary concern for these transnational corporations and their lobbyists in Washington and Brussels alike, is whether the new rules will recognize them as European firms, or as foreigners. This is particularly important with respect to the liberalization of public procurement in the member states as EU-based American firms seek to share in this sector.

While the fortunes of American transnationals with investments in the EU are significant, there is also concern in the U.S. over their relationship to American exports. As Bergsten et al. noted: "Over time...foreign investment becomes less and less the complement of, and more and more the substitute for, U.S. exports," (1978, p. 97) and so there may be a divergence in the interests of U.S. business and the U.S. economy. Hufbauer (1990) raises this same concern by noting the comment of former Secretary of Defense, Charles E. Wilson, who said that "what's good for the country is good for General Motors, and vice versa". (p. 48) While that may well have been true in 1953 when GM's profits were almost entirely generated in the U.S, in 1988 merely 44 percent were accounted for by its American operations, while fully 37 percent came from its European divisions.

U.S. Policy Considerations in the Wake of EC-92

American policy towards the European Union and the EC-92 program has progressed beyond the reactionary, "Fortress Europe" scare mongering. It is now widely recognized that the EU has at least as much at stake in an open international trading system as the U.S. and so is unlikely to pursue protectionist policies. In place, specific positive and negative implications now form the topics of discussion. Of the former, both U.S. exporters and firms with European operations should gain significantly from the single market although, on the negative side, these gains may be limited by new incarnations of residual restrictions on public procurement and possibly some protectionist policies for specific sectors. Ginsberg (1989, p. 8) noted the potential for American exports to be inadvertently harmed by EU anti-dumping duties, quotas and voluntary restraint agreements targeted for Japan, inasmuch as they affect the exports of Japanese transplant firms operating in the U.S. On balance, however, U.S.-EU trade relations continue to be mutually-beneficial and the general thrust of EU trade policies--discriminating against Japan--should strike a familiar tone to most U.S. policymakers.

However, a number of specific issues remain and an exhaustive list is provided by Cooney (1989, p. 1). The setting of EU-wide technical and environmental standards are a concern as they affect U.S. exports, but increasingly U.S. firms and standards-setting bodies are being invited to participate on a reciprocal basis. The opening-up of public procurement in the EU affects a sizeable part of the European economy but most likely, "national" will be replaced by "European" as the criteria for contract tendering. It is, however, unclear how European affiliates of U.S. firms will be treated. The concept of *reciprocity* in the granting of market access for non-EU firms remains an important issue, but since this policy is very much akin to the U.S.'s, and given the already sizeable American presence in European markets, it is likely to prove acceptable in practice. Similarly, the debate over how to define the "rules of origin" in dealing with products with components from many sources and the related definitional problem of "local content," also threatens to significantly affect the operations of U.S. affiliates in the EU.

Other issues are more universal and not specifically tied to EC-92. These include the EU's treatment of intellectual property which is of particular concern to American computer software, publishing and entertainment firms. Perennial areas of concern and the basic stock of trans-Atlantic economic diplomacy also include: the social dimension, which threatens to add business costs to U.S. affiliates; competition policy, which favorably prohibits subsidies for local, national champions; and monetary policy which is already closely-linked to the U.S.'s. In addition, there remain some particular sectoral issues such as automobiles, telecommunications, information technology, electronics and agriculture where there are the greatest internal pressures on the European Union for industrial policies, and which may lead to de facto protectionism (Harrison 1988, 24, Buchan et al. 1991, p. 12).

The influence of the U.S. on the proceedings of the EC-92 program is the greatest of any non-member country. An example of the resolution of U.S.-EU trade conflicts is found in the compensation received by the U.S. for its lost trade when Portugal and Spain joined the EU.[5] Clearly the importance of the U.S.-EU trading relationship is such that the EU is prepared to make significant bilateral accommodations to the U.S. However, U.S. Commerce Secretary Robert Mosbacher's suggestion that the U.S. should be granted a role in the EC-92 deliberations were going too far (Ludlow, 1991: 226). As Ginsberg (1989) points out, this would not be acceptable to the EU "since we would not afford the Europeans the same treatment when we deliberate" (p. 11). There are, therefore, limits to the United State's role in internal European affairs, and that this role may in fact be diminishing.

European economic and, should it occur, political integration clearly poses a new challenge for American foreign policy. As Ginsberg (1989) notes, with the process of progressive European economic unification since the 1950s (encouraged by the U.S.) "Europe has come of age" (p. 8). The U.S. must brace itself in the 1990s for a more self-confident, independent-minded, and assertive economic and political partner in Europe. This in itself provides a significant challenge to American foreign policy, particularly as it coincides with a similar ascension on the world stage of another "civilian power," Japan (Ginsberg 1989, p. 9). Hufbauer (1990) suggests that the U.S. may be compelled to relinquish its role as the sole "custodian of the international economic system" (p. 49) to a U.S.-EU-Japan triumvirate.

The lead taken by the European Union in supporting the restructuring the eastern European economies following the collapse of the "Iron Curtain" in 1989 portends the future limited role of the U.S. in this region. The EU's desire to forge ties with its eastern neighbours and the independent diplomacy undertaken by western European countries in response to former Soviet president Gorbachev's call for a *common European home*: "tear(s) at the contours of U.S. security policy in Europe" (Ginsberg 1989, p. 10). While these concerns belong primarily in the political realm they do parallel, as they always have done, the realities of the economic realm, in addition to affecting the general course of U.S.-EU relations. Thus, while EC-92 is a program addressing the economic structure of Europe, it has significant political implications that are only compounded by its coincidence with the restructuring of the international political balance.

A final implication of EC-92 for the U.S. strikes much closer to home and echoes the earlier discussion of the role of American transnational firms in substituting the products of their overseas affiliates for U.S. exports. Hufbauer (1990) asserts that "a significant offshoot of the European state will be further disassociation between firms and nations, as transatlantic and transpacific mergers and alliances redraw the map of global business" (p. 47). The growing internationalization of the world economy, of which EC-92 will be a substantial contributor, will lead to increasingly divorced corporate and national entities. Already, it is difficult to talk of General Motors as a U.S. company rather than a European company, and the same process is even occurring with Japanese firms such as Honda, as they spread themselves internationally. "Like baseball teams of today, national champions of tomorrow may prove surprisingly 'disloyal' to their local supporters" (Hufbauer 1990, p. 48).

The Potential Impacts of EC-92 on the Trade of the U.S. States and Regions

The exposure of U.S. states and regions to trade with the European Union and the latter's contribution to their manufacturing growth have been analyzed in detail in Chapters 2 and 3, respectively. Upon these bases, the potential impacts of EC-92 on trans-Atlantic trade and the states' economies may be evaluated. As has been discussed above the analysis will be restricted to exports only; since these events are occurring in the internal EU market, they will be most directly affecting the realm of U.S. exports. The impacts upon imports, however, will be indirect and are, at this stage, very difficult to foresee. It is conceivable that the European Union's exports may be severely disrupted as European producers lose their sheltered national markets and are compelled to focus on their domestic sales. On the other hand it is also quite conceivable that in the longer-term, EU producers may be able to realize greater domestic economies of scale through the enlarged local market, and so compete more effectively with American and other foreign firms. The actual outcomes depend upon the strategies pursued by European firms in their restructuring responses. In both cases, the impacts are likely to be evident in only the medium and longer-terms, in contrast to those affecting exports, many of which may occur in the immediate aftermath of EC-92.

Evaluating the impact upon exports necessitates the examination of several issues and depends upon the availability of secondary information. First, estimates are required for the anticipated expansion of the European Union's markets with the single market program. Since these markets represent the destination for U.S. goods, any change in their size will have a commensurate effect upon the demand for U.S. exports. Second, while these markets may grow with EC-92, the effect on exports will depend upon the level of penetration of U.S. goods in the European markets. The existing level may be sustained or changed markedly with an increase in demand and if the demand for U.S. products is comparatively elastic, then an increase in European demand with EC-92 may, for instance, result in a proportionately greater increase in the demand for U.S. exports. Third, the issue of trade creation versus trade diversion is pertinent in assessing the effects of EC-92. The extent to which the integration of the European economy diverts trade from U.S. to other European partners is of major consequence to U.S. exporters and the U.S. government. The experience of previous integration events may enable a consideration of this issue. Finally, the persistence or even the creation of new barriers to U.S. trade with the EU will necessarily have a significant effect on the degree to which any growth in European demand is translated into demand for U.S. goods. For each of these issues, the effects will be differentiated by sector since the impacts on demand and the imposition of trade barriers will themselves vary by industry sector.

Estimating the Impacts of EC-92 on U.S. Exports by Industry Sector

In the following discussion, each of the four issues introduced above will be considered in evaluating the probable sectoral-level impacts upon trade. In this way, a range of impacts by sector will reveal a profile of potential trade effects that may be utilized in the shift-share forecasting model. This model will be estimated twice: first, using growth rates from the lower range of estimates; and second, using those of the higher range. Taken together, these two scenarios demarcate the upper and lower bounds of the likely impacts of EC-92 on the states' exports and, hence, their economies. These results--based upon imperfect data--are necessarily tentative and need to be regarded with caution. However, with such qualifiers they are nevertheless both illuminating and informative and a valuable contribution to the issue of international trade and regional economics.

The Expansion of EU Markets for Industrial Goods. As has been discussed above, it is widely assumed that the single market program will be responsible for a significant increase in the European Union's gross domestic product. The Cecchini (1988) report estimates an increase of between 4.3 and 6.5 percent, figures which have been challenged and revised both upwardly and downwardly. When one considers that these estimates represent a one-time real increase then they can be appreciated as being a significant boost to the European economy, particularly if Baldwin's (1989) assertions that dynamic effects will magnify these gains still further prove to be true. These estimates, however, measure gains from a welfare perspective and represent economic benefit to European consumers. They do not directly imply a growth in the demand for goods in the European market and so are not directly relevant for U.S. exporters. Undoubtedly, however, a growth in GDP of five percent will increase the demand for most or all products, with the actual relationship depending upon the income elasticity of demand for individual goods.

The estimated welfare gains for individual sectors are reported in Emerson (1988) and in Table 4.5 above, although these are not directly comparable to the U.S. SIC categories. The twenty-one European sectors approximate to the 20 manufacturing SIC categories and are included in Table 4.7 which reports the welfare gains as a percentage of output. These data are adapted from those contained in Emerson (1988) and indicate the relative magnitude of EC-92's anticipated effects across different industry sectors. Evidently, the effects of the program vary greatly: from less than 2 percent for Oil, Gas and Petroleum to as high as 14.2 percent for Office Machinery. Other sectors with high estimated effects include Electrical Goods, Motor Vehicles and Other Transport, Mechanical Engineering, and Other Manufactures.

The Effects of the Removal of Internal Barriers by Sector. An additional source of information on the sectoral impacts of EC-92 is found in Buiges et al.'s (1990) study. This project identified the manufacturing sectors most likely to experience the greatest impacts from the completed internal market. Attention was paid to those sectors which currently experience the greatest intra-EU non-tariff trade barriers and, hence, those which are presumed to be most affected by their removal. It is presumed that the liberalization of controls on public procurement will cause formerly closed markets to be open to firms from other EU members and possibly, also, to those of non-

TABLE 4.7 Welfare Gains from EC-92 by Sector and Share of GDP

	Equivalent SIC Sector	Gains from barrier removal and integration ($ billion)	Share of Total Output, 1985 (%)
Dairy products	20	2.0--4.9	2.7--6.7
Meats, preserves	20	1.2--3.7	2.0--6.1
Beverages	20	1.6--2.1	2.3--3.1
Other food products	20	4.5--9.5	2.3--4.8
Tobacco products	21	1.6--2.3	3.2-4.6
Textiles, clothing	22 / 23	3.8--4.1	2.4--2.6
Timber, furniture	24 / 25	1.8--2.0	2.1--2.3
Paper and products	26 / 27	3.4--6.3	2.1--3.8
Chemicals	28	11.5--19.0	3.9--6.5
Oil, gas, petrol	29	1.5--4.5	0.5--1.5
Rubber, plastics	30 / 28	1.4--3.6	1.6--4.2
Leather	31	1.7	5.3
Non-metallic minerals	32	1.3--3.3	1.3--3.3
Ores, metals	33	0.6--5.6	0.3--2.8
Metal articles	34	2.5--6.4	1.5--3.8
Mechanical engineering	35	14.2--17.5	7.2--8.8
Office machinery	35	8.3--8.6	13.7--14.2
Electrical goods	36	19.7--24.6	10.2--12.7
Motor vehicles	37	17.6--22.3	9.6--12.2
Other transport	37	4.6--7.5	8.1--13.2
Other manufactures	38 / 39	1.7--2.0	7.2--8.4

Source: Adapted from Emerson pp. 1988, 235-237 and 246-247.

members. From a global trade perspective therefore, "new" markets will be effectively created.

Forty sectors out of 120 are included in the study and these are separated into four types. First, high-technology, public-procurement sectors including Telecommunications, Computers and Medical Equipment are those in which state and public authorities are generally major customers and the proliferation of *national champions* has left a number of European producers that are comparatively small in comparison to their American and Japanese competitors. Traditional public-procurement and regulated sectors are those which are often state-owned. These include *natural monopolies* such as Energy-Generation, and Railways, and other sectors which have been deemed to have strategic significance such as Shipbuilding and Electrical

Engineering. Finally, a large group of consumer and capital goods sectors are identified where, for various reasons, there presently exists substantial non-tariff barriers; in many cases, these result from different national technical standards. Table 4.8 includes the 40 sectors most affected by EC-92. For the first three types, the non-tariff barriers are estimated to be high and, for the fourth group, they are deemed to be moderate. While in theory EC-92 should see the removal of all non-tariff barriers in all sectors, it is possible that in the public-procurement sectors, in particular, there may remain a degree of national preference in purchasing policies that will discriminate against both other EU producers and U.S. exporters.

Of the sectors identified in Table 4.8, it is apparent that there are particular types of industry comprising those which are most likely to be affected by the removal of the remaining non-tariff barriers. In particular, Industrial Machinery and Electrical and Electronic Equipment comprise a large share of the 40 sectors identified by Buiges et al (1990). In the case of the former, these are mostly in the commercial sector wherein the non-tariff barriers are largely technical barriers. For the latter, these also include sectors that are dominated by public-procurement and presumably many national champions comprise these sectors. In addition, the Food Products sectors are often subject to government regulation and several are listed in the traditional public-procurement or regulated markets groups. Other notable sectors include Chemicals, Textiles and Apparel, the former of which is an important exporting sector for the U.S. This is also one which is often highly regulated and, in the case of Pharmaceuticals, is one dominated by the purchases of public health authorities in Europe.

Estimates of Sales Growth by European Industries. Neither of the former two sources of sectoral-level estimates of the impacts of EC-92 focuses directly upon the demand potential for individual sectors; in both cases, they merely offer indications of those sectors most affected. A third source, however, deals directly with the anticipated effects upon sales of the completion of the internal market. One component of the comprehensive project, the "Research on the Cost of Non-Europe" project--the results of which were ultimately incorporated into the Cecchini (1988) report--was an extensive survey of European industrialists' views on the effects of the internal market. This survey was undertaken in each of the 12 members of the European Union by national consultants, industry organizations or banks and compiled by Nerb (1988). As part of the survey, the respondents were asked about their expectations of the effect of EC-92 on their sales and from their

TABLE 4.8 The European Industrial Sectors Most Affected by EC-92

European Industries	Equivalent SIC classes
Group 1: High-technology Public-procurement Sectors	
Office Machines	Industrial Machinery (35)
Telecommunications Equipment	Electrical and Electronic Goods (36)
Medico-surgical Equipment	Instruments (38)
Traditional Public-procurement or Regulated Markets	
Group 2	
Wine and Wine-Based Products, Brewing and Malting, and Soft drinks & Spa Waters	Food Products (20)
Pharmaceutical Products	Chemicals (28)
Boilers and Sheet-metal Products	Fabricated Metal Products (34)
Railway Equipment	Transportation (37)
Group 3	
Spaghetti, Macaroni, Cocoa, Chocolate & Confectionery	Food Products (20)
Electrical Wires and Cables and Electrical Equipment	Electrical and Electronic Goods (36)
Shipbuilding	Transportation (37)
Group 4: Sectors with Moderate Non-tariff Barriers	
Wool Industry, Cotton Industry, and Carpets and Floor Coverings	Textiles (22)
Footwear, Clothing, and Household Textiles	Apparel (23)
Basic Industrial Chemicals, and Other Chemical Products	Chemicals (28)
Rubber Industry	Rubber (30)
Glassware and Ceramics	Stone, Glass and Clay Products (32)
Agricultural Machinery, Machine Tools for Metals, Textile and Sewing Machines, Machines for Foodstuffs Plant for Mines, and Other Specific Equipment	Industrial Machinery (35)
Electronic Equipment, Domestic Electrical Appliances, Transmission Equipment, and Lamps and Lighting	Electrical and Electronic Goods (36)
Motor Vehicles, and Aerospace Equipment	Transportation (37)
Photographic and Cinematographic Laboratories	Instruments (38)
Jewellery, Gold and Silver, and Games, Toys and Sporting goods	Miscellaneous Manufactures (39)

Source: Adapted from Buiges et al. (1990), p. 24.

responses quantitative estimates were developed for individual industry sectors. These estimates are reported in Table 4.9.

These estimates, too, reveal a varied sectoral pattern. Once again, Industrial Machinery, Electrical and Electronic Equipment, Instruments and Food Products appear among the sectors most affected. In addition Textiles, Apparel, Lumber and Furniture are also expected to have comparatively large increases in sales. While the variation among the estimates is not particularly large, these data reinforce the contention that certain sectors are likely to experience greater growth than others.

These estimates, however, are probably not accurate predictions of the sectoral growth rates resulting from EC-92; they are the estimates of European industrialists and may be quite different from the effects experienced by foreign (ie, U.S.) exporters, particularly in sectors for which they have a comparative advantage or disadvantage.

The Penetration of U.S. Exports in the European Market. There is a concern among EU policymakers that benefits of the single European market may be reaped by foreign firms, particularly in sectors where American and Japanese firms already benefit from existing economies of scales over domestic firms. This issue has typically been raised with reference to international trade agreements and reciprocity in bilateral trade relations. Among the many studies of EC-92 and its implications, however, there does not appear to have been any examination of the potential effects of the program on the rates of penetration of foreign imports in the European market. Any change in penetration rates would have significant implications for the degree to which U.S. exports may share in the growth of EU demand.

Recent trends in import penetration are documented by the European Commission (D.G. External Relations, 1989) for the period 1973-85. This period was chosen as it spans the years since the first oil shock in 1973 and those between the accessions of Denmark, Ireland and the United Kingdom, and more recently, by Greece, Portugal and Spain. Import penetration rates for manufactured goods are calculated as the proportion of domestic demand that is satisfied by imports. It is evident that these rates are very similar for the EU and the U.S. alike, at 13.1 and 12.3, respectively, in 1985. For Japan, however, the comparable rate is only 4.8 percent and is virtually unchanged since 1973, indicating the comparative insularity of the Japanese economy with respect to imports.

This study reported EU penetration rates for three subsets of manufacturing sectors, strong, moderate and weak-demand sectors were identified based upon prevailing levels of domestic demand over the same period: "between 1972 and 1985, demand in the OECD countries increased by more than 5% (strong demand), around 3% (moderate

TABLE 4.9 European Industrialists' Perceived Effects on Sales of the Completion
of the Internal Market, by Major Industry Group

European Industry Group	Nearest Equivalent SIC	Net Effect on Total Sales (%)
Food, Drink and Tobacco	20 / 21	6
Textiles	22	7
Man-made Fibers	22	3
Footwear and Clothing	23	7
Timber and Furniture	24 / 25	7
Paper Products, Printing and Publishing	26 / 27	5
Chemicals	28	4
Plastic products	28	6
Oil Refining	29	3
Rubber Products	30	5
Leather Goods	31	6
Non-metallic Minerals	32	5
Primary Metals	33	4
Fabricated Metals	34	6
Mechanical Engineering	35	6
Office and Data Processing Machinery	35	6
Electrical Engineering	36	7
Motor Vehicles and Parts,	37	4
Other Transport	37	5
Precision Engineering, Optics, etc.	38	6

Source: Adapted from Nerb (1988), Tables 3.5.3--3.6.19.

demand), or less than 2% (weak demand)" (European Commission, D.G.
External Relations, 1989, p. 33). Table 4.10 contains import penetration
rates for these subsets and for all manufacturing sectors, with changes
from 1973 to 1985.

The recent history of import penetration for the EU suggests that the
strongest- and weakest-demand sectors have had the highest rates
and, for the former in particular, these rates have increased markedly.
One may infer from this that for the Chemicals, Industrial Machinery
(some sub-sectors only) and Electrical and Electronic Equipment sectors
in particular, the effects upon U.S. exports of an expansion in EU
demand may be amplified. In contrast, for those sectors with lower
levels of import penetration, an increase in demand resulting from EC-
92 may be diminished in its change in import demand.

TABLE 4.10 European Union Import Penetration Rates for Manufacturing Sectors, 1973-1985

European Sectors	Nearest Equivalent SIC	Import Penetration, 1985 (%)	Change 1973-85 (%)
All Manufacturing Sectors		13.1	+ 2.7
Strong-Demand Sectors		19.9	+ 6.9
Chemicals and pharmaceuticals	28		
Office machines and data-processing equipment,	35		
Electrical and Electronic equipment	36		
Moderate-Demand Sectors		9.7	+ 2.0
Foodstuffs, beverages, tobacco	20 / 21		
Paper, printing	26 / 27		
Rubber, plastics	28 / 30		
Industrial and agricultural machinery	35		
Transport equipment	37		
Weak-Demand Sectors		13.8	+ 1.3
Textiles, leather, clothing	22 /23 31		
Non-metallic minerals	32		
Ores, ferrous and non-ferrous metals	33		
Metal products	34		
Miscellaneous industrial products	39		

Source: Adapted from European Commission (D.G. External Relations, 1989), Tables 23 and 24.

These postulates are based upon the presumption that import penetration rates themselves will be unchanged by EC-92, and this may not be the case. Since a major component of the program is the cessation of restrictive national industrial policies, particularly in the public-procurement-dominated sectors, it is highly likely that, for certain industries, import penetration may be increased sharply. In particular, the public-procurement sectors identified by Buiges et al. (1990)--groups 1, 2 and 3, in Table 4.8--are those in which this may be the case.

Trade Creation and Trade Diversion

In the discussion above the two theoretical outcomes of an international economic integration event were discussed: *trade creation*, where the event results in a net increase in global trade such that the trade of third countries is also increased; and *trade diversion*, where trade is diverted from third countries to partners. When considering an event such as EC-92, there is inevitably a concern for the impacts upon existing trade relations and, in particular, those with third countries not participating in the integration process.

Truman's (1975) division of trade into three basic components--domestic consumption, trade with partner countries, and trade with non-members--enables the identification of six possible cases resulting from an economic integration event and these are described in Table 4.1, above. Third countries such as the U.S. fear Cases 3 and 4 in particular, in which their trade with members is diminished. In his analysis of the experience of the EEC's formation, however, Truman (1975) found that there was a net trade creation.

In their more recent study, Jacquemin and Sapir (1988) found that for the four largest European Union members, the majority of industry sectors experienced Case 1, Double Trade Creation from 1975 through 1982. Unfortunately, only summary data is reported and it is not revealed which actual industrial sectors experienced each case.

In an *ex ante* study, Haaland and Norman (1992) analysed the potential impacts of EC-92 and the proposed extension to include the EFTA countries (European Economic Area) on the EC, EFTA, Japan, the United States and the rest of the world. They found that their "most important conclusion...is that the internal market in Europe poses no threat to Japan or the U.S.A." (p. 85) In contrast, however, Milner and Allen (1992) highlight the trade diversion potential of EC-92. For this, quantitative estimates are offered although in their discussion they acknowledge that these may be more than offset by resultant growth in the European economy. In addition, they identify the important--and unpredictable--role played by diplomacy and commercial policies in affecting future trade patterns.

The prospects for U.S. trade, therefore, appear to be quite positive: based upon past experience at least, there is little evidence to suggest that an integration initiative such as EC-92 will result in trade diversion and negative consequences for U.S. exports. Indeed, the official line of the U.S. Department of Commerce is that American exporters are likely to benefit from the 1992 program (U.S. International Trade Administration, 1990).

Barriers to U.S. Exports to the European Union

There are relatively few visible barriers to U.S. exports of manufactured products. This may appear, at first, quite surprising given the recent history of contentious trade issues between the European Union on the one hand and the United States and the Cairns Group of agricultural exporters on the other. The stand-offs between these groups delayed agreement of the Uruguay round of the General Agreement on Tariffs and Trade (GATT), which was finally completed at the eleventh hour in late 1993. Certainly, trade appears to be the primary subject of trans-Atlantic diplomacy in the early 1990s, but the points of contention center mainly upon agricultural products, services and intellectual property, and do not generally include manufactured goods. Obstacles to U.S. manufactures are generally found in the realm of technical standards and public procurement policies. A purview of the U.S. Trade Representative's *1991 National Trade Estimate on Foreign Trade Barriers* (United States Trade Representative, 1991) reveals few barriers to manufactured goods. Much of the concern, however, centers not upon existing restrictions but the fear of future barriers, particularly if the European Union should develop dirigiste industrial policies or erect new barriers to regulate the degree to which foreign firms benefit from the enlarged market. An overview of the prospects for trade barriers to manufactured goods is therefore necessarily brief.

Some manufactured agricultural products, such as Food Products (SIC 20) and Tobacco Products (21), are subject to variable levies which are tariffs that comprise part of the EU's protection of its agricultural interests (USTR, 1991). In addition, from time to time new EU regulations threaten to erect new technical barriers to U.S. products. In 1991, concern was raised over regulations that would have effectively excluded some wines and distilled spirits from the European Union. In general, these cases arise from the EU's attempts to set common definitions for particular products. As a result, in some cases a product may not conform and hence be prohibited by default. In most cases such "aberrations" are resolved through negotiation.

The area of standards, testing and certification is of major concern for almost all sectors, and comprises approximately half of the almost 300 directives constituting the program. It is also an arena of intense lobbying by U.S. government and industry representatives. In general, U.S. interests are being attended to in the process of setting EU-wide technical standards, etc., and there is no evidence of an explicit intention to use these to exclude the products of non-member countries. However, as Milner and Allen (1992) point out, there is a history of problems caused by just such a process of harmonizing European standards. One of the more vitriolic recent disputes between the U.S. and EU concerned the potential exclusion of almost all meat imports from the U.S. The cause was an EU-wide ban on meat from hormone-fed cattle which was the result of the harmonization of the separate, national standards, many of which had no concern for this issue.

One of the most important areas where barriers to U.S. products exist presently is in the area of public procurement. As is the case elsewhere, including the United States, "buy national" is a long-standing feature of government and public-authority procurement policy. As discussed above, a major component of the EC-92 program is to address these, but they may be replaced by "buy European" policies with little effective change for U.S. exporters. The EU, however, has expressed an interest in loosening these policies further on a bilateral and reciprocal basis. It remains to be seen what progress can be made on this highly visible and politically-sensitive issue. Public procurement represents an important component of a number of sectors including Chemicals (SIC 28), Machinery (SIC 35), Electrical and Electronic Equipment (SIC 36) and Transportation Equipment (SIC 37). Within these broad sectors, Electrical Generating and Transmission Equipment and Telecommunications Equipment are especially restricted industries. In the latter, widespread state ownership of the national telecommunications providers tends to favor domestic equipment suppliers, and although the American firms have some significant comparative advantages in this growing sector there is considerable political pressure within the EU to maintain a domestic European industry. This is one area in which *national champions* may continue to be protected from unregulated international competition, although "national" may be replaced by "European" as the operating criterion.

Finally, a major issue in U.S.-EU trade relations concerns aircraft manufacture and Airbus Industrie, in particular, a consortium of several European aerospace firms and the world's second largest producer of commercial aircraft. Owing to intense lobbying by American civil aircraft firms (who, together, dominate the industry worldwide) the U.S. government has lodged complaints with the GATT regarding the support given Airbus and its affiliates by several EU members.[6] It should be noted, however, that there exist no barriers to U.S. exports in this sector and that the issue, as with the shipbuilding industry, concerns state support to producers and is thus on the supply side. Automobiles have also become an area of interest even though the U.S. presently exports very few vehicles or parts to the EU. The EU is likely to maintain discriminatory restrictions on the importation of Japanese automobiles and, with the growth of Japanese-owned plants in the U.S., several of whom have indicated an intention to export, it is feared that the EU policy may therefore affect U.S. exports by default.

EC-92 Growth Estimates by Sector

From the issues considered above, estimates of the potential growth in demand for U.S. exports may be developed. These are presented in Table 4.11 and are necessarily given as a range of percentage increases by sector. Although estimated in a somewhat subjective manner their value is, perhaps, best viewed from a comparative perspective. Given the available information, the relative sector-by-sector growth estimates reflect the anticipated differential effects of EC-92 on individual sectors. In Table 4.11, growth estimates for each sector are reported taking into account the information presented in Tables 4.7--4.10 above.

The estimates of welfare gains by sector (percentages of 1985 output) are taken directly from Table 4.7, adjusting as necessary to obtain values for the 20 SIC categories. For the effects of internal barrier removal, however, a more subjective scale is necessary since Buiges et al. (1990) did not offer quantitative estimates. In accordance with that analysis, the effects upon each sector are specified as either great, moderate or slight corresponding to Buiges' Groups 1, 2 and 3 (great), Group 4 (moderate), and all other sectors (slight), respectively. Once again, converting these estimates into SIC categories requires a subjective evaluation. Although some food products sub-sectors are included in Groups 2 and 3 in Table 4.8, much of this sector is not likely to be greatly affected by EC-92 (the program does not address the Common Agricultural Policy which severely restricts agricultural commodities markets) and so the net effect of barrier removal is judged to be moderate overall. Similarly, the effects upon Fabricated Metal Products is deemed to be moderate. The Textiles, Apparel, Rubber Products and Miscellaneous manufactures sectors are placed in Group 4 and are presumed to be affected moderately as well. Five sectors, Chemicals, Industrial Machinery, Electrical and Electronic Equipment, Transportation Equipment and Instruments are represented by sub-sectors listed in Groups 1, 2 and 3, and each is presumed to be affected greatly by the removal of the internal barriers. For the remaining sectors, which are not identified in Table 4.8, the effects are deemed to be slight.

The anticipated growth in sales reported in Table 4.9 is included in column 5 of Table 4.11. While the estimates of welfare gains and the effects of barrier removal correspond quite closely, the estimated sales increases are somewhat at odds with the former two considerations. Relatively low sales increases are anticipated for the Chemicals and

TABLE 4.11 A Summary of the Potential Impacts of EC-92 by Industry Sector.

Industry Sector	SIC	Welfare estimate (%)	Effects of Barrier Removal	Sales Growth (%)	Import Penetration (Type A, B or C)	Range of Growth Estimates
Food Products	20	2.0–6.7	Moderate	6	B	2–4
Tobacco Products	21	3.2–4.6	Slight	6	B	2–4
Textiles	22	2.4–2.6	Moderate	3–7	C	2–3
Apparel	23	2.4–2.6	Moderate	7	C	2–4
Lumber	24	2.1–2.3	Slight	7	(1)	1–3
Furniture	25	2.1–2.3	Slight	7	(1)	1–3
Paper	26	2.1–3.8	Slight	5	B	2–3
Printing/Publishing	27	2.1–3.8	Slight	5	B	2–3
Chemicals	28	3.9–6.5	Great	4–6	A	5–8
Petroleum/Coal	29	0.5–1.5	Slight	3	(1)	1–2
Rubber	30	1.6–4.2	Moderate	5	B	2–3
Leather	31	5.3	Slight	6	C	3–5
Stone/Glass/Clay	32	1.3–3.3	Slight	5	C	1–3
Primary Metals	33	0.3–2.8	Slight	4	C	0–2
Fabricated Metals	34	1.5–3.8	Moderate	6	C	1.5–4
Industrial Machinery	35	7.2–14.2	Great	6	A / B	8–15
Electrical and Electronic Equip.	36	10.2–12.7	Great	7	A	10–14
Transportation Equipment	37	8.1–13.2	Great	4–5	B	8–13
Instruments	38	7.2–8.4	Great	6	C	7.5–9
Miscellaneous	39	7.2–8.4	Moderate	5.5 (avg.)	C	5–8

(1) These sectors were not explicitly identified in Table 4.7.

Transportation sectors even though the predicted welfare gains are quite large and the effects of barrier removal are thought to be great. For a number of other sectors the opposite case is found, where substantial increases in sales are anticipated in sectors thought to be only slightly affected by EC-92. For the Industrial Machinery, Electrical and Electronic Equipment, and Instruments sectors, however, comparatively large increases in sales are forecast which correspond to the anticipated welfare gains and barrier effects. In general, the sales growth estimates do not vary greatly across the sectors but these values do provide reasonable benchmark estimates of the approximate percentage increase in the demand for U.S. exports from the EU.

The rates of import penetration in the European market reported in Table 4.10 are summarized as types A, B and C in column 6 of Table 4.11. These correspond to the three classes of sectors grouped according to levels of international demand which have, respectively, high and increasing; low and stable; and high and stable penetration rates. These qualitative measures are relevant in that they indicate the extent to which increases in the size of the European sectors may be translated into demand for U.S. goods.

The remaining considerations are not readily incorporated into such a tabular form and instead provide a background reference. Through a consideration of each of these previous reports, estimates of the growth in demand for U.S. manufactures are made. Given the imprecise nature of this exercise, they are necessarily expressed as ranges. For Food Products , the welfare gains and effects of barrier removal may be quite substantial for some sub-sectors, but given that many food products are subject to EU-wide import controls, the anticipated increase in demand for U.S. goods is estimated to be relatively slight, between 2 and 4 percent. Estimates for the remaining sectors are made similarly, being considered quite low for SIC categories 21 through 27, and 29 through 34, owing to either low estimates of the impacts of EC-92 or low levels of import penetration. For several other categories, however, the effects upon the demand for U.S. goods are estimated to be quite substantial. For Chemicals substantial impacts of EC-92 and a high level of import penetration suggest a fairly large increase in demand for U.S. goods in this sector (between 5 and 8 percent) although this is tempered somewhat by the possibility that the high-level of public procurement in many of its sub-sectors will reduce the net effect upon U.S. exports. For the Industrial Machinery, Electrical and Electronic Equipment, Transportation Equipment, Instruments, and Miscellaneous sectors, the overall impacts on exports are estimated to be quite large. In each case, large estimates of welfare gains, moderate or great effects of barrier removal, with varied values for the other factors, collectively suggest substantial increases in the EU's demand for U.S. exports in these sectors. In particular, Industrial Machinery and Electrical and Electronic Equipment are already important exporting sectors for the U.S. as a whole and with the anticipated removal of technical barriers within the EU and the opening up of public-procurement, these sectors are anticipated to grow by 10-14, and 8-13 percent, respectively.

Clearly, these estimates of the growth in U.S. exports resulting from EC-92 are tentative and founded upon a subjective analysis. However, as was noted above, the primary objective is to develop realistic and justifiable estimates to reflect the differential effects of EC-92 by sector recognizing the limitations of the available data. Thus, while specific estimates may be altered according to a different interpretation or as more appropriate data become available, the profile of growth estimates by sector is unlikely to vary greatly. Furthermore, when incorporating these estimates in the shift-share forecasting model below it needs to be recognized that the results do not represent definitive statements for the effects of EC-92 on U.S. states, but rather the most likely scenarios.

Modelling the Impact of European Integration

The shift-share model employed in Chapter 3 may also be utilized as a forecasting tool to examine the impacts of EC-92 on individual state and regional economies. Much of the controversy surrounding the shift-share method, however, is directed towards its use in estimating future regional economic trends. The model presumes that national economic growth--in this case, growth (or decline) in international trade--will be spread among the subnational regions (states) according to their industrial structures. In addition, use may also be made of the regional shift component necessitating the assumption that previous trade biases will be perpetuated in future regional patterns.

In a review of shift-share forecasting models, Stevens and Moore (1980) described many distinct specifications of the model, and decried the inconstancy of the notation and the widely varying definitions of the components. In spite of this, however, it is apparent that a consistent logic is employed in all specifications. Simpler models consider only national and industrial-mix shift components which are assumed to be constant and ignore the existence of particular, regional shifts. Models such as the Ingrow and Super Ingrow (Brown, 1969) assume the regional shift component to be zero and that regional growth is due to just national and industrial shifts. Other models incorporate the regional shift components: in some cases, it is not explicitly identified and the effects are embodied in a larger all-embracing component, for instance, Hellman's "Constant Share" and "Fixed Ratio of Employment to Regional Population" models (Stevens and Moore 1980, p. 425, Hellman, 1976). In other models, including Hellman's "Implicit-" and "Explicit Shift-Share" models (Stevens and Moore 1980, p. 426, Hellman, 1976), and Zimmerman's (Stevens and Moore 1980, p. 426, Zimmerman, 1975) and OBERS' models (Stevens and Moore 1980, p. 428), the regional shift is explicitly specified and estimated from previous patterns. In each of these cases, regional shift in the future is assumed to follow past trends.

Perhaps the most devastating criticism of shift-share models as forecasting tools is their naive assumptions that industrial sectors in each region will experience the same economic stimuli in equal measure, and that any differentials (identified in regional shifts) will be consistent with past trends. For the present topic, a shift-share forecast assumes that the effects of EC-92 will be felt in the 38 states and regions in equal proportion to their industrial mixes and past regional biases toward the EU. It is a leap of faith, however, to suppose, for instance, that a predicted increase in U.S. exports of a particular industry to the EU will be accounted for in equal measure by all firms in that industry, throughout all the states and regions, and where regional differences occur, these will be foreseen from past trends. However, acknowledging such deficiencies and recognizing the technique's limitations, it may still be usefully applied in the present analysis and is a powerful device with which to identify the structural dimensions of regional economies and their growth.

The examination of the impacts of EC-92 on U.S. states and regional economies is an attempt to estimate the one-time effects of a particular international trade event assuming all other variables remain unchanged. What is proposed, therefore, is a *partial* analysis employing the *ceterus paribus* assumption that all other factors remain constant. In this framework, the shift-share methodology may be particularly appropriate to model the effects of exogenously obtained estimates of changes in U.S. trade relations with the EU on the existing structure of state and regional trade contained in the compiled database. The model will be developed from that used in Chapter 3 to analyze the trading experience of the states and regions over the period, 1983-1990. The regional shift component will also be estimated from that obtained in the earlier analysis, and the forecast will be enabled with the inclusion of sectorally-specific estimates of growth in U.S.-EU trade developed above.

The impacts specific to EC-92 will be multifarious and the sources referenced for quantitative estimates may often address only certain sectors. On balance, these may be considered as being of two types. Positive impacts of EC-92 may affect both exports and imports as the program leads to growth in the European economy as a whole and differentially in individual sectors. This growth may occur directly as barriers to trade are removed or indirectly as the liberation of production factors spurs economic activity. These may similarly result in a positive impact on exports from U.S. states as well as upon the exports of the European Union, that is, U.S. imports. The latter, however, will most likely be less immediate and inherently long-run in nature. For this reason, the analysis will focus solely upon the impacts to exports which may be estimated as a short-run scenario through a shift-share model.

A second group of impacts, however, may have negative consequences for bilateral trade. Although the European Union has a vested interest in liberal world trade and has forsworn any protectionist intentions, it is noted below that there remains the possibility of restrictions on imports to the EU in some sectors. This may come about as EU-wide commercial policy replaces those of the separate nations in which the net effect may be an increase in trade barriers for third parties, ie, the U.S. There is thus the possibility that, in certain sectors, U.S. exports may be negatively affected by the 1992 program. For imports, on the other hand, these too may be negatively affected by EC-92 if the cold blast of international competition sweeps into formerly protected European sectors, causing the retrenchment of certain EU industries and a resultant decline in exports to the U.S. This may be a difficult phenomenon to estimate not least because it is a politically-charged scenario in Europe and secondary sources may not be reliable, if even available.

Since the forecasting model will limit its concern to only a partial analysis of the changes in the exports of states and regions to the EU, several of the components in the analytical shift-share model developed above will be unaffected. Of the 13 shift components in the original model, just three would be affected by a change in exports to the EU. These would be the national, industrial-mix and regional EU export shift components, described in Figure 4.1. For the former two, the anticipated EC-92 total and sectoral growth rates, xe_{92} and xe_{i92}, are obtained from the scenarios discussed above. For the latter, a value for xer_{i92}, the actual regional sectoral growth rate for exports needs to be estimated from those found in the 1983-90 analysis of EU export change. This was obtained by extracting the mean deviation of the xer_i and xe_i values for each region-by-sector cell over the 1983-1990 period and applying these to the anticipated xe_{i92} values.

FIGURE 4.1 The EC-92 Regional Impact Model

National Exports Shift

$$NXE_{92} = \sum_i Q_{ri90}\left[\frac{XE_{90}}{Q_{90}}\,xe_{92}\right]$$

Industrial Mix Exports Shift

$$IXE_{92} = \sum_i Q_{ri90}\left[\left(\frac{XE_{i90}}{Q_{i90}}\,xe_{i92}\right) - \left(\frac{XE_{90}}{Q_{90}}\,xe_{92}\right)\right]$$

Regional Exports Shift

$$RXE_{92} = \sum_i Q_{ri90}\left[\left(\frac{XE_{ri90}}{Q_{ri90}}\,xe_{ri92}\right) - \left(\frac{XE_{i90}}{Q_{i90}}\,xe_{i92}\right)\right]$$

Where:

Q_{ri90} is the total manufacturing output of region r, and industry i, in 1990.

XE_{90} is the total U.S. exports to the EU in 1990.

Q_{90} is the total U.S. manufacturing output in 1990.

xe_{92} is the growth rate of total U.S. exports to the EU with EC-92.

XE_{i90} is the total U.S. exports to the EU for industry i in 1990.

XE_{ri90} is the exports of region r to the EU, by industry sector, i, for 1990.

and other variables follow the same notation, except:

xe_{ri92},   which is the growth rate of exports to the EU from region r and industry i, estimated from 1983-90 trends.

As noted above, the regional EU export shift component is contentious since one may question its stability in the past and hence, its applicability for forecasting purposes. This issue will be addressed in developing the forecast below. The forecast of net impacts to the states' and regions' manufacturing output is therefore obtained as the sum of these three components.

A Shift-Share Forecasting Model of the Effects of EC-92 on the Exports of U.S. States to the European Union

The shift-share forecasting model was estimated twice using the profile of sectoral growth rates resulting from EC-92 (developed above) and the exports and output data for the states and regions in 1990. The model contains three components that were described in Figure 4.1. Two runs of the model were conducted using, respectively, the lower and upper ranges of growth estimates. In accordance with the above discussion of the objective of developing scenarios rather than definitive estimates of regional export growth, specifying the upper and lower bounds of the likely effects of EC-92 will derive the most likely range of outcomes for the individual states. The results of the two estimates are displayed in Tables 4.12a and 4.12b. The values represent the increase in exports to the EU for each state and region and are measured as both thousands of 1990 dollars and as proportions of the states' total exports to the EU in 1990.

The National and Industrial-Mix Shifts

The national and industrial-mix shifts represent the anticipated growth in exports by state and region given the average anticipated growth in exports to the EU, the differential industry growth rates, and the industrial structures of the states. In effect, these two components represent the expected outcome of EC-92 assuming there are no unique regional variations. In addition, these shifts represent the benchmarks against which states can measure their actual EC-92-related growth to determine their relative performance vis-à-vis the European Union.

Since a net increase in U.S. exports is anticipated, the national shifts are large and positive for each state and in proportions equal to their existing exports to the EU. The total shift for the U.S. as a whole amounts to $4.8 and $7.9 billion for the lower and higher growth estimates, respectively. These estimates of the effects of EC-92 on exports suggest that substantial increases may be anticipated. For individual states and regions, the national shifts vary between $22.7 million for West Virginia and $497.0 million for California for the lower range of estimates, and $37.2 and $814.2 million for the higher estimates, respectively.

The industrial-mix shifts illustrate the effects of EC-92 once differential sectoral growth estimates and different industry structures are taken into account. As before, these represent deviations from the national shift such that both positive and negative shifts are reported. Together, these should sum to zero for the U.S. as a whole, and the small negative U.S. totals result from rounding.

Some notable states which appear to be well-suited to benefit from EC-92 include California, Massachusetts, Michigan and Ohio with $96.1, $51.6, $117.2 and $41.0 million industry-mix shifts respectively (lower range of estimates). On the other hand, states with industrial structures less-oriented to EC-92 include Alabama (-$31.5m), Louisiana (-$38.7m), Pennsylvania (-$55.8m), and Texas (-$62.3m).

In column 6 of both Tables 4.12a and 4.12b, the national and industry-mix components are summed and expressed as percentages of the states' 1990 exports to the EU in order to enable a comparative consideration. For the U.S, the national and industry-mix shifts (by definition, effectively the former alone) represent 6.3 and 10.4 percent of total manufacturing exports to the EU for the low and high sets of growth estimates, respectively. The outcome for individual states may be compared to these U.S. averages, and the state-wide patterns are displayed in Figures 4.2 and 4.3. These values, based as they are on the national and industry-mix shifts combined, represent the expected effects of EC-92 in the absence of the regional shift components. In effect, therefore, these measure the growth of states' exports if each state conformed to national and sectoral trends.

A very similar and distinct pattern is evident for both sets of growth estimates. Above-average shifts are found in the states of the Midwest, Middle Atlantic and the Southeast, exclusively. These regions therefore appear to be best poised to reap the benefits of EC-92 while the West, South, South Atlantic and New England regions have industrial bases apparently less-compatible to the European export stimulus.

From the shift-share analysis of the states' manufacturing growth experience since 1983, it was evident that the national and industrial-mix shifts alone accounted for only part of the states' and regions' growth. It appeared that with respect to exports in particular, a state's exports of a certain sector was only partially related to its total output and that apparent regional effects contributed much to the total growth. In addition, the level of aggregation of the sectors was found to mask considerable variations in the export activities of constituent sub-sectors. In the case of Transportation Equipment, for example, sub-sectors such as aircraft and missiles are major exporters whereas automobiles are not, yet they are all subsumed in a single sector at the 2-digit SIC level employed in this analysis.

TABLE 4.12a Lower Forecasts of Growth in Exports to the European Union Resulting from EC-92 (and as a percentage of 1990 exports to the EU)

	National ($)	Industrial-Mix ($)	Regional ($)	Total ($)	National & Ind-Mix (%)	Regional (%)	Total (%)
Alabama	80,435,658	-31,512,086	-1,267,320	47,656,252	6.2	-0.2	6.1
Arkansas	49,769,089	-13,021,358	-13,991,302	22,756,429	9.8	-3.7	6.1
California	497,010,060	96,130,297	149,294,911	742,435,268	5.8	1.5	7.2
Colorado	45,695,133	5,958,526	20,077,035	71,730,694	5.7	2.2	7.9
Florida	111,333,103	5,697,577	-30,406,356	86,624,324	9.1	-2.4	6.8
Georgia	148,887,796	-34,637,963	-23,485,290	90,764,543	7.2	-1.5	5.8
Illinois	259,989,629	-10,936,471	-7,226,094	241,827,064	7.1	-0.2	6.9
Indiana	164,775,163	-1,866,453	-87,709,360	75,199,350	12.2	-6.6	5.7
Iowa	69,633,656	-5,493,186	-14,810,891	49,329,579	7.6	-1.8	5.8
Kansas	61,073,550	-6,331,464	-12,898,077	41,844,009	11.0	-2.6	8.4
Kentucky	82,256,116	7,459,792	27,871,128	117,587,036	5.1	1.6	6.7
Louisiana	99,704,746	-38,666,762	-23,657,046	37,380,938	5.3	-2.1	3.3
Massachusetts	123,488,501	51,566,969	67,894,102	242,949,572	5.5	2.1	7.6
Michigan	287,785,983	117,286,035	-291,115,367	113,956,651	22.7	-16.3	6.4
Minnesota	93,616,625	6,695,084	78,973,017	179,284,726	4.4	3.4	7.8
Mississippi	47,946,271	-14,666,849	-10,653,774	22,625,648	4.8	-1.5	3.3
Missouri	117,776,781	19,295,099	-35,166,967	101,904,913	9.0	-2.3	6.7
New Jersey	162,146,049	-15,310,041	-49,973,581	96,862,427	8.8	-3.0	5.8
New York	286,444,385	22,320,972	-14,556,675	294,208,682	6.4	-0.3	6.1

(continues)

Table 4.12a (*continued*)

North Carolina	187,448,589	-34,954,932	463,646	152,957,303	5.2	0.0	5.2
Ohio	311,819,885	41,005,902	-46,506,113	306,319,674	7.8	-1.0	6.7
Oklahoma	47,343,122	5,396,800	1,575,776	54,315,698	7.2	0.2	7.4
Oregon	49,856,208	-18,098,628	11,948,295	43,705,875	4.6	1.7	6.3
Pennsylvania	233,336,053	-55,845,974	-42,163,434	135,326,645	7.5	-1.8	5.8
South Carolina	81,045,886	-21,711,547	36,697,749	96,032,088	3.7	2.3	6.0
Tennessee	113,575,391	-13,245,589	-21,817,994	78,511,808	6.9	-1.5	5.4
Texas	320,061,800	-62,259,265	-6,501,189	251,301,346	6.1	-0.2	6.0
Virginia	102,069,356	-18,790,570	17,728,230	101,007,016	4.4	0.9	5.4
Washington	91,508,260	-2,854,308	455,825,152	544,479,104	1.3	6.7	8.0
West Virginia	22,735,177	-7,948,543	5,829,132	20,615,766	3.9	1.5	5.4
Wisconsin	136,865,338	7,361,973	-8,693,435	135,533,876	8.0	-0.5	7.6
Delmar	76,183,333	-1,007,023	-20,927,900	54,248,410	8.9	-2.5	6.5
Lower New England	91,576,893	28,044,573	65,632,370	185,253,836	4.5	2.5	7.0
Mid Mountain	24,975,892	-2,221,900	4,666,967	27,420,959	6.0	1.2	7.2
Southwest	49,133,099	13,851,499	29,136,986	92,121,584	5.7	2.7	8.4
Upper Mountain	24,733,413	-12,870,908	69,626,451	81,488,956	2.6	15.3	17.9
Upper New England	54,333,312	10,210,048	5,227,243	69,770,603	6.3	0.5	6.8
Upper Plains	44,265,433	-14,043,871	-1,833,485	28,388,077	7.7	-0.5	7.3
U.S.	4,852,634,734	-14,545	283,106,540	5,135,726,729	6.3	0.4	6.7

TABLE 4.12b Upper Forecasts of Growth in Exports to the European Union Resulting from EC-92 (and as a percentage of 1990 exports to the EU)

	National ($)	Industrial -Mix ($)	Regional ($)	Total ($)	National & Ind-Mix (%)	Regional (%)	Total (%)
Alabama	131,765,107	-49,155,588	-4,168,314	78,441,205	10.5	-0.5	10.0
Arkansas	81,528,883	-20,861,645	-23,028,131	37,639,107	16.2	-6.1	10.0
California	814,173,533	133,744,675	275,043,178	1,222,961,386	9.2	2.7	11.9
Colorado	74,855,160	4,474,257	41,927,756	121,257,173	8.7	4.6	13.3
Florida	182,379,539	5,599,840	-58,602,030	129,377,349	14.7	-4.6	10.1
Georgia	243,899,496	-57,201,577	-39,828,438	146,869,481	11.8	-2.5	9.3
Illinois	425,900,182	-5,364,969	-25,504,816	395,030,397	12.0	-0.7	11.2
Indiana	269,925,274	519,248	-147,962,186	122,482,336	20.3	-11.1	9.2
Iowa	114,069,884	-2,718,010	-29,955,747	81,396,127	13.2	-3.5	9.6
Kansas	100,047,206	-8,989,522	-23,205,677	67,852,007	18.3	-4.7	13.6
Kentucky	134,747,278	16,371,373	48,833,032	199,951,683	8.6	2.8	11.4
Louisiana	163,330,629	-64,096,230	-36,524,865	62,709,534	8.7	-3.2	5.5
Massachusetts	202,291,819	76,317,185	100,437,914	379,046,918	8.7	3.2	11.9
Michigan	471,434,583	207,884,326	-487,458,753	191,860,156	38.1	-27.3	10.8
Minnesota	153,357,415	18,394,762	130,505,082	302,257,259	7.5	5.7	13.1
Mississippi	78,542,846	-23,223,137	-18,379,921	36,939,788	8.0	-2.7	5.3
Missouri	192,935,206	29,896,727	-56,741,516	166,090,417	14.7	-3.7	10.9
New Jersey	265,618,410	-34,072,386	-78,323,253	153,222,771	13.8	-4.7	9.2
New York	469,236,855	5,931,191	-10,477,271	464,690,775	9.9	-0.2	9.6

(continues)

Table 4.12b (*continued*)

North Carolina	307,067,587	-51,974,657	-652,824	254,440,106	8.7	0.0	8.7
Ohio	510,805,551	80,885,458	-85,843,270	505,847,739	13.0	-1.9	11.1
Oklahoma	77,554,803	9,162,505	6,958,678	93,675,986	11.9	1.0	12.8
Oregon	81,671,596	-28,795,057	17,398,217	70,274,756	7.6	2.5	10.1
Pennsylvania	382,237,813	-88,220,108	-71,409,823	222,607,882	12.5	-3.0	9.5
South Carolina	132,764,748	-34,181,027	63,090,963	161,674,684	6.2	4.0	10.1
Tennessee	186,052,728	-19,517,482	-41,719,128	124,816,118	11.5	-2.9	8.6
Texas	524,306,985	104,637,775	399,750,775	420,068,960	10.0	0.0	10.0
Virginia	167,204,197	-31,455,747	40,265,851	176,014,301	7.2	2.1	9.4
Washington	149,903,612	-4,479,085	739,045,626	884,470,153	2.1	10.8	12.9
West Virginia	37,243,470	-11,968,003	9,688,356	34,963,823	6.6	2.5	9.2
Wisconsin	224,204,991	22,309,320	-16,055,597	230,458,714	13.7	-0.9	12.8
Delmar	124,799,192	-6,862,811	-35,449,849	82,486,532	14.0	-4.2	9.8
Lower New England	150,016,044	43,343,738	114,343,639	307,703,421	7.3	4.3	11.6
Mid Mountain	40,914,081	-3,995,120	9,842,744	46,761,705	9.7	2.6	12.3
Southwest	80,487,040	21,218,437	43,454,649	145,160,126	9.3	4.0	13.2
Upper Mountain	40,516,867	-19,540,562	109,796,499	130,772,804	4.6	24.1	28.7
Upper New England	89,005,733	17,541,099	12,509,279	119,056,111	10.4	1.2	11.6
Upper Plains	72,513,107	-22,295,541	-8,221,922	41,995,644	12.8	-2.1	10.7
U.S.	7,949,309,450	-11,898	863,378,907	8,413,325,434	10.4	1.1	11.5

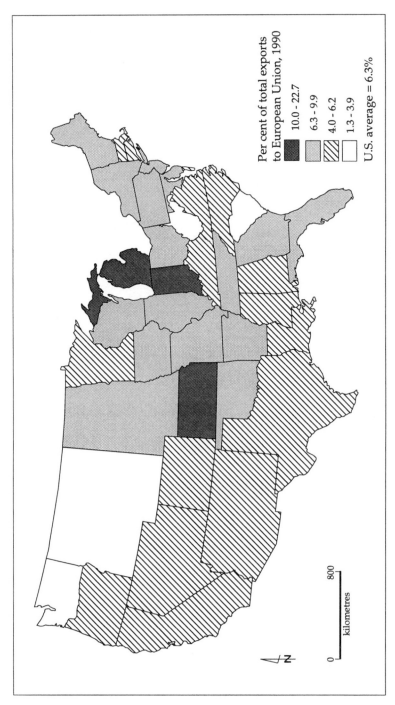

FIGURE 4.2 Forecast national and industrial-mix shifts due to EC-92: lower sectoral estimates.

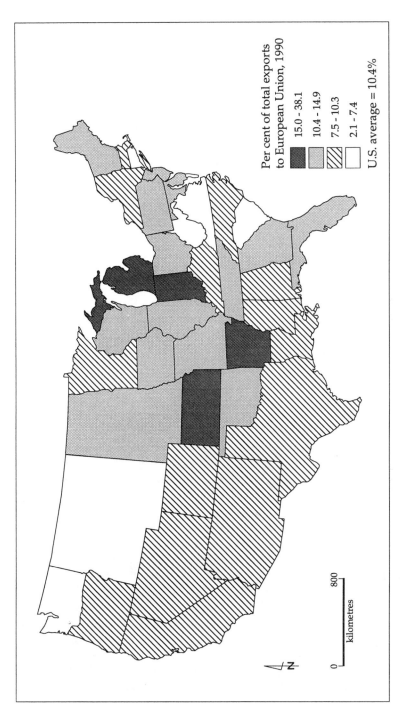

FIGURE 4.3 Forecast national and industrial-mix shifts due to EC-92: upper sectoral estimates.

The Total Shifts

The former shift-share analysis of earlier trade and manufacturing growth highlighted the significant contribution of differential regional shifts. In most cases, the regional shifts were considerably larger than the industry-mix shifts and contributed substantial portions of the total growth over the period. These regional shifts, however, are only evident as the residual growth not accounted for by national and industry-mix shifts. Although the model applied in Chapter 3 isolated the regional shift attributable to exports to the EU, this was based upon the residual growth in actual state exports as a component of total manufacturing growth. In forecasting the potential impacts of EC-92, the national and industry-mix shifts can be estimated, but the residual growth constituting the regional shift is not known.

Clearly, however, the regional shift component is a substantial part of the shift-share explanation and to omit it would be detrimental to the analysis. In accordance to the specification of the model above, the regional shift component is estimated using a regional EU-export growth rate (xe_{ri92} in Figure 4.1) developed from the previous experience in the 1983-90 analysis. For this, the average $xe_{ri}:xe_i$ ratio for the seven incremental years (1984-1990) was taken and applied to xe_{i92} in the forecast shift-share model to obtain values of xe_{ri92}. This variable is then utilized in the regional shift component.

In this manner, the regional shift resulting from the export growth effects of EC-92 is estimated for each state to be most closely conforming to past trends. Herein lies the weakness of this component, and with it, of the utility of the shift-share model as a forecasting technique. Since regional effects are clearly significant and of particular interest, they must necessarily be included but in forecasting but one is making the assumption that past trends in regional shifts will persist. The regional shift components estimated in the two forecasts reported in Tables 4.12a and 4.12b therefore represent the state growth in exports attributable to regional effects that may be anticipated given past experience. To a greater or lesser extent, past regional patterns will most likely prevail in the future, even after an event such as EC-92, but the extent to which they do will clearly affect the accuracy of the regional shift component and also, the forecast as a whole.

The regional shift components reported in column 4 of both Tables 4.12a and 4.12b are similar in sign and magnitude to those estimated for the states' 1983-90 experience (the regional EU-export shift component). However, owing to the differential sectoral growth estimates, and the fact that xe_{ri92} is unique to each state-by-sector observation, these shifts are not equal even in a relative sense. Indeed, in the cases of Colorado, Iowa, Oklahoma and Oregon, the regional EU export shifts were negative for the period 1983-90, but for the estimated effects of EC-92, they are positive. This is entirely consistent with the flexibility of the shift-share model, the components being merely the sum of individual sectors' shifts.

The regional shifts represent deviations from the national shift component and so summing all three shifts derives the total EC-92 export growth anticipated for each state. Once again, this may be viewed in comparative terms by expressing the total shift as percentages of the states' 1990 exports to the EU. These values are given for the low and high growth estimates in column 8 of Tables 4.12a and 4.12b, respectively. The U.S. growth in exports due to EC-92 (and hence, the average) is 6.7 and 11.5 percent, respectively for the lower and upper growth estimates. Once again, these may be viewed as a nationwide pattern, displayed in Figures 4.4 and 4.5.

For the total shifts due to EC-92, a very different pattern is revealed. Throughout the western states and regions (excepting only Oregon) above-average shifts are found. In New England, and the two northern states of Minnesota and Wisconsin as well, an above-average growth in exports to the EU are forecast to result from EC-92. For the lower growth estimates, Illinois, the Upper Plains region and Florida also benefit disproportionately from the export stimulus of EC-92, but their advantage apparently disappears in the forecast using higher growth estimates--presumably due to the specific effects of different sectoral growth rates and industrial-mixes.

It is clear from these two instances that the Middle and South Atlantic, south eastern and southern states, as well as several in the Midwest are likely to receive a less than average export stimulus from EC-92, the lowest shifts being recorded for Louisiana and Mississippi (3.3/3.3 and 5.3/5.5 percent of 1990 exports for the low and high estimates, respectively). While the actual sectoral profile of growth rates may, of course, be quite different from either of these two extreme cases the broad regional patterns of the impacts of EC-92 on state exports are evident.

The inclusion of the regional shift component radically alters the pattern of states' gains from EC-92 and this necessarily brings into question the validity and stability of the forecasting model. Two issues, in particular, arise. First, it is likely that the regional shift component effectively captures some of the variation due to industrial effects but which are subsumed by the level of sectoral aggregation. For instance, that Washington has such a large regional shift component is not due exclusively to the trade-orientation of this state, but in large measure also to the presence of the high-exporting aircraft industry. However, since this industry is merely a sub-sector of SIC 37

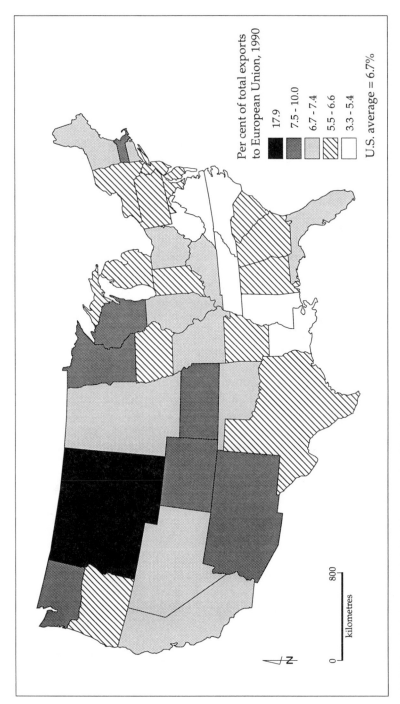

FIGURE 4.4 Forecast total shifts due to EC-92: lower sectoral estimates.

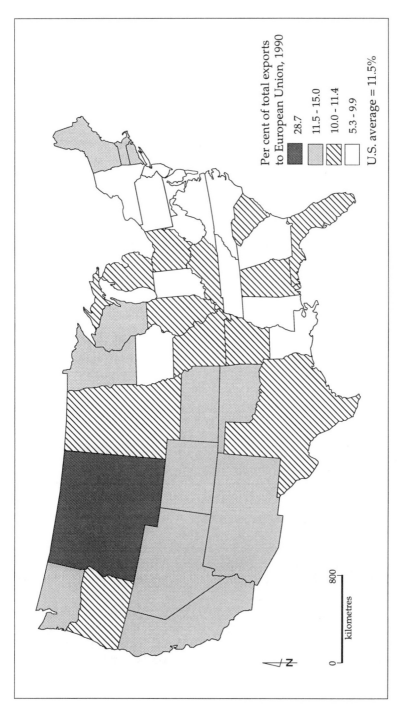

FIGURE 4.5 Forecast total shifts due to EC-92: upper sectoral estimates.

(Transportation Equipment) the export-growth effects attributable to this sub-sector are not entirely accounted for by the industry-mix shift. In a model with a greater degree of sectoral disaggregation, it is likely that the industry-mix shift will become more prominent to the detriment of the regional shift.

Second, the shift-share forecast highlights the importance of the regional shift component and hence the persistence of regional effects becomes a key issue in estimating future regional growth. The stability of regional shifts over time can only be gauged with hindsight and so the regional shift component effectively embodies a major source of error for this model.

The Impacts of Export Growth on Regional Economies

While the impacts of EC-92 on the states' exports to the EU reveal significant implications for the states' trading relations, another measure of the disproportionate effect of EC-92 is through considering the shifts as impacts upon the regional economies directly. This may be achieved by simply expressing the shifts as percentages of total 1990 manufacturing output for each state, the values for which, are given in Table 4.13.

From the values reported in Table 4.13, the growth in exports to the EU resulting from EC-92 clearly amounts to only a fraction of the total manufacturing output in each state; as little as 0.06 or 0.10 percent in Louisiana and as much as 0.98 and 1.59 percent in Washington (respectively, for the lower and higher growth estimates). The U.S. average is also noted in the table and it is sorted to indicate which states have above- or below-average shifts.

While the values of these shifts appear to be negligible to the total regional economies, one should note that real growth rates of these magnitudes would, in fact, represent substantial one-time contributions to regional output. Furthermore, in introducing this forecasting exercise it was noted that, given the imprecision of the available data, that relative results are of more interest; there is evidently a considerable variation in these shifts among the states and regions in relative terms. Once again, these are illustrated graphically in Figure 4.6. Since the patterns for both lower and higher growth estimates are very similar, only that for the latter is shown.

The state by state pattern of EC-92 shifts as shares of total output reaffirms the greater impact of EC-92 being felt by the western and New England states. Throughout the West (except Oregon) above-average impacts of EC-92 are forecast. For Washington state, it is estimated that the growth in exports to the EU may be as much as 1.6 percent of total 1990 production. In the New England states as well,

TABLE 4.13 The EC-92 Shifts in Exports as Percentages of Total 1990 Manufacturing Output

	Total Shift: Lower Growth Estimates	Total Shift: Higher Growth Estimates
Washington	0.98	1.59
Upper Mountain	0.54	0.87
Lower New England	0.33	0.55
Minnesota	0.31	0.53
Massachusetts	0.32	0.50
Southwest	0.31	0.48
Colorado	0.26	0.44
California	0.25	0.40
Kentucky	0.23	0.40
Upper New England	0.21	0.36
South Carolina	0.19	0.33
Oklahoma	0.19	0.32
Mid Mountain	0.18	0.31
United States total	0.17	0.30
Virginia	0.16	0.28
Wisconsin	0.16	0.28
New York	0.17	0.27
Ohio	0.16	0.27
Illinois	0.15	0.25
West Virginia	0.15	0.25
Missouri	0.14	0.23
Oregon	0.14	0.23
North Carolina	0.13	0.22
Texas	0.13	0.22
Florida	0.13	0.19
Iowa	0.12	0.19
Kansas	0.11	0.18
Tennessee	0.11	0.18
Delmar	0.12	0.18
Alabama	0.10	0.16
Georgia	0.10	0.16
New Jersey	0.10	0.16
Pennsylvania	0.10	0.16
Upper Plains	0.11	0.16
Mississippi	0.08	0.13
Arkansas	0.08	0.12
Indiana	0.07	0.12
Michigan	0.06	0.11
Louisiana	0.06	0.10

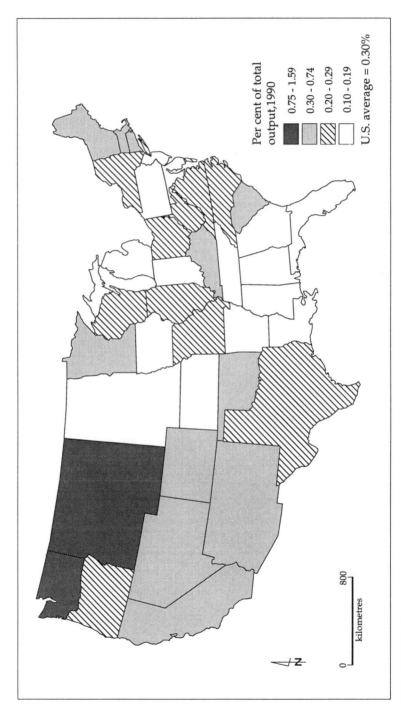

Per cent of total
output,1990

0.75 - 1.59

0.30 - 0.74

0.20 - 0.29

0.10 - 0.19

U.S. average = 0.30%

kilometres

0   800

N

FIGURE 4.6 Forecast total shifts due to EC-92: upper sectoral estimate, (as a percentage of total output).

above-average impacts are predicted and also in Minnesota, Oklahoma, Kentucky and South Carolina. Throughout the South, Southeast and South Atlantic, however, as well as the Middle Atlantic and Midwest, the export stimulus of EC-92 appears to amount to a negligible proportion of existing output. Clearly the economic effects of EC-92 are going to be felt disproportionately among the states.

Summary of the Forecast EC-92 Impacts

The totals shifts forecast as resulting from the EC-92 export stimulus are summarized in Table 4.14. The states are sorted according to their total shifts expressed as percentages of manufacturing output, and the U.S. averages are included as well to provide a benchmark for evaluating the relative impacts upon each state. In addition, the states are grouped (by means of the shading pattern) to identify those with above or below average shifts as a proportion of existing exports, and above or below average shifts with respect to output.

The first group headed by Washington are those states and regions which are forecast to experience an above-average increase in exports to the EU as a contribution to both existing levels of exports as well as total manufacturing output. For these states, the effects of EC-92 are anticipated to have the most significant boost to their regional economies. For the second group also, including Kentucky and South Carolina, the export stimulus provided by EC-92 represents an above-average boost to their total output but has less significant effect on their patterns of exports.

For the third and fourth groups, the growth in exports to the EU represents a below average share of their manufacturing output and hence, one may infer that the effects of EC-92 will be less evident for these states. This is particularly so for the fourth group--from Virginia to Louisiana--for which the shifts are below average with respect to both existing output and existing exports. For the third group, however, the impact upon EU exports is above average and so the impacts of EC-92 will be appear to be quite significant although they will not contribute greatly to their local economies.

Discussion: Modelling the Regional Impacts of External Trade Events

An explicit purpose of the analysis reported in this chapter is to demonstrate a methodology for examining the regional economic impacts of an exogenous event. The extended shift-share model estimated an actual value to anticipated increases in trade from the

152

TABLE 4.14 A Summary of the Forecast Shifts due to EC-92

	Total Shift (dollars)		Percentage of Exports		Percentage of Output	
	Lower Growth Estimate ($)	Higher Growth Estimate ($)	Lower Estimate (%)	Higher Estimate (%)	Lower Estimate (%)	Higher Estimate (%)
Washington	544,479,104	884,470,153	8.0	12.9	0.98	1.59
Upper Mountain	81,488,956	130,772,804	17.9	28.7	0.54	0.87
Lower New England	185,253,836	307,703,421	7.0	11.6	0.33	0.55
Minnesota	179,284,726	302,257,259	7.8	13.1	0.31	0.53
Massachusetts	242,949,572	379,046,918	7.6	11.9	0.32	0.50
Southwest	92,121,584	145,160,126	8.4	13.2	0.31	0.48
Colorado	71,730,694	121,257,173	7.9	13.3	0.26	0.44
California	742,435,268	1,222,961,386	7.2	11.9	0.25	0.40
Upper New England	69,770,603	119,056,111	6.8	11.6	0.21	0.36
Oklahoma	54,315,698	93,675,986	7.4	12.8	0.19	0.32
Mid Mountain	27,420,959	46,761,705	7.2	12.3	0.18	0.31
Kentucky	117,587,036	199,951,683	6.7	11.4	0.23	0.40
South Carolina	96,032,088	161,674,684	6.0	10.1	0.19	0.33
U.S.	2,291,251,000	3,753,123,042	6.7	11.5	0.17	0.30
Wisconsin	135,533,876	230,458,714	7.6	12.8	0.16	0.28
Ohio	306,319,674	505,847,739	6.7	11.1	0.16	0.27
Illinois	241,827,064	395,030,397	6.9	11.2	0.15	0.25
Missouri	101,904,913	166,090,417	6.7	10.9	0.14	0.23

(continues)

Table 4.14 (*continued*)

Florida	86,624,324	129,377,349	6.8	10.1	0.13	0.19
Kansas	41,844,009	67,852,007	8.4	13.6	0.11	0.18
Upper Plains	28,388,077	41,995,644	7.3	10.7	0.11	0.16
Virginia	101,007,016	176,014,301	5.4	9.4	0.16	0.28
New York	294,208,682	464,690,775	6.1	9.6	0.17	0.27
West Virginia	20,615,766	34,963,823	5.4	9.2	0.15	0.25
Oregon	43,705,875	70,274,756	6.3	10.1	0.14	0.23
North Carolina	152,957,303	254,440,106	5.2	8.7	0.13	0.22
Texas	251,301,346	420,068,960	6.0	10.0	0.13	0.22
Iowa	49,329,579	81,396,127	5.8	9.6	0.12	0.19
Tennessee	78,511,808	124,816,118	5.4	8.6	0.11	0.18
Delmar	54,248,410	82,486,532	6.5	9.8	0.12	0.18
Alabama	47,656,252	78,441,205	6.1	10.0	0.10	0.16
Georgia	90,764,543	146,869,481	5.8	9.3	0.10	0.16
New Jersey	96,862,427	153,222,771	5.8	9.2	0.10	0.16
Pennsylvania	135,326,645	222,607,882	5.8	9.5	0.10	0.16
Mississippi	22,625,648	36,939,788	3.3	5.3	0.08	0.13
Arkansas	22,756,429	37,639,107	6.1	10.0	0.08	0.12
Indiana	75,199,350	122,482,336	5.7	9.2	0.07	0.12
Michigan	113,956,651	191,860,156	6.4	10.8	0.06	0.11
Louisiana	37,380,938	62,709,534	3.3	5.5	0.06	0.10

EC-92 program in the European Union. More importantly, however, it is quite transparent in identifying the components of the impact. The sources of each state's fortune can be traced and identified as being derived from either its industrial structure or some regional, competitive advantage. It is anticipated that this aspect of the model will be of more value than the summarised value of the impact. Certainly, this should be the case for the discerning reader concerned for the structural dimensions of the regional-international trade linkage.

With respect to the empirical analysis at hand, it is evident that the trade impacts of EC-92 will fall differentially on the individual states and regions of the U.S. It should be noted, however, that the objective is not simply to identify the winners and losers from this event but to indicate the states' respective stakes in the program. The imputed data are acknowledged to be far from perfect and hence an upper and lower range of estimates were utilized. With this caveat, the results of the forecast models should be taken as an indication of the range of impacts an individual state may experience. Obviously, alternative, even improved, estimates of the effects of EC-92 on European demand for industrial products would yield different results. For an individual state these may differ from those presented above although for the U.S. as a whole the state-by-state pattern would be unlikely to change.

Clearly, this is a partial analysis which omits any consideration of interregional trade that may diffuse the economic stimulus of a exogenous event such as EC-92. The analysis, therefore, is constrained to addressing the goal of estimating the direct effects of an exogenous economic event on regional economies. Subsequently, these findings may be included into specific models of regional economic activity, such as regional or interregional input-output analyses, or general equilibrium models. In contrast to previous statements on the likely impacts of EC-92, this analysis explicitly refrains from using subjective assessments where possible, and avoids basing its findings on "expert" opinions. Instead, the model is completely transparent and is readily replicable, and reproducible with updated estimates or, indeed, for use in another context.[7]

Notes

1 A general discussion of the conclusions of the Cecchini Report can be found in Cecchini (1988) and a more detailed report in either Emerson et al. (1988) or European Commission, Directorate-General for Economic and Financial Affairs (1988).

2 EUR 9 includes the first nine members of the European Union: Belgium, Denmark, France, Germany, Ireland, Italy, Luxembourg, the Netherlands and the United Kingdom.

3 For instance, Volkswagen and Ford recently made an EU-assisted investment in a new automobile plant in Setubal, Portugal. See *Financial Times* (7-19-91) p. 2.

4 For instance, the "New Global Role for the EC" was a major item in a report prepared for the Committee on Foreign Affairs of the U.S. House of Representatives. U.S. Congress, House Committee on Foreign Affairs (1989).

5 The U.S. was granted continued preferential access to export feed grains to Spain. This agreement was due to expire at the end of 1990 and caused a significant trade dispute, with the U.S. threatening to retaliate by reducing imports from the EC by $440 million, before it was extended another year. It remains an issue, however. (U.S. Representative to the European Community 1990, p. 3)

6 From its inception, Airbus has received considerable political and financial support from European governments. An example was the 1989 decision of the German federal government to provide exchange rate risk coverage to the Daimler-Benz corporation, a stakeholder in Airbus Industrie (Ludlow, 1990: 230).

7 For example, see Hayward and Erickson (forthcoming).

5

Summary: International Trade and Regional Policy

This study has focussed specifically upon the role of United States-European Union trade in manufactured goods, and the potential impacts of the EU's EC-92 program on this trade, from the perspectives of the individual U.S. states. The background for this topic is the changing international economic arena in which multinational economic integration is becoming commonplace and, simultaneously, sub-national entities are taking greater responsibility for their own economic fortunes in the global marketplace. EC-92, therefore, is an example of a major contemporary event that poses both a significant threat as well as an opportunity to U.S. industries and to their host states.

The main purpose of this work, however, is to explore the external dimensions of regional economies. It was noted in Chapter 1 that individual U.S. states and other regional entities have increasingly assumed responsibility for their own international relationships. To a large extent the competitive state has replaced federal agencies in this arena. States have effectively included international trade promotion and the solicitation of foreign direct investment in their development planning tool kits. The anticipated positive contribution of trade to regional economies has gone largely unquestioned. Where differential impacts of trade have been considered these are usually applied to industry sectors. Extending this concern to the regional dimension is a challenge that has in the past been hampered by poor or absent data. The research reported in the foregoing chapters is a contribution to this deficient area of our knowledge. In so doing, some empirical support--or otherwise--will be now available to complement states' trade policies and programs.

A secondary and altogether more insidious purpose of this book is to contribute to an important contemporary concern among industrial geographers (in particular); namely, the evident global-local dialectic in economic globalization. Processes operating at the supranational level--such as an integration event like EC-92--necessarily compromise the role of national agencies, and especially their ability to operate independently. The impacts of such processes, therefore, are concentrated at the sub-national--local or regional--levels, where the realities of economic change are manifest. The emergence of competitive states--regional agencies pursuing independent policies-- complement and compound the effects of globalization. In the present, limited study, international trade is examined directly with respect to the individual U.S. states' industrial economies. The national level is all but ignored. So, in addition to being a pragmatic response to the evident need to inquire into the trade relations of states, this research also seeks to contribute to a new perspective on regional economies: one in which regions are seen to exist in an international as well as a national environment.

The Regional Economic Impact of Trade

The economic significance of trade for individual states was examined in Chapters 2 and 3. In the former this was evaluated as the relative value of trade to total production, and then the specific importance of trade with the European Union. In Chapter 3, an extended shift-share model was employed to estimate the contribution of EU trade in the recent experiences of the states. In each case, new and improved data were revealed. Additionally, appropriate and replicatable analytical tools were demonstrated, with the goal of improving our handling of this topic.

It is evident from the data portrayed in Figures 2.2 and 2.3 that the relative importance of trade to total industrial production varies markedly among the states. Using the U.S. average as a base, states may be identified as being above or below average in their engagement with international trade. The summarized data illustrated in Figure 2.4 reveal the regional patterns to this. At one extreme are those states comparatively heavily involved with respect to both exports and imports. These include those in New England and the south west, as well as Ohio and Kentucky. On the other hand, those with below average engagements to both are found throughout the east coast, the south east and Midwest.

The particular contribution of trade with the European Union adds a further dimension to this analysis as it reveals the state-by-state patterns of trade orientations. Measures of *exposure* are used which express each state/region's trade with the European Union as a proportion of either their total international trade (*trade exposure*) or their total industrial output (*production exposure*). These measures have the advantage over simple trade data in that they simultaneously represent trade levels and the importance of these to regional economies.

A distinct pattern of comparatively high *export trade* exposures were found for the north east, South Atlantic and south western regions (Figure 2.8). With the addition of some isolated central states as well, the states of these regions appear to be particularly EU-oriented in their export trade relations. For imports, too, there is a definite regional pattern with European competition in the form of imports being relatively larger for the states in the Middle and South Atlantic regions and in the heartland (Figure 2.9). Evidently, the international trade relations of individual states are highly varied and reveal distinct regional patterns.

The consideration of the production exposure values incorporates an evaluation of the importance of these trade orientations to the states' manufacturing economies. In Figure 2.13, the pattern of export and import production exposure was summarized and five types of state were identified. These, too, reveal regional patterns. States with positive economic exposures attributable largely to high export production exposures include Washington, the Upper Mountain region and Minnesota in the north, and Virginia and the Carolinas in the South Atlantic region. For these, the EU represents a significant component of demand for local industrial output and relatively little competitive threat. On the other hand for states in the eastern Great Lakes regions, the Middle Atlantic and several in the Central Plains, EU trade makes a significant, but negative economic contribution with a low export exposure and a major competitive threat posed by imports. Another identifiable category includes those states with both high export and import exposures, but a positive balance overall. These include New England (including New York), Kentucky and West Virginia, and the south western region (including California). For these states, trade with the EU is a substantial component of their regional economies and is of a bilateral nature. Finally, two categories identify states with relatively little exposure to EU trade and with either positive or negative balances, respectively. These include most of the states of the Southeast, South Central, western Great Lakes and Pennsylvania, and for them trade with the European Union has much less economic significance. These results illuminate the nature of state-level trade more accurately than that resulting from raw trade flows.

Beyond a static analysis of the importance of trade, its contribution to regional manufacturing growth is analyzed in Chapter 3. An extended shift-share model was employed for the years 1983 through 1990. This model identifies the independent contribution of exports and imports, and even those specifically attributable to the European Union. Although it is found that domestic demand remains the major contribution to growth in all states, trade nevertheless accounts for a varied but significant share. The balance of the EU trade contribution to the regional growth is displayed in Figure 3.15. The states west of the Rockies, those of the South Atlantic, parts of New England, Minnesota and Mississippi, all benefited from a positive contribution to their manufacturing economies. For the remainder, the experience of trade with the European Union was, on balance, negative.

These findings will almost certainly provoke some reassessment of individual states' trade promotion programs. The patterns and the individual experiences revealed may differ from--contradict, even-- those which are currently thought to exist. In all cases, they indicate the significant contribution of trade, and trade with the EU in particular, to states' economies.

The Practicalities of Regional Trade Analysis

This book is an attempt to link two interrelated but usually disconnected fields of study: regional economic growth and international trade patterns. It has been argued that on both theoretical and pragmatic grounds it has become necessary for regional analysts to attend to the international realm. Furthermore, for geographers and others, the process of globalization creates an imperative to link the global and local--international and regional-- levels of inquiry. In pursuing the present study, some significant methodological issues were addressed.

As has been discussed at several points in the analysis, a number of constraints were imposed upon this research by limitations in the data available. The elaborate procedure to alleviate the known biases in the published state-by-state export data was described in Chapter 2 and Appendix 1. It is believed that this method produces the best estimates of true state export patterns yet available. It is understood that efforts are under way to produce more accurate data at the Massachusetts Institute of Social and Economic Research through a laborious procedure of matching shippers' export declarations with individual firm identification numbers obtained from the U.S. Social Security Administration's files. In this way, it is hoped that more precise locations for the origins of exports will be obtained. It will be interesting to compare these estimates (when available) to those generated by the procedure developed for this study.

Similarly, it is understood that the Bureau of the Census plans to release state-by-state imports data to complement the exports data available since 1987. However, it was argued in Chapter 2 that these may be of little value to regional economic analysis as they will, presumably, record the states of first destination (in the U.S.) of foreign imports. Once in the United States, state boundaries pose no barrier to imports and so they effectively compete with domestic producers in all states. Unless this data can be modified to account for inter-state trade it will not be possible to identify specific state or regional targets for imports, and so it will be of little value for regional analysis. Data produced by apportioning national imports by states according to their sectoral production levels--the method used in this research--will therefore remain more appropriate.

In two other ways, however, improvements in the data may significantly enhance this line of research. First, the analysis would be greatly improved by the availability of less-aggregated data. It was noted in the shift-share analysis above, that the regional shift components in part accounted for some sectoral variation that was disguised by the 2-digit SIC level of aggregation. In particular cases such as Washington and Michigan, the industry-mix shift components were skewed by the Transportation Equipment sector which includes both Aircraft and Motor Vehicles. The former of these is a major net exporter, and the latter a net importer. With more disaggregated data greater accuracy would be obtained by the shift-share model.

The second area in which improved data would be particularly valuable is in obtaining estimates for industries other than manufacturing. For the United States, the agricultural and service sectors account for much of the nation's international trade. In the former, much of the actual exported goods are commodities for which it is notoriously difficult to identify a state of origin. This may be illustrated by just one observation from the MISER state-by-state export data: that much of the exported agricultural products of the Mid western farm states are attributed wrongly to port states such as Louisiana. In the case of the latter, service exports are identified in the merchandise trade statistics. This is due to the major problem of recording and valuing intangible trade. This is, however, an area of great interest and it is likely that detailed estimates of services trade will become available in the future.

In pursuit of this research, some methodological advances were made which have a value beyond their particular application here. The extended international shift-share model is a relatively simple but revealing device for examining trade patterns. The disaggregation of the regional shift component in particular, represents an innovative extension of the simpler version of the model. It is hoped, therefore, that this methodological construction may be utilized further.

Trade Events and Regional Outcomes: the Case of EC-92

The first two parts of the analysis reported in this book successfully established the significance of trade in regional economic growth first, in a static form (Chapter 2) and then in a dynamic form (Chapter 3). Furthermore, techniques have been demonstrated to facilitate such an analysis. In the final section (Chapter 4) attention shifted to employing these techniques to evaluate the potential impacts of an external trade event. In this, the extended shift-share model was reformulated as a forecasting tool to estimate the range of likely impacts of the EC-92 program.

A major deficiency in this analysis is acknowledged to be the limited and poor quality of information on the external trade impacts of EC-92 and hence, the impacts on U.S. trade with the European Union. While numerous studies have considered the internal, domestic European dimensions of the program and the impacts upon trade among members of the European Union, there has been little attention paid to its external effects. In this research, a variety of available estimates of the sectoral growth effects of EC-92, import penetration levels and trade barriers were utilized. Much of this information was qualitative and typical of the type available for this topic which necessarily constrained its applicability in an explicitly quantitative analysis of such as this. There is a great need for more research on the external impacts of international economic integration events such as EC-92, especially as they are an increasingly common phenomenon in late twentieth century. Owing to the limited data on the trade effects of EC-92 the results of the forecast in Chapter 4 are presented as scenarios, indicating the potential range of impacts on individual states rather than firm estimates.

EC-92 is solely an internally-oriented program--internal to the European Union. It is a package of some 270 initiatives with the common purpose of eliminating the remaining barriers to trade among the 12 member states. These are non-tariff barriers, including customs formalities which impose an administrative burden on intra-EU trade, technical barriers that perpetuate a fragmented European economy of separate, national markets, and fiscal barriers that distort prices between members and necessitate the regulation of cross-border commerce. The removal of these barriers is the sole objective of EC-92; current deliberations on full monetary union, a European currency, the

Social Charter and even political union are, as Hufbauer (1990: 13) describes them, the "outer-wrapping." The fact that the European debate has moved on to theses issues is itself testimony to the progress of EC-92 and the enthusiasm for deeper European integration that it has engendered. Of even greater relevance is the likely expansion of the European Union by the accession of the members of the European Free Trade Association (EFTA) and possibly some of the nations of the erstwhile Soviet bloc. The former have already acquired "honorary" EU status as part of the European Economic Area (since January, 1994). Effectively, therefore, the objectives of EC-92 are being simultaneously extended to the EFTA members and so creating an even larger, unified European economy. Hence, the impacts of EC-92 are being magnified as it is itself merely a stage in an on-going historical process.

While the EC-92 program contains no direct considerations for external trade relations its external impacts will nevertheless be quite profound. Given the size of the emerging European economy, complex ramifications will undoubtedly reverberate throughout the global economy. For the U.S., the most direct effects are likely to be on exports as it is anticipated that the program will cause an expansion of European demand for many goods--dramatically so, in many cases. Such an export stimulus will have regional economic consequences and these are pursued in Chapter 4. However, although the program is a classic example of a free-trade initiative, it may paradoxically increase barriers to goods from non-members including the U.S. Despite much concern for this issue at the federal level, there is relatively little evidence to suggest that discrimination against U.S. exporters will actually increase. In fact, within the EU, most trade issues concern (as is the case in the United States) that with Japan and other East Asian countries and, given the long-established and substantial transnational corporate operations between North America and Europe, few instances of increased obstacles to U.S. manufactured exports can be foreseen at this stage. Nevertheless, numerous other, indirect consequences of EC-92 are being postulated, including the impact upon global capital markets, exchange rates and the global competitiveness of European industries--and, hence, their import penetration in the U.S.--but the impacts of these are not tackled in this research.

The potential impacts of EC-92 on the regional economies of these states are forecast using the extended international shift-share model. This is a *partial analysis* with no explicit modelling of interregional trade or of any multiplier effects--although it should be noted that the regional shift component is an ex post estimate and partially embodies these effects. Furthermore, given the earlier discussion of the range of potential impacts, this forecast was made only for the effects upon

exports. Two forecasts are reported using both the lower and higher
ranges of export growth estimates. In interpreting the results, emphasis
is placed upon relative regional impacts and the shift-share model
specifically identifies the separate effects of industry structure and
regional competitive advantage.

The net impact of EC-92 in relative terms was presented in Figure 4.6
and revealed a pattern similar to that for the EC export trade stimulus
in the earlier period, 1983-1990. State-by-state differences are due to
the varied sectoral impacts estimated in the first part of Chapter 4
and from these forecasts, a very distinct regional pattern of impacts
from EC-92 is revealed. For most states west of the Rockies and those in
New England (plus four outliers) an above average regional growth
stimulus is forecast. For the remainder the EC-92 stimulus to their
manufacturing economies is forecast to be minimal, including those
states in the Middle Atlantic and Southeast despite their geographic
proximity to the European Union.

These findings identify those states and regions with the greatest
stake in the European Union's EC-92 program. While it indicates for
whom the growth stimulus may be the greatest, it also implies that
those same states have the most to lose should the program fail to
engender the anticipated growth in U.S. exports. In particular, this
may occur should new protectionist barriers be erected and so these
findings simultaneously indicate the regional impact of such an event.
For those states which appear to benefit little from EC-92 these
forecasts should cause them to re-evaluate their trade promotion
programs, especially with respect to the EU. In particular, for some
states, the very different values of the industrial-mix and regional
shifts suggest that the growth stimulus of EC-92 is potentially
substantial but that this is offset by (negative) regional effects. While
it is acknowledged that the level of aggregation of the data may
exaggerate the regional shift components, it is also evident that low
levels of export orientation towards the EU reduces the stimulus that
might otherwise be received from EC-92.

In sum, the analysis identified the differential nature of regional
trade relations with a foreign partner and indicates the degree to
which an event such as EC-92 is likely to have highly discriminatory
impacts. Furthermore, it provides a model with which the a real
value can be estimated for the role of European trade in regional
economic growth, and for the potential regional growth stimuli that
may be anticipated given a certain change in external demand.

The interdependence of the global economy and the implications of
international events are likely to be leading areas of concern in the
future. The heightened awareness of the external dimensions of

regional economies against the backdrop of global economic realignments creates a enticing realm of inquiry. For geographers and regional economists the emergent global economic interdependence affords an opportunity to introduce their unique spatial and regional perspectives to the study of an arena in which the main actors--nation states--have long been conceived of as independent, unitary and aspatial.

The European Union's EC-92 program is but one of a number of contemporary economic integration events that promise to radically realign the patterns of global trade. The proposed North American Free Trade Area (NAFTA) and its possible future extension into Latin America will also have significant implications for state economies in the U.S. Beyond these, however, the impacts upon other world regions and, particularly, the smaller nations such as those in the Caribbean may be quite profound. Similarly, developments in the former Soviet bloc as it re-integrates with the capitalist world, and the growing economies of the Pacific Rim and their renewed interest in regional trade associations, also contribute to the rapidly changing global economy.

The formation of regional trading blocs and international trade policy have become major components of contemporary international relations. More than ever, these events are guided by economic rather than political concerns and they have implications that extend to many other fields of inquiry. For instance, a major concern arising with the proposed NAFTA is the environmental impacts of the industrial and agricultural restructuring that may follow in its wake-- particularly, on the Mexican side. The regional economic impacts of such international events are of primary concern therefore to those whose interests lie in the environment, rural sociology among many other fields of inquiry.

The External Imperative for Regional Policy

This research has sought to support the case for extending regional analysis and policy to encompass the international dimension. It is argued that regions can no longer be conceived of as entities within national bodies alone; sheltered from external events. While the national context remains an important consideration as national institutions, labor practices and modes of production constrain the paths of regional development, regions are nevertheless increasingly impacted directly by international events. So, while as Ettlinger (1994) argues, the national context stamps a distinct imprint which characterizes regional development, the European Union (for one) is actively pursuing integration which will have the effect of diminishing this. For European regions, a *European context* is displacing the separate, national contexts. In the United States on the other hand, an open economy and laissez-faire national agencies (with respect to regional policy) render the *international context* the more relevant for individual states.

The analysis reported in this book does not consider regions' internal economies. These findings are intended to contribute to the various applied regional economic models, in which they would be incorporated as exogenous impacts upon region's export sectors. In this way, this research is entirely complementary with that in the mainstream of regional economic analysis, which are concerned with endogenous economic relationships.

In Chapter 2, the ill-informed but popular attention to state trade balances was noted. As states are increasingly perceived as separate and internationally competitive entities comparisons will become an imperative. Benchmarks are necessary for evaluating both individual states' trade balances as well as the relative performances between states. It is hoped that the limitations of the current data--the MISER state exports series--will become more widely appreciated. The exposure measures developed in Chapter 2 and the shift-share components reported in Chapter 3 both yield more reliable statistics for such purposes.

In the spirit of trying to "sell" the techniques employed in this research, a few notes should be made on further refinements. First, it has been acknowledged above that the shift-share model--even in its extended international form--is a fairly crude device. More importantly, it is highly susceptible to the level of disaggregation contained in the data; both sectorally and spatially. In this research, some states were amalgamated to overcome weaknesses in the data. Clearly, it would be preferable to disaggregate these and this will become possible when a longer time series of MISER exports data become available.[1] The 2-digit SIC level of aggregation, however, has been forced upon us in this analysis. The availability of more disaggregated data would substantially improve the results of the shift-share analysis. In particular, it is anticipated that the regional shift components would be reduced. These could then be more reliable interpreted as reflecting regional competitiveness whereas, at present, they incorporate some sectoral effects.

In addition, it should be acknowledged that this analysis has taken an *extensive* approach to the external dimensions of regional economies. In considering individual industry sectors, we have relied upon the quantitative data and have given no attention to qualitative aspects.

These latter might include technological developments and product life cycles, comparative regional or national productivities, corporate structures and the operation of local industrial networks. All of these concerns are valid and necessary for a complete appraisal of a region's competitive position. The present findings provide the platform upon which such *intensive* research may build. The methods reported in this book may be used to reveal regional competitive patterns and to highlight the regions and sectors which appear to be succeeding, or not. Thus, the targets for intensive analysis are revealed.

Finally, an important area of concern which has been noted but excluded in this research are the impacts of international capital movements on regional economies. In particular, a valuable extension of this analysis would be to consider the relationship between trade and investment at the level of individual states and regions. Foreign direct investment (FDI) in the U.S. has become a major factor in many state economies and this coincides with an increasing concern for the effects on regional economies of U.S. investment being transplanted abroad (to Mexico, for instance). The extent to which trade and investment are substitutes or complements for each other is of great interest. Logic would imply that the spatial transfer of capital embodied in FDI is a substitute for the transfer of material goods, the two being motivated by the same uneven distribution of the factors of production. On the other hand, anecdotal and even empirical evidence suggests that the opposite relation occurs.[2] This is an important area requiring further attention.

We must now recognize that regional economies are operating in an *international context*; furthermore, it is an environment which is undergoing dramatic change in the 1990s. The research here is an attempt to contribute some empirical understanding of the U.S. states' role in this environment, and to provide some tools for the analysis of this situation. From the outset--the construction of the data set--the intention has been to provide a comprehensive and rigorous approach, and to rectify the evident ignorance of individual states' situations.

The findings, however, provoke more questions than answers. While revealing the contribution of industrial trade in the states' economies questions arise over the causes of an individual state's trade performance. The evidence presented here merely suggests where to look.

Finally, the analysis focussed upon the potential impacts of the European Union's EC-92 program, and a methodology for examining such an event was demonstrated. This is just one of a number of contemporary trade events that may be examined in such a manner. Indeed, EC-92 has itself been succeeded by first, the European Economic

Area, and more recently, the Maastricht Treaty on European Union, each of which are integration events having external trade implications. Closer to home for the U.S. states, the North American Free Trade Area promises even more profound trade impacts, and is itself further evidence in support of the central contention of this research: that international trade and regional economies are irrevocably entwined and demand our attention.

Notes

1 Hayward and Erickson (forthcoming) specify an extended shift-share model for all 48 contiguous states.

2 Erickson and Hayward (1991) found that FDI was positively related to U.S. regional flows of exports.

Appendix 1:
Constructing the Data Set

The data utilised in this analysis are essentially derived from two sources. While both are, in fact, produced by the U.S. Bureau of the Census they originate from very different observations and are compiled separately. The only data sources to include both origin and destination data for the U.S. states is that based upon U.S. customs declarations and distributed after some processing by the Massachusetts Institute of Social and Economic Research (MISER). These are available for exports only, and only since 1987.

Although enthusiastically employed in state level analysis the MISER data is well-known to contain some serious biases which inflate the values of states with major ports, and to deflate those of the interior states. A solution was developed which reduced thses biases by merging the MISER data with another series, the Census of Manufactures and Annual Survey of Manufactures. These contain the state values for exports but with no destinations declared. Nevertheless, it is felt that the state-by-state relativities would be more accurate than for the MISER data.

A protracted and complex procedure is employed in which the CM/ASM data are used as the basis for a new set of state-by-state exports, and are apportioned by destinations according to the data contained in the MISER series. In addition, the total value of exports by sector is taken from the MISER series which is deemed to be the more accurate as it is taken from flow measures rather than the CM/ASM's stock (survey) measures. Several stages are involved in the construction of the data set which is illustrated schematically in Figure A1.1. In this diagram, the source data sets are identified and their structures and contents described, and arrows indicate the merging and manipulation process.

The first stage was to obtain a complete set of export and production data based on the 1987 Census of Manufactures (CM) and the 1983-1986 Annual Survey of Manufactures (ASM). These sources are subject to the disclosure rules established by the U.S. Congress that protect

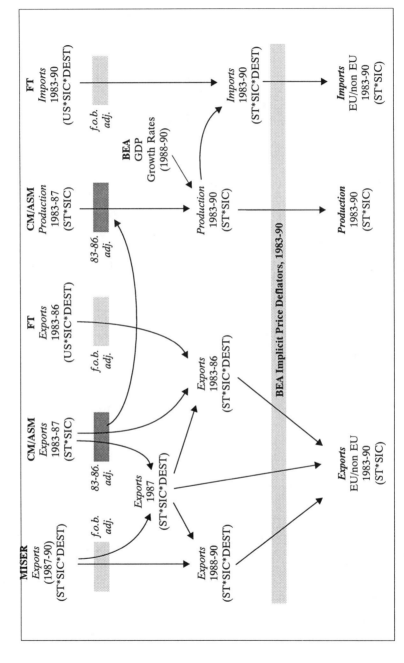

FIGURE A1.1 The construction of the U.S. state-EU trade database.

Legend (Figure A1.1)

MISER	State by state exports prepared by the Massachusetts Institute for Social and Economic Research.
CM/ASM	State level exports from the Census of Manufactures and Annual Survey of Manufactures.
FT	National exports and imports obtained from shippers' customs declarations and prepared by the Bureau of the Census.
BEA	Data obtained from the Bureau of Economic Analysis.
f.o.b.	Adjustment coefficients to convert the MISER and FT data to a "freight on board" basis, for compatibility with the CM/ASM data.
Index variables	
ST	U.S. state
SIC	Industry code
DEST	Foreign country

individual establishments and firms (just as for individual persons in the Census of Population) from being identified in published data. Before publication, therefore, data for industrial sectors in a number of states are omitted. For each state, the combined size of the omitted ("disclosed") sectors is evident from a comparison of the state totals and the sums of the published sectors. Many "disclosures"--ie, effectively gaps in the data--occur and some are quite glaring. For instance, in published Census reports Washington state, the home of the Boeing aircraft company (one of the U.S.' largest single exporters) includes no Transportation Equipment sector (SIC 37)! Similarly, one may point to the absence of data for the Tobacco Products sector (SIC 21) for Virginia. Fortunately, the full data matrix of 1987 exports from the CM has been made available elsewhere.[1] From the complete set of export values, estimates for undisclosed production values were imputed. Then, using the values obtained for 1987, estimates were made for prior years and a complete set of CM and ASM export and production estimates was obtained.

It would be possible to evaluate the accuracy of these estimates by comparing them with the actual data compiled by the Census Bureau. However, to do so would be a violation of the rules protecting this data. The author has had privileged access to the unedited data at the Bureau, but wishes to emphasize that in no way has any protected data or information been employed in obtaining these estimates; they are derived solely from published data. Indeed, an important objective of this discussion is to demonstrate this procedure.

The second stage of the data manipulation procedure is perhaps the most crucial for this research. It was noted above that the MISER data contains biases towards states with ports although one may presume that, with respect to SIC classes and destinations, the aggregate data are sound. Also, it was suggested that the CM/ASM data more accurately reflect the states' relative shares of exports. The chosen solution to obtain more accurate state-by-foreign destination trade data therefore was to blend the two data series. First, from the MISER data, the manufacturing SIC categories alone were selected and the export values adjusted with the Freight on Board (f.o.b.) adjustment factors reported in Appendix B of the 1987 Census of Manufacturing export report (U.S. Bureau of the Census 1991). These factors are needed to adjust the values from MISER's Free Alongside Ship (f.a.s.) basis, in which shipping and insurance costs are included, to the CM/ASM's f.o.b. basis. Second, the CM exports data were adjusted such that they match the MISER exports at aggregated 2-digit SIC levels, since the latter is presumed to report the more accurate total export dollar values. Third, the CM's export values are apportioned by foreign destination in the same proportion by state of those of the MISER data. In this way, a STATE-by-SIC-by-DESTINATION export data matrix is obtained as an *alternative* to the MISER data set; one that more accurately reflects the states' shares of exports. Finally, this data set is aggregated to a state-by-SIC level, with export values summed for EU and non-EU destinations.

The data set developed with the above procedures contains 744 state-by-SIC observations, each with an EU and non-EU export value. These export figures may be compared to the corresponding MISER values and a simple ratio derived which itself may be used as an adjustment coefficient for the conversion of the latter to the former. Since no CM/ASM data are available more recently than 1987, in the third stage of the data manipulation process these adjustment coefficients were used to effect a conversion of the 1988-1990 MISER data. Accordingly, a unique adjustment ratio is obtained for each state-by-SIC cell and these are applied to the post-1987 MISER data to get comparably adjusted export data. In many cases these adjustment ratios have extreme values: in excess of 500 or even 1,000 percent, and less than 50 percent (where 100 percent implies no adjustment to the MISER data). These extreme cases generally occur for sectors with particularly small trade flows and so some conservative criteria were applied: for cases where the sector's exports amounted to less than 5 percent of the state total, or where either the MISER or final adjusted 1987 total exports were less than one million dollars in value, the *mean* state adjustment coefficient was substituted for the unique cell value. With these coefficients, adjusted exports data were obtained for the years since 1987 for which CM data are not available.

The fourth stage was to complete the export data series prior to 1987. Again, this was achieved with adjustment ratios derived from the 1987 data set. In this case, the key values are the proportions of each state-by-SIC cell's export attributed to the EU and non-EU destinations. For the years 1983-1986, the U.S. total exports by foreign destinations (FT) are merged with the corresponding ASM state-by-SIC data. Having adjusted the latter to equal the former at the SIC levels (i.e., U.S. totals), the ASM exports may be apportioned to either EU or non-EU destinations according to the 1987 proportions. Finally, these individual export values were adjusted according to the total U.S. (SIC) exports to the EU and non-EU destinations, respectively. This method of essentially apportioning values according to aggregate totals and known 1987 proportions was deemed to be the best method by which to estimate earlier state export patterns in the absence of detailed, real data.

The fifth stage in this data manipulation, is to obtain state-level imports. As noted above, imports are available only for the U.S. as a whole by SIC category but for the present purposes this is not considered to be a problem since, were accurate state-level imports available, they would at best be measures of the states' consumption of imports. In obtaining such data, serious problems are encountered since import shipments enter one state are usually broken down into smaller lots and distributed elsewhere, to either secondary distributors or final consumers who are quite likely in another state. The present concern, however, is for the external trade impact upon states' industries and so foreign imports are of concern only where they compete directly with the industries of a particular state. The relevant measure is one that represents import competition not consumption, and this may be obtained by apportioning total U.S. imports across the individual states according to the state patterns of industrial production. The most significant assumption of this procedure is that imports into the U.S. market equally affect domestic competitors throughout the U.S. While this assumption may be simplifying, in the absence of more detailed estimates of import penetration patterns, it is the most relevant procedure.

For the years 1983-1987, the availability of CM/ASM industrial production data, i.e., the total values of shipments data, matches the available FT imports data but for subsequent years, CM/ASM data are not yet available. Estimates of total manufacturing output for the years 1988-1990, therefore, were made by inflating the 1987 values by the same rates as those of total U.S. goods production recorded in the *Survey of Current Business* (U.S. Bureau of Economic Analysis, 1989, 1991). In this manner, state-by-SIC output values were obtained and used to estimate imports from the EU and non-EU sources for the years

1988-1990, thereby complementing the exports data described above and completing the data set.

A final stage in this procedure is to apply price deflators to render the values from successive years comparable to one another. Implicit price deflators for the manufacturing sectors were obtained by personal communication from the U.S. Bureau of Economic Analysis.

The objective is to evaluate the potential impacts of EC-92 on the regional economies of the United States. In most cases, these are individual states although some contiguous states are grouped into multi-state regions. It was felt that smaller values of trade flow were more prone to error and so combining some of the smaller states was a pragmatic method of reducing the risk of erroneous results. To this end, the criterion applied was to merge states with total 1987 manufacturing exports of less than one billion dollars. For similar reasons of data reliability, only the 48 contiguous states were included and the resulting 38 states and regions are depicted in Figure 2.2.

The data set therefore contains absolute trade figures (both exports and imports) between 38 states and either the European Union or all other world regions combined, and the total value of their industrial output (of which exports are a part). Furthermore, these data are disaggregated to the two-digit Standard Industrial Classification (SIC) categories for the years 1983 through 1990.

The procedure described above produces a unique database of bilateral trade flows between the 38 states and regions and the European Union. It is, of course, too large to be reproduced in its entirety in printed form. In order that it be made available for further analysis or replication of the present analysis, these data may be obtained from the author at the Department of Geography, The University of Auckland, PO Box 92019, Auckland, New Zealand.

Notes

1 The appendix to Risha's (1991) comparison of the two manufacturing trade data series contains a complete set of 1987 CM state export values. This report was distributed externally by the Foreign Trade Division of the U.S. Bureau of the Census. It is presumed that the inclusion of formerly "disclosed" exports values from the 1987 CM was an oversight. However, they have now officially entered the public realm and the author wishes to emphasize that only such public data has been used in this analysis.

Appendix 2:
The European Union:
Evolution and Integration

The research reported in this book concerns the impacts of European integration on U.S. state economies, and specifically the EC-92 program. This event is one in a series of deepening rounds of integration in post-war European history. Even before its completion, the EC-92 program was succeeded by a further initiative, the Maastricht Treaty on European union.

This book takes the perspective of the third parties to these developments, the individual U.S. states. However, in support of this analysis this appendix offers some supplementary discussion of recent European history and contemporary issues. This will be particularly valuable as a complement to Chapter 4, especially for those readers who require clarification of the actors and agencies in the European political economy.

Post-War European Integration

The European Union, as it is now titled, came into being when six western European nations signed the first Treaty of Rome in March 1957. The essential goal of the Treaty was the formation of an integrated, pan-European free market--a "coalition of self-interest" (Dudley 1989, p. 25). Central to this were the so-called "four freedoms", the pursuit of the free movement of: goods, services, capital and labor (Hufbauer 1990, p. 1). The Treaty established the European Economic Community (EEC) as of January 1, 1958, which, along with the existing European Coal and Steel Community (ECSC, founded in 1951) and the European Atomic Energy Community (Euratom, founded by the second Treaty of Rome, 1957) integrated the major economies of western Europe and laid the framework for post-war European economic development. The six founding members were the previously-associated BENELUX countries (Belgium, the Netherlands and Luxembourg) and the three largest continental economies: France, Italy and the Federal Republic of Germany. From 1968, the three parallel institutions were merged and came to be known jointly as the European Communities (EC or, simply, the Community).

From the outset, the EEC received warm encouragement from the rest of the western world and, especially, the United States. In addition to its economic goals, its foundation served two strategic objectives. First, European integration was politically desirable to preclude another disastrous European war. In particular, it was felt that if Germany could be economically integrated with its neighbors its expansionist tendencies would be curtailed. Second, founded at the height of the Cold War, the Community was seen by the U.S. and its western allies as an important pillar in the rebuilding of capitalist western Europe and as a bulwark against further expansion of the Soviet bloc. United States' support for the EC, therefore, was complementary to the other major geopolitical initiatives: the Marshall Plan (1947) and the North Atlantic Treaty Organization (1949).

Given the U.S.'s dominant position in the world economy of the early post-War years, the re-emergence of the western European economies posed little economic threat. To the contrary, the re-industrializing Europe provided a profitable market for both American consumer goods and investment. U.S. firms, as much as their European counterparts, were major beneficiaries of the gradual removal of tariffs between the six founding members of the EEC. Indeed, firms such as General Motors and Ford established continental-scale operations in Europe with considerable advantages in economies of scale over their European competitors--advantages which remain to this day (Dicken, 1992).

U.S. concern for the competitive potential of the European Community first surfaced in President Kennedy's address to Congress in 1962, in which he warned of the emerging single economy across the Atlantic.[1] His response to this challenge set the tone for subsequent U.S. trade policy which was to negotiate multilateral reductions in trade barriers through the proceedings of the General Agreement on Tariffs and Trade (GATT). The U.S.-EC trading partnership was viewed on both sides as being mutually beneficial and the Kennedy Round of the GATT (1963-68) resulted in the reduction in the EC's Common External Tariff. The Community's importance in world trade was already apparent. Indeed, Hufbauer (1990) makes the assertion that "without the prior formation of the EC, there would not have been a Kennedy Round at all" (p. 5) as individual European countries-- France and Italy in particular--would individually have been unwilling to make the necessary concessions to free trade. The EC, therefore, was an active accomplice in the U.S.'s post-War policy of liberalizing world trade and, between the two, a largely harmonious trading relationship existed.

From the late 1960s through the 1970s, the Community became distracted from its pursuit of a true common market--the original 'four freedoms'. This neglect resulted from a preoccupation with geographic (membership) expansion and the twin oil shocks of 1973 and 1979. Following lengthy negotiations Denmark, Ireland and the United Kingdom acceded to the European Community on January 22, 1972. Norway, too, was a signatory to the Treaty of Accession but withdrew after a referendum on membership. The oil shocks and subsequent periods of inflation restrained the EC's trade-liberalizing tendencies and the period of the 1970s and early 1980s has been described by Hoffman (1989) as the Community's "dark age" (p. 29). Disharmony among the members over budget contributions, the European Currency Unit (ECU), the Exchange Rate Mechanism (ERM) and the Common Agricultural Policy (CAP) contributed to a general malaise; *eurosclerosis* and *europessimism* gained wide currency as by-words for the EC's performance at this time.

The Community received a jump-start which initiated a renewed period of optimism with the 1985 White Paper (policy document), "Completing the Internal Market" (European Commission 1985). This identified the numerous non-tariff barriers (NTBs) to intra-EC trade, that remained as obstacles to the four freedoms and proposed 300 legislative acts to remove these and finally create a truly unified European market. The White Paper was followed by a number of studies which forecast a significant economic benefit accruing from the adoption of these proposals. Most influential was the Commission-sponsored Cecchini Report[2] which estimated a boost to the Community's gross domestic product (GDP) of between 4.3 percent and 6.4 percent, or about $270 billion, numbering new jobs in the millions as well as substantial budgetary gains. Other estimates varied but generally fed the enthusiasm for the project still further.

The White Paper identified three categories of barriers: physical, technical and fiscal. Physical barriers include the frontier posts and customs controls. Although serving only administrative functions they nevertheless add an overhead cost to intra-Community trade. Technical barriers, including health and safety, packaging, product definition and other standards are regarded as the most significant barriers since, in many cases, they effectively exclude one member's goods from another's market thereby protecting and perpetuating separate national markets. Finally, fiscal barriers result from the members' different excise and indirect (sales) duties on goods which present a barrier as individual governments necessarily regulate cross-border trade which might otherwise undermine different tax regimes.

The Single Europe Act (SEA) of July 1, 1987, acted on the White Paper's proposals and amended the Treaty of Rome to create a true common market. It also set a deadline for the completion of this program, the now infamous December 31, 1992 which gave rise to the widely used terms for the project: "EC-92", "Europe 1992" or just "1992."

The continuing progress of the EC-92 program owes much to the coercion applied by the SEA but also to a number of other factors not least the leadership of the President of the European Commission, Jacques Delors. Progress has been also smoothed by assuaging peripheral members' concerns with an increase in the EU's structural funds which are granted to economically-backward areas (Gardner 1991a). In addition, a new approach to the harmonization of technical standards has expedited the program. The principle of *mutual recognition* wherein a product accepted by one member country's standards authorities is automatically accepted EU-wide has reduced exhaustive harmonization of a multiplicity of member rules and individual product categories. Finally, a key characteristic of the EC-92 program which distinguishes it in particular from the arduous process employed by the GATT is that from the outset, the package was accepted as a whole; leaving the working-out of the details to be accomplished later but within a specific timetable.

The Primary Features of the EC-92 Program

The program spelled out in the Single European Act is an attempt to finally create a true customs union as envisaged by the founding Treaty of Rome. That this had not previously been achieved is noted by Cooney (1989) in his retelling of one U.S. executive's aphorism: "On January 1, 1958, the original six members of the Common Market took down their signs at the internal borders that said 'customs.' They then put up new signs that said 'taxes'" (p. 9). In addition to differential taxes that necessitate an administrative burden in order to redress them on cross-border shipments, different national technical standards, public procurement policies and national fiscal regimes have perpetuated a degree of market fragmentation that had diminished the earlier gains of economic integration.

The major causes of this fragmentation have been identified by the European Commission[3] as:

1. The high administrative costs of dealing with differential national bureaucracies.

2. The higher transport costs due to frontier formalities
3. The increased costs of meeting different national technical standards, necessitating smaller product runs.
4. The welfare costs of duplicated research and development efforts by different national firms
5. The higher costs incurred by consumers of uncompetitive, regulated national markets, especially in those sectors dominated by public procurement.
6. The higher costs and reduced choice to consumers confined to domestic markets for goods and services.
7. The opportunity costs discouraging productive activity from locating optimally in the EC and from benefiting from the full market.

In order to address these problems, the EC-92 program proposed actions on three fronts: the removal of physical barriers, technical barriers and fiscal barriers.[4] These three areas are discussed in some detail below and should be noted as the full extent and the limits of the EC-92 program. The many other programs being initiated or debated within the European Union, including monetary union (EMU), political union and the Social Charter, are complementary to EC-92. They are not a part of EC-92 proper, but are what Hufbauer (1990, p. 13) refers to as the "outer-wrapping" and should be considered separately. However, as they may impinge upon the success of EC-92 they are also discussed below.

The Removal of Physical Barriers

The physical obstacles to the free movement of goods and people are perhaps the most visible. Prior to EC-92, the frontier posts on the internal borders of the member states were the most obvious indicators of continued division within the Community. The customs, immigration controls, passports and baggage searches represent a nuisance to individual travellers but these and the administrative burden added a real cost to intra-EU commerce. The Single Administrative Document of 1988[5] reduced the paperwork burden but the bureaucracy still exacted a toll and a major the goal of EC-92 was to eliminate frontier controls altogether (European Commission 1985, p. 9).

Economic gains therefore may be realized from the removal of the border controls but equally as important is the political dimension. The elimination of restrictions on the movement and activities of EU citizens would be an important step in creating a true European community. Although customs duties and trade restrictions within the Community were eliminated by 1968, frontier posts remained and have even assumed additional roles as a direct result of EU policies. The EC-92 program calls for the complete elimination of all internal border controls and so each of their several roles have needed to be addressed individually.

One of the most important uses of frontier controls has come to be to ensure that as goods travel from one member country to another correct adjustments are made to the indirect taxes levied against them (value added tax and excise duties). Without such physical controls the differential fiscal regimes of member states would be undermined. However, with the harmonization of fiscal policies among members (discussed below) this particular raison d'étre for frontier posts is expected to vanish.

A second role of frontiers is as instruments of individual members' commercial policies. Under the Treaty of Rome, there are no restrictions on trade between members, but instances remain of individual members' national policies towards particular third country goods. Under Article 115 of the Treaty, members are allowed to introduce protectionist measures against non-members' goods arriving via another member (Ó'Cléireacáin,1990). A good example of the use of Article 115 is Italy's restrictions on the importation of Japanese cars. Other members, including Germany, have no restrictions, and France and Britain have had voluntary export restraint agreements. Thus, in the absence of Article 115 and the internal customs controls it authorizes, Japanese cars could enter the Italian market by the back-door, via Germany or France. The White Paper, however, explicitly states that the abolition of all national trade restrictions are a goal of the EC-92 program (European Commission 1985, p. 11). This effectively renders Article 115 inoperable and compels the members to harmonize their commercial policies.

Frontier controls are also employed to apply countervailing charges to commodities in transit between members where no Community-wide policy has been established and these are allowed under Article 46 of the Treaty. Again, the White Paper envisages an extension of the Common Agricultural Policy (CAP) and similar programs for other commodities to obviate the need for future recourse to this provision and thereby removing a further function of frontiers.

The internal frontiers are also used in the front line against the spread of animal and plant diseases, and to ensure that products in transit meet national health standards. The EC-92 program calls for the harmonization of all national health standards and the mutual acceptance among members of each other's certification procedures. With this is achieved, the need for frontier inspections will be removed.

The regulation of transportation itself has been another major function of the frontier posts. Much of the intra-community transport operators are subject to quotas. These necessitate vehicles carrying authorizations and checks upon these permits are generally made at the border crossings. If transportation in the EU is to be de-regulated, as discussed below, then these controls will also become unnecessary. Similarly, safety inspections made at the borders should become unnecessary when the national road-safety inspections are harmonized (European Commission 1985, p. 13).

Another role of the customs posts is in the recording of trade statistics required by both the members' statistical agencies and those of the European Commission itself. If border posts are to be removed then an alternative method of data collection will become necessary, and surveys will replace the flow measures currently used.

Finally, the frontier controls are a primary tool for intra-EU police activity. Individual member states have declared their legitimate concerns over terrorism, the smuggling of drugs and other prohibited goods, and the immigration of non-EU nationals. To address these concerns, a common European passport has been proposed (European Commission 1985, p. 15) and progress has been made towards a Convention on External Frontiers (*Financial Times* 6-27-91a, p. 1) which will enable the removal of internal border checks. This issue, however, remains contentious and provokes continuing dissent among member states. For example, progress has depended upon Britain being assured that it would not have to remove its border checks, and upon Spain and Britain agreeing to disagree over the status of Gibraltar. Clearly the removal of frontier posts is a sensitive issue for many countries. An example of potential progress occurred in June 1989, when five members (Belgium, France, Germany, Luxembourg and the Netherlands), out of impatience towards the remainder of the Community, signed the Schengen convention agreeing to remove all of their internal frontiers and to adopt common immigration and visa policies (Sallnow 1991, p. 40). Portugal and Spain acceded to the convention in June 1991 (Buchan 1991c, p. 2) which serves as a model for the whole EU despite the recalcitrance of the remaining members.

The intra-EU border controls presently perform a variety of functions and each of these have needed to be addressed before the barriers can be removed. Fortunately, however, many of these functions are the direct result of the necessity to enforce existing technical and fiscal barriers. If these are eliminated then the removal of the physical barriers will be made much easier.

The Removal of Technical Barriers

Technical barriers to the free movement of goods and people within the Community are less visible than formal border controls but are more complex and more obstructive. They arise from the individual national regulations for health and safety, packaging, product definitions and technical specifications. Their importance is acknowledged in the White Paper:

> barriers created by different national product regulations and standards have a double-edged effect: they not only add extra costs, but they also distort production patterns; increase unit costs; increase stock holding costs; discourage business cooperation, and fundamentally frustrate the creation of a common market for industrial products. (European Commission 1985, p. 17)

In effect companies are often confined to national markets and unable to achieve the production efficiencies afforded by economies of scale. Indeed, technical barriers have been estimated by the Cecchini Report to be the costliest, the estimated the gains from their removal being $240 billion (Cecchini 1988, Table 9.2).

In its 1985 White Paper, the European Commission proposed the removal of all technical barriers except for those absolutely necessary on health or safety grounds. Its guiding principle is that "if a product is lawfully manufactured and marketed in one member state, there is no reason why it should not be sold freely throughout the Community" (European Commission 1985, p. 17). This principle was upheld by the European Court of Justice as long ago as 1979, in its landmark "Cassis de Dijon" decision. In this case, the French liqueur of that name had been banned from sale in Germany because its alcohol content was *below* that required by the 1922 *Branntweinmonopolgesetz* statute which established the German definition for a liqueur (Hufbauer 1990, p. 12). In its decision, however, the Court determined that the German law was both contrary and inferior to Article 30 of the Treaty of Rome. Henceforth, the liqueur could be sold in Germany because it was legally produced and sold in another member country, ie. France. This particular piece of jurisprudence had a profound effect upon the European Commission's ability to confront member countries on matters of internal competition and has provided the legal basis for much of the EC-92 program.

With respect to the removal of obstacles created by technical barriers, EC-92 adopted a "new approach" to the harmonization of national standards. In the past, progress had been very slow as harmonization was conducted under Article 100 which required unanimous agreement by the European Council. Agreements took a very long time to implement and proved to be over-regulatory as the quirks of each member's existing standards and national industry lobbies had to be accommodated. The effect of this process was that EU-wide regulations could not even keep pace with the development of new technologies and thus stifled innovation. Judging from past performance, therefore, it would be impossible to meet the goals of EC-92 under the existing procedures. The new approach calls for the harmonization under Article 100 of only the minimum regulations which are then incorporated into national codes. Following the acceptance of essential minimum standards, the precedent set by the Cassis de Dijon decision and Articles 30 to 36 of the Treaty prohibiting national measures from restricting the free movement of trade are then employed to compel member states to mutually recognize each others' national standards. In this somewhat devious and legalistic manner European technical standards are created de facto, and with them a free market, too.

A second important dimension in the streamlining of the process of setting EU-wide technical standards has been to remove the issue from the political arena. Much of the task has been delegated to existing non-governmental European standards agencies (this mechanism being allowed by Article 155). The Comité Européen de la Normalisation (CEN) and associated bodies CENELEC, UEAtc, RILEM, and CEPT (in telecommunications) are quasi-private organizations comprising both government and industry members. Delegating the burden of setting technical standards to such bodies removes it from the congested agenda of the European Council and the process has been expedited greatly. Indeed, progress can be measured almost daily. For instance, in 1991 a draft standard for the new generation high-definition television (HDTV)--a technology not yet implemented--was proposed (*Financial Times* 6-27-91c, p. 2).

A further proposal of the White Paper addressed the potential for the future imposition of national technical standards. It was proposed that members would be required to submit future national regulations to the European Commission to be reviewed for conformity with EC provisions prior to its implementation. An issue most likely to put this policy to the test will result from the rise of environmental concerns and the moves by some members, notably Germany, to legislate "green" standards for products (*Economist* 6-15-91b, p. 61). These include the use of recyclable materials in products and packaging, environmentally-friendly chemicals and a minimum recyclable component in automobiles. There is much concern that such environmental regulations, implemented by individual member states, will effectively--and cynics may say, intentionally--create new technical barriers even as the old ones are being removed.

In addition to product standards, other barriers of a technical nature were identified by the White Paper. Of particular concern is the significant part of the EU's economic activity that is part of public (i.e., government) procurement or which takes place in highly regulated industries. Throughout the European Union the energy, transport, water and telecommunications industries have remained aloof from the free trade precepts of the Treaty of Rome (especially Articles 30 and 59 addressing the free movement of goods and services), and in many other public procurement sectors EU directives on public works and supply contracts have generally been ineffective (Cooney 1989, p. 20).

Tenders for public contracts that are restricted to national firms effectively cloister those firms from competitive forces and necessarily raises the costs to both governments and consumers alike. Cecchini (1988, p. 16) has estimated public-sector procurement to amount to 15 percent of the Community's gross domestic product of which only 2 percent is open to intra-EU competition (Ginsberg 1989, p. 2). Under the EC-92 program, public authorities in the member countries will be required to make their bidding processes completely transparent--that is to say they will be public, with adequate notice, and open to tenders from all sources. To ensure the success of this initiative the Commission will be acquiring new legal powers to nullify contracts that are found to be in violation of these precepts (Cooney 1989, p. 20).

A number of other, mostly service, sectors are highly regulated; some are public- or semi publicly-owned and others are private but subject to government regulation that inhibits cross-border commerce, and some of the most prominent EC-92 initiatives address sectors such as financial services and transport. The White Paper underscores its concern for the service sector by reporting that in 1982 these sectors accounted for 57 percent of total Community value added, compared to only 26 percent for manufacturing industries (European Commission 1985, p. 26), and its share is widely believed to be rising. In the financial services sector it is proposed that "financial products" experience the same free flow as goods. There needs to be some coordination of rules governing these sectors but it is proposed that after harmonization, the supervision of the market will be devolved among the members using the *home country* principle in which the state of an institution's headquarters will be responsible for the necessary oversight (European Commission 1985, p. 28). The effectiveness of such a regulatory approach has been called into question with the 1991 fraud-laden collapse of the Bank of

Credit and Commerce International (BCCI). BCCI was a "stateless" bank: its ownership based in the United Arab Emirates, its management in Pakistan, chartered in Britain and Luxembourg, with operations based in the Cayman Islands (*New York Times* 8-12-91, p. A1). Its fraudulent operation and precipitous collapse highlighted the deficiencies of the existing regulatory mechanisms and the weakness of national-level authorities when dealing with transnational firms.

Transport services are to be similarly afforded free passage throughout the EU. This was required under the Common Transport Policy of the original Treaty of Rome (European Commission 1985, p. 29) and so most of the measures specified in the White Paper called for their immediate or swift implementation. Broadly, these include the removal of national restrictions and quotas on the provision of transport services, especially by operators from other member countries. An example of the progress of the EC-92 program on this area is the recent accord of the members' transport ministers on the break-up of national monopolies in rail transport (Gardner and Tomkins 1991, p. 15). This agreement will allow for rail companies to offer services throughout the EU with automatic rights of usage of the existing European rail network. Furthermore, this will enable the development of combined transport services in which road and rail (and maybe also air and sea) systems are integrated.

The EC-92 program also seeks to create a single market for emerging new technology service sectors such as audiovisual services, information and data processing, computerized marketing and distribution services, and electronic banking (European Commission 1985, p. 30). To this end EU-wide technical standards will be established requiring the harmonization of existing technologies and EU standards for new ones.

Two components of the "four freedoms," the free movement of labor and capital, are currently subject to barriers of a technical nature. EC-92 will enforce the mutual recognition of educational and professional qualifications by member countries, removing the last significant obstacle to an open European labor market. The liberalization of capital movements will also be required post-1992 of those members who have not already opened up their capital markets. This requirement will be facilitated by the deregulation of the financial services sector, but it also raises the need for exchange rate stability and necessitates discussion of the European Monetary System or even full monetary union upon which members have differing positions.

Finally, the White Paper called for the Community to create suitable conditions for industrial cooperation. These include the harmonization of company law, and of intellectual property and copyright laws, etc. (European Commission 1985, pp. 34-37). Progress in many of these areas has been made prior to EC-92 but the current program should provide the impetus to finish the process where it has stalled (Cooney 1989, pp. 35-36).

The Removal of Fiscal Barriers

The fiscal dimension of the EC-92 program addresses the disparate national systems of indirect taxation utilized by the individual member countries. At present, there are widely varying rates of sales and excise taxes on goods within the European Union. If these differential taxes are not redressed at the internal frontiers then there would be an incentive for consumers to make their purchases in the lower-tax countries, and national taxation regimes would be undermined. The corollary of this is that the removal of these frontier posts--a fundamental goal of EC-92--has inescapable implications for the national systems of indirect taxation.

In 1967, the EC members decided to replace their existing systems of sales taxes with value added tax (VAT) regimes that, while differing in actual levels, employed a similar structure among the members (European Commission 1985, p. 41). The standard rate of VAT varies from 12 percent in Luxembourg and Spain to between 18.5 and 22 percent in Denmark, France, Holland, Ireland and Italy (European Commission 1985, 49; *Economist* 6-15-91c, p. 70). Furthermore, VAT rates vary on different products such that luxury goods may be taxed at rates of 25 to 38 percent in Belgium, France, Italy, Greece, Portugal and Spain but at only standard rates in the other countries. Similarly, goods considered as necessities (food, children's clothing) are usually taxed at lower rates of 2 to 7 percent while in Britain and Ireland, these are zero-rated.

The second type of indirect tax is the excise tax, levied on particular goods such as alcoholic beverages, tobacco products, and gasoline products. It is usually justified as by social concerns rather than simple revenue generation. Here again, however, there is a wide variation in the levels imposed by the individual members. The differences are widest on tobacco and alcohol products; Germany, Portugal and Spain having no duties on wine at all (Buchan 1991c; European Commission 1985, p. 50). In general, there is a marked difference between the northern and southern member states with respect to levels of excise duties, and these tend to reflect cultural traits.

The EC-92 program calls for the approximation in national levels of VAT and excise duties among the members in order to facilitate the removal of frontier posts and the present bureaucratic burden of redressing different rates. This burden amounts to some 50 million customs forms each year and at an estimated total cost to companies and governments of \$9.5 billion in 1988 (*Economist* 6-15-91c, p. 70) The harmonization of taxes and duties has proved a difficult task for the members as this issue makes the twin challenges to their sovereignty by: (1) removing their frontier posts, as well as (2) limiting their freedom to levy taxes. In the original White Paper, it was proposed that VAT would be collected only by the country of origin, to be distributed later among members through the use of a clearing-house system (Hufbauer 1990, p. 9). In December 1990, it was decided to revert to a modified "destination" system since an acceptable means of disbursing tax revenues could not be found. Typically the debate divides the net producers and net consumers among the member states over who should benefit most from tax receipts (*Economist* 6-15-91c, p. 70).

The removal of fiscal barriers is one of the most important components of the EC-92 package and to many observers provides the greatest test of the program as a whole. Britain for instance, rejects the idea of establishing minimum levels of VAT arguing that this infringes on its sovereignty and that, in any case, it should be left to the market to force a convergence of tax rates. On the other hand, it has no such qualms about excise duties, since apparently they are perceived as an instrument of public health and welfare policy (*Economist* 6-15-91c, p. 70). Such concerns, and the resistance of many members to raise or lower duties on specific products, has hampered agreement on fiscal barriers. On June 24, 1991, however, European finance ministers finally agreed on minimum rates of VAT and excise duties, fudging the issue (for Britain's sake) of whether they were laws, or merely agreements, and allowing a number of exclusions for those countries not willing to tax certain goods (Buchan 1991c, p. 2).

Progress of the EC-92 Program

Despite successive pronouncements that the EC-92 program was behind schedule, particularly with respect to the performance of the Council of Ministers (Hufbauer 1990, p. 13) and the progressively louder cries of anguish from individual members as their peculiar interests are sacrificed for the common good, progress was sustained. Of the 282 proposals tabled by the European Commission by mid-1991--ie, with eighteen months remaining--193 have been voted into EU law by the Council (Buchan 1991a, p. 4). Many of these, however, only take effect once accepted into national legislation by each member's parliament, and here there is a wide variation in the performance of individual countries. For instance, of the 126 measures sent to the member states for ratification by mid-1991, Italy has managed to turn only 52 into national law whereas its partners have managed at least 81, and Germany and France, 107 and 101, respectively. The process has benefited from the European Council's six-month rotating presidency as each successive President seeks to distinguish its own term by substantial progress on EU business.

On the removal of physical barriers, the 12 have agreed on the elimination of customs formalities and inspections of the health of animals and plants at the place of origin rather than borders. There remain some unresolved issues concerning the flow of third country goods throughout the EU and of the flow of agricultural products. Also Britain, and to a lesser extent Denmark, Greece and Ireland, maintain that they require border controls for security reasons.

A useful measure of the progress of EC-92 is perhaps its effect on the activities of European firms and of foreign investment in the EU. In the high-technology electronics, aerospace and telecommunications sectors in particular, company reorganizations, mergers and acquisitions, partnerships and other collaborative ventures have been occurring apace in anticipation of the single market (Ginsberg 1989, p. 32). Also, Heitger and Stehn (1990) report that Japanese direct investment in a broad spectrum of industries has been stepped-up apparently as a result of the EC-92 program. Evidently, both European and foreign firms are convinced of the inevitability of the single market and are preparing for it.

Some of the main obstacles to progress, however, remain: in particular, the concern of some members over issues of sovereignty and national security, and others over industrial policy and the potential for significant unemployment in particular industries as national subsidies and protection are eliminated.[6] The success of EC-92 is not assured but it is nevertheless clear that progress has been made on this ambitious project. Furthermore, if one recognizes that 1992 is itself an arbitrary deadline and that the program is on-going, then its impact on both the European and global economy should not be ignored.

Further Integration Beyond EC-92

With the EC-92 program well under way in the early 1990s, the headlines have been captured by a series of new initiatives that, to varying degrees, complement or grow out of the single market project. These are not, however, parts of the EC-92 program proper but they may have significant impacts on its progress. This "outer-wrapping" (Hufbauer 1990, p. 13) may be grouped under three types: (i) initiatives to extend the EU's intervention in the European market; (ii) initiatives to extend the process of integration beyond the economic realm; and (iii) moves to expand the geographic coverage of the EU. While there is broad agreement on the direction and progress of EC-92, these additional initiatives expose some serious divisions among the members.

Extensions Beyond EC-92

Moves to direct the EU into a greater interventionist role in the European economy have taken two tracks. The first of these is generally referred to as the social dimension. Because one of the sacred four freedoms concerns the free movement of people (i.e., labor) it is generally accepted by all members that EU citizens should have the right to free mobility within the European Union. However, it is widely feared that this very same freedom, when also applied to capital, will lead to a greater exploitation of labor if capitalists are able "divide and rule," playing workers in one region off against those in another. There is a particular concern that health and safety regulations as well as the bargaining position of labor vis-á-vis industry will be undermined. To counter this, a second component of the social dimension concerns the need for EU-wide regulations on health, safety, social security, sexual equality and worker participation in firms. The European Charter of Fundamental Social Rights was proposed at the summit of EU leaders held in Madrid in June, 1989, and was accepted by all the members except Britain (Hufbauer 1990, p. 15). Similarly, the Commission's adoption of a resolution calling for European Works Councils to enable worker participation in European firms was also rejected by the British government (U.S. Representative to the European Community, 1990, p. 5). Britain's position--stated most forcefully by former Prime Minister Thatcher--finds sympathy to varying degrees elsewhere in the EU and stems largely from an ideological position which views EU social policy as smacking of welfare statism and corporatism:

> We have not successfully rolled back the frontiers of the state in Britain only to see them reimposed at a European level with a European superstate exercising a new dominance from Brussels.[7]

The second track along which greater interventionism has been proposed is in the area of industrial policy. The EC-92 program exudes a liberal-economic ideology: the dismantling of national and sectoral restrictions on trade in favor of the broad gains of free trade. This, however, challenges the former tendencies of most European governments for dirigiste economic management. Although interventionism fell out of favor in the 1980s, the political realities of economic recession in the early 1990s and the suffering of particular industrial sectors has promoted a resurgence of the dirigiste camp. The view found its most vociferous advocate in the brief tenure of Edith Cresson as prime minister of France from mid-1991 until early 1992, but is held by many throughout the EU (Buchan et al. 1991, p. 12). Cresson led the call for the EU to establish an industrial policy to protect and nurture specific industrial sectors that are presently suffering foreign competition, particularly from Japanese firms (her main bête noir). Again, the split among the members over the need for an industrial policy falls mainly along ideological lines as countries with free-trade-oriented administrations such as Germany and Britain oppose any retrenchment on trade liberalization, while those with more dirigiste or labor-oriented perspectives, as well as those with industries under particular threat (such as France and Italy) are its main advocates.

An industrial policy would effectively reverse the European Commission's previous stand against members' support of *national champions*--national firms receiving preferential support from their own governments[8]--and their replacement by *European champions*. Pressure, however, is growing from certain industries who perceive the greatest threat from foreign (especially Japanese) competition. These include many sectors long accustomed to national protection and patronage such as automobiles[9] and others widely regarded as having strategic importance such as the electronics sector, where Japanese firms have already been gaining a European presence through the acquisition of European firms.[10] Indeed concern is growing that despite the Community's efforts to allay fears of a "Fortress Europe" (*New York Times* 10-23-88, p. A1) it may yet be "created not by design but by default in response to protectionist lobbying by individual interest groups" (Buchan et al. 1991, p. 12). However, since the EU's flagship industrial policy, the Common Agricultural Policy, already consumes fully 56 percent of its total budget, it is unlikely to willingly embark on further intervention.

Initiatives to extend the process of European integration beyond the free-market EC-92 program are generally led by those who see this as merely a stage in an evolutionary process towards the grand goal of European unification. A single European market, therefore, is to be complemented by a single monetary system and a single currency. This initiative has been led by Jacques Delors, President of the European Commission and an April, 1989 report outlined a staged process toward achieving this goal. In the first stage, each members' national currencies will be linked in the European Exchange Rate Mechanism (ERM)[11] and national monetary policies will be more closely coordinated. In the second stage, monetary union and a single currency will be undertaken, and this was represented by the 1991 Maastricht Treaty (below). At the time, all members were part of the ERM but several dropped out during the September 1992 currency markets debacle. While the Maastricht Treaty was eventually adopted by all twelve members, the most notable effect so far has been the change in the Community's title--European Union--and promised economic union has yet to be achieved.

Extensions Beyond the Economic Realm

A second front on which greater European integration is being pursued is towards political union. This is less advanced than monetary union but has been gathering pace in the aftermath of the recent political developments in Eastern Europe and the demise of the Soviet Union in 1991. In the Rome summit of EU leaders in December, 1990, the Intergovernmental Conference (IGC) on Political Union was launched to draft amendments to the Treaty of Rome to extend the EU's jurisdiction to cover immigration, the environment and energy, as well as enhance the EU's legislative process and develop a common foreign and security policy. This initiative has similarly uncovered significant differences in the visions of the member states. Britain, once again, but supported to a lesser extent by Denmark and Portugal, leads the resistance to political union as it has been proposed, particularly where it specifies a future "federal" structure.[12] The transfer of sovereignty to a supranational authority which is implied by the concept of a federal structure is the main issue in the discussion over political union. Nevertheless, an agreement was reached among all 12 members' governments in Maastricht in December, 1991, to work towards political union (*New York Times* 12-10-91, p. A1).

The initiatives to extend European economic intervention further into social and political realms have thrown the divisions within the European Union into high relief. Giovannini (1989) identified the different historical experiences of the members as a partial explanation. For France, Germany, Italy and Spain, the disruptions of the mid-twentieth century brought on by Nazism, Fascism, and World War II, have meant that "the initiative for European unification is viewed....as a most welcome opportunity to overcome the political nightmares of fifty years ago" (Giovannini 1989, p. 364). For other members not sharing the same experience, such as Britain for instance, their enthusiasm for EC-92 is limited to the aspects of free-trade, while political integration and the implied subordination of national autonomy is viewed with great suspicion. On a more ideological plane, Gardner (1991b) suggests that Britain's dissent on such issues as the

Social Charter stem from a fundamental disagreement on the role of the European Union (p. 18). For the British, the goal of EC-92 is purely economic, to boost economic growth through a liberated and integrated market. For other members, most often lead by France, EC-92 should also entail a level playing field for European labor and industry alike, for which interventionist policies may be required. These are two different and conflicting perspectives. In addition, the fact that Britain often finds itself outside the mainstream of EU policy owes much to its belated entry and the traditional dominance of the Paris-Bonn axis in setting the European agenda.

The other major rift within the EU which is frequently exposed is between: (a) the richer, industrial and northern members; and (b) the poorer, rural and mostly-southern countries. This core-periphery dichotomy appears in a variety of issues, including agricultural and industrial policy, regional policy, the level of members' contributions to the EU's budget, and the Community's policy towards non-member countries, especially Eastern Europe.

Geographical Expansion of the European Union

The third identifiable component of the outer-wrapping is the future geographic extent of the European common market including expansion of the EU's membership and its relations with the European Free Trade Association (EFTA).[13] A queue has developed of states wishing to join the existing 12 members, and their number has increased with the advent of EC-92 and the disintegration of the former Soviet bloc. At the head of the queue are the EFTA members, followed by Turkey (Hufbauer 1990, p. 16), Malta (*Financial Times* 6-20-91c, p. 2) and the newly-capitalist nations of Eastern Europe, led by Hungary and Czechoslovakia. The issue of expansion was put on hold through the EC-92 program but with its completion discussions are being renewed apace.

In addition to the slew of applications for membership, the EU has recently completed negotiations with the seven members of EFTA on the creation of a joint European Economic Area (EEA, *Financial Times* 6-20-91b, p. 2, *New York Times* 10-23-91, p. A1 and Hufbauer 1990, p. 16). came into effect along with the 12 member single market on December 31, 1992, creating a single, free market of 19 separate nations and approximately 380 million people.

External Trade Relations

External trade is not directly addressed in EC-92. Indeed it is often referred to as the *missing element*:

> The most controversial aspect of the 1992 Plan from the point of view of non-Europeans is the omission of any discussion of the extra-European effects of the plan. (Harrison 1988, p. 14).

As the project began to be taken seriously by the outside world in 1988, a widespread fear developed that the EU was planning to create a free market surrounded by external trade barriers. This fear and the widely-used term "Fortress Europe" were fuelled by comments made in August, 1988 by the Commissioner for external relations, Willy de Clercq, that the EU was not obliged to extend the benefits of the single market to non-EU firms.[14] This position was quickly restated by the Commission to say that access to the enlarged EU market would not be *unilaterally* extended to third countries but could be secured with *reciprocity* on their part (Hufbauer 1990, p. 20). This and subsequent events have allayed fears of the "Fortress" but:

> ...attention (has) shifted to ramparts, moats and drawbridges, rather than the large fortress on the hill" (Hufbauer 1990, p. 21).

The European Union has been a leading, and often isolated, player in the most recent GATT negotiations. In the protracted Uruguay round--which was originally due to have been completed in December, 1990, but was finally resolved in late 1993--it has resisted the liberalization of the trade in farm products. Given the significant divisions over the Common Agricultural Policy among its own members, it is remarkable that it has continued to speak with a single voice in the GATT negotiations. Furthermore, it is somewhat ironic, given the Community's liberal attitude towards internal trade, that its record on external trade has received some severe criticism. The GATT's April, 1991, review of the Community's trade policies highlighted the European Commission's "penchant for pursuing individual industries' interests separately" (Dullforce 1991, p. 6) which is contrary to the GATT's fundamental principles of multilateral and cross-sectoral trade policy. Furthermore, the EU has been one of the most enthusiastic users of "anti-dumping" penalties (allowed under the GATT) to discriminate against specific products of particular countries (*Economist* 6-15-91a, p. 20; *Financial Times* 4-17-91, p. 6). Future GATT decisions on the validity of anti-dumping actions, therefore, may seriously constrain the Community's ability to protect key industries.

The European Union's trade relations with the U.S. remain particularly important. For the U.S., too, the EU is its single largest trade partner and, perhaps more importantly, it is a major importer of high-technology products.[15] The U.S., therefore, is particularly concerned about possible protectionist actions in these sectors as well as the traditional bugbear, agriculture. With respect to U.S. firms operating in Europe, the effects of EC-92 are being monitored very carefully. However, most U.S. transnational firms are well-established in Europe and, as Hufbauer notes: "Community officials have all but publicly said that their immediate target (on trade issues) is Japan, not the United States" (1990, p. 36).

Trade relations with Japan are markedly different and quite confrontational. The penetration of Japanese firms in the European market remains a major concern to the EU following, as it does, their successful forays in North America which has raised alarm over the potential effects of opening the single market to such competition. Clearly, the effects of Japanese firms' global success and the perception of their trade practices will have a significant impact upon the direction of EC-92, particularly as it provokes a vigorous internal debate between protectionists and free-traders.

The European Union's trading relations with countries of the Third World are, to a large extent, governed by long-standing trade agreements. The Generalized System of Preferences (GSP) and Lomé Convention (now in Round IV) owe much to several members post-colonial responsibilities. In addition, the Multifiber Agreement (MFA) governs the trade in many textile and apparel sectors. EC-92 is less likely to affect these agreements than will the Uruguay round of the GATT, but may yet have some impact on the Community's trade with the Third World. Koekkoek, et al. (1990) and Langhammer (1990) agree that the long-run trade creation[16] effects of EC-92 will be beneficial to Third World trading partners but Emmerij (1990) suggests that the disruption to existing trade patterns brought about by the enlarged European market will have negative repercussions in some cases. In addition, preferential trade agreements with individual members may be lost with EC-92 but as Davenport (1990) notes, "one developing country's preference is another's adverse tariff margin."

The direct effect of EC-92 on trade with third countries will result from the necessary elimination of Article 115 of the Treaty of Rome. As noted above, this allowed members to pursue individual commercial policies and restrict imports from members if their origins were in non-member countries. The single market, however, will undermine the enforcement of this Article with the net result being trade-liberalizing. In most of its external trade relations, the EU is employing the concept of *reciprocity* in deciding whether third-country firms will have equal access to the single market. Traditionally, this term has implied that firms from two countries are ensured equal 'new' access to the markets in each other's country when each's firms start from an equal base. Disputes may arise, however, when foreign firms start with a considerable European presence while EU firms have a negligible base in third countries. In this respect attention is again directed towards Japan in particular (Hufbauer 1990, p. 34). The EU, therefore, is applying a subjective and bilateral concept of *meaningful* reciprocity but which is, in fact, similar to the U.S. concept of "level playing fields" as espoused in the Omnibus Trade and Competitiveness Act of 1988.

This interpretation of the concept of reciprocity raises concern among the EU's trading partners in that it may be used as an instrument of trade protectionism. A good example of the problems that can arise is that of market access to the European banking sector. If the concept is strictly applied U.S. banks will be barred from the single market because European banks cannot be offered reciprocal access to the U.S. market. The U.S.'s Glass-Steagall and McFadden Acts respectively separate banking and commerce, and impose geographic restrictions on banks' operations. European banks operating in the U.S. will naturally be subject to the same restrictions and but will therefore be unable to operate on the continental scale that U.S. banks would enjoy in Europe (Hufbauer 1990, p. 35). In this case, however, the EU has redefined its test of reciprocity away from a "mirror image" test to one of "market access and competition opportunities comparable to those granted by the Community".[17] While the concept of reciprocity threatens to raise some disputes between the EU and its trading partners "it is important to note that the United States has also increasingly moved in the direction of establishing reciprocity as a guiding principle for determining who will gain (or lose) access to the U.S. market" (Harrison 1988, p. 26).

The Contemporary European Scene

The dissolution of the former Soviet, East-European bloc since 1989[18] has significantly altered the international environment midway through the EC-92 project. It is quite possible that with European leaders' attention diverted towards the unfolding events in the east, momentum for EC-92 may be diminished and the thornier issues of the single market program may be starved of attention. Alternatively, with the project well under way, it may be the outer-wrapping initiatives that are be adversely affected.

Perhaps the most fundamental impact of the post-Cold War era is the change it brings about in the North Atlantic political and economic relationship. For Hufbauer (1990), there is under way a "shifting center of gravity from shared security interests to shared economic interests" (p. 19) with a concomitant diversion of attention from London and NATO to Bonn and the EU. In addition, the removal of a political and military adversary in the east will most likely lead to a loosening of the EU's ties to the U.S., and moves towards establishing an independent foreign and security policy are already under way (Buchan 1991d, p. 16).

The revolutions in Eastern Europe since 1989 have brought with them new responsibilities. Prompted by Germany--itself undergoing significant changes with reunification--the EU is taking a leading role in welcoming the newly-capitalist states of eastern Europe to the western fold. Economic aid, trade and investment programs are under way at both the firm level and at the state level; for instance, the European Bank for Reconstruction and Development (BERD).[19] These developments, however, may lead to further tensions within the European Union, as the northern members' attention (in particular) is redirected towards the east, and away from the southern and peripheral members who have formerly been the recipients of northern capital.

The changing international environment also creates new political challenges for the European Union as its economic might brings concomitant responsibilities.[20] Increasingly, the EU is being viewed as a political and even military entity in international diplomacy. The 1991 Gulf War and the break-up of the former Yugoslavia have posed challenges to the EU and its members. These new responsibilities are already producing tensions that can be identified on two fronts. First, in the debate over the EU's role in security matters and its relationship to the U.S., France leads the call for an independent, pan-European security organization while Britain and Germany urge the continuation of the present North Atlantic alliance with a stronger European role through the previously titular Western European Union (WEU). Secondly, another tension finds Britain and France on the same side of the issue as the only two who are permanent members of the United Nations' Security Council. In this capacity, they are coming under pressure to subordinate their national interests to those of Europe as a whole, and to act as representatives of the EU. These two tensions are becoming more important and will undoubtedly affect the pace of European integration, although perhaps more so for the outer-wrapping such as political union than for the purely economic program of EC-92.

Notes

1 "Special message to the Congress on foreign trade policy," in Kennedy, J.F. 1962, pp. 68-77.

2 This was reported in three sources: briefly in Cecchini (1988) and in more detail in Emerson et al. (1988) and European Commission, Directorate-General for Economic and Financial Affairs (1988).

3 European Commission (1987), and Harrison (1988), p. 3.

4 These are described in detail in the European Commission's 1985 White Paper (European Commission 1985).

5 This is discussed in Hufbauer (1990), p. 8.

6 It has been estimated that in the short-term more than 550,000 jobs may be lost as a result of a reduction in both private and public sector employment. See Harrison (1988) p. 12.

7 Part of Margaret Thatcher's speech in Bruges, Belgium September 20, 1988. Reported in *New York Times* (9-22-88) p. A5.

8 For instance, France was recently compelled to withdraw its proposed support for Thomson, an electronics firm, after a warning from the EU Trade Commissioner. See, *Financial Times* (6-20-91a) p. 1 and Financial Times (6-25-91) p. 6.

9 European auto-makers have formed a lobby group, ACEA, to press their case with the EC. See *Financial Times* (6-27-91b) p. 1.

10 For instance, Fujistu's takeover of both ICL, the British computer-maker, and Nokia Data of Finland. See Buchan et al. (1991). Also, a more detailed analysis of Japanese direct investment in the EC is found in Heitger and Stehn (1990).

11 Each of the eleven members who have joined the ERM (Greece being the exception) have pegged their currencies to the European Currency Units (ECU)-- the EU's incipient currency which is a specific composition of EU member's national currencies. The ERM allows fluctuations of only 2.25% around its peg, 6%, in the case of Britain, Portugal and Spain (Wolf 1992).

12 This term first entered an official Community document with the description of the EU as a "union with a federal goal" in a draft treaty proposed by Luxembourg at the June leaders' summit. See, Buchan (1991b) p. 1. The issue of sovereignty is thought to be key in the rejection of the Maastricht accord by the Danish electorate on June 2, 1992. See *New York Times* (6-4-92) p. A14.

13 Following several recent defections to the EU, the seven remaining members of EFTA are Austria, Finland, Iceland, Liechtenstein, Norway, Sweden and Switzerland.

14 Reported by Calingaert (1988a, p. 120) from *1992: The Impact on the Outside World*, a speech by EU Commissioner, Willy de Clercq at the Europaeisches Forum, Asprach, August 29, 1988.

15 Of U.S. exports to the EU, 46 percent are classified as high-technology, against only 29 percent for Japan (Hufbauer 1990, p. 21).

16 *Trade creation* as a result of the EC-92 program is considered below in the discussion of customs union theory.

17 The European Commission, quoted by Dullforce (1989) p. 6.

18 The Council for Mutual Economic Assistance (Comecon), the Soviet bloc's common market, was finally disbanded in April, 1991. See *Financial Times* (6-29-91) p. 3.

19 The Banque Européen de Reconstruction et Developpement was established in 1991 with $12.2 billion capital. See *Financial Times* (4-16-91) p. 1; *Science et Vie Economie* 72 (May, 1991) p. 14; *Financial Times* (6-26-91) p. 18.

20 The rise of Europe as an independent and significant player in international affairs was predicted by Paul Kennedy (1987) in his concluding chapter written *prior* the end of the Cold War.

Bibliography

Allen, David N. and David J. Hayward. 1990. The role of new venture formation/entrepreneurship in regional economic development: A review. *Economic Development Quarterly* 4(1):55-63.

Archer, Stephen H. and Steven M. Maser. 1989. State export promotion for economic development. *Economic Development Quarterly* 3(3):235-242.

Balassa, Bela. 1975. Trade creation and diversion in the European Common Market: An appraisal of the evidence. In *European Economic Integration* ed. Bela Balassa, 3-40. Amsterdam, The Netherlands: North-Holland.

Baldwin, Richard. 1989. The growth effects of 1992. *Economic Policy* (October) 247.

Barff, Richard A. and Prentice L. Knight, III. 1988. Dynamic shift-share analysis. *Growth and Change*, 19(2):1-10.

Bergsten, C. Fred, Thomas Horst, and Theodore H. Moran. 1978. *American multinationals and American interests*. Washington, DC: The Brookings Institution.

Brown, H. J. 1969. Shift-share projections of regional growth: Empirical test. *Journal of Regional Science* 9:1-18.

Buchan, David. 1991a. Twelve slip into unflagging pace in frontiers marathon. *Financial Times*, 17 June, 4.

_____ 1991b. Britain rejects EC treaty 'with a federal goal'. *Financial Times*, 18 June, 1.

_____ 1991c. European dream begins to take real shape. *Financial Times*, 26 June, 2.

_____ 1991d. Horse-trading before high noon. *Financial Times*, 28 June, 16.

Buchan, David, Andrew Hill, and Guy de Jonquières. 1991. The battle within Fortress Europe. *Financial Times*, 17 June, 12.

Buiges, P., F. Ilkovitz, and J-F. Lebrun. 1990. The impact of the internal market by industrial sector: The challenge for the member states. *European Economy--Social Europe*, Special Edition.

Business Week. 4-10-78. The reluctant exporter. 54-66.

Calingaert, Michael. 1988a. *The 1992 challenge from Europe*. Washington, DC: National Planning Association.

_____ 1988b. A bigger market for U.S. Exports. *Export Today*, 4(6):18-20.

Cecchini, Paolo. 1988, *The European challenge, 1992*. Aldershot, England: Gower.

Cooney, Stephen. 1989. *EC-92 and U.S. industry*. Washington, DC: National Association of Manufacturers.

199

Coughlin, Cletus C. and Phillip A. Cartwright. 1987a. An examination of state foreign export promotion and manufacturing exports. *Journal of Regional Science* 27(3):439-449.

_____ 1987b. An examination of state foreign exports and manufacturing employment. *Economic Development Quarterly* 1(3):257-267.

Coughlin, Cletus C. and Oliver Fabel. 1988. State factor endowments and exports: An alternative to cross-industry studies. *The Review of Economics and Statistics* 70:696-701.

Davenport, Michael S. 1990. The external policy of the Community and its effects upon the manufactured exports of the developing countries. *Journal of Common Market Studies* 29(2):181-200.

Dicken, Peter. 1992. Europe 1992 and Strategic Change in the International Automobile Industry. *Environment and Planning A* 24:11-31.

Dudley, James W. 1989. *1992--strategies for a single market*. London: Kogan Page.

Dullforce, William. 1989. Brussels stands firm on Banking access. *Financial Times*, 21 September, 6.

_____ 1991. Poor marks for EC external trade practices. *Financial Times*, 17 April, 6.

Dutton, John C. and Edward W. Erickson. 1989. The North Carolina World Trade Index. *The North Carolina World Trade Association 1989 directory*. Raleigh, NC: The North Carolina World Trade Association.

Economist. 6-15-91a. Repeal the protectionist's charter. 20.

_____ 6-15-91b. Free trade's green hurdle. 61-62.

_____ 6-15-91c. The last frontier. 70.

Economists Advisory Group, Ltd. 1987. *The likely impact of deregulation on industrial structures and competition in the Community*. Luxembourg: Office for Official Publications of the European Communities.

Emerson, Michael, Michel Aujean, Michel Catinat, Phillipe Goybet, and Alexis Jacquemin. 1988. *The economics of 1992*. New York, NY: Oxford University Press.

Emmerij, Louis J. 1990. Europe 1992 and the developing countries: Conclusions. *Journal of Common Market Studies*, 29(2):243-253.

Erickson, Rodney A. 1989. Export performance and state industrial growth. *Economic Geography* 65:280-292.

_____ 1992. Trade, economic growth, and state export promotion programs. In *Economic development strategies for state and local governments*. ed. McGowan, R. P. and E. J. Ottensmeyer. Chicago, IL: Nelson-Hall.

Erickson, Rodney A. and Susan W. Friedman. 1990. Enterprise zones I: Investment and job creation of state government programs in the United States. *Environment and Planning A* 8(3):251-267.

Erickson, Rodney A. and David J. Hayward. 1991. The international flows of industrial exports from U.S. regions. *Annals of the Association of American Geographers* 81(3):371-390.

_____ 1992. Interstate differences in relative export performance: A test of the factor endowments theory. *Geographical Analysis* 24 (forthcoming).

Ettlinger, Nancy. 1994. The localization of development in comparative perspective. *Economic Geography* 70(2): 144-166.

European Commission. 1985. *Completing the internal market.* Luxembourg: Office for Official Publications of the European Communities.

_____ 1987. *Europe without frontiers.* Luxembourg: Office of Official Publications of the European Communities.

_____ 1988. *Research on the cost of non-Europe.* Luxembourg: Office for Official Publications of the European Communities.

_____ Directorate-General for Economic and Financial Affairs. 1988. The economics of 1992. *European Economy* 35.

_____ Directorate-General for External Relations and Directorate-General for Economic and Financial Affairs. 1989. International trade of the European Community. *European Economy* 39.

Eurostat. 1992. *Europe in Figures* Third Edition. Luxembourg: Office for Official Publications of the European Communities.

Farrell, Michael G. and Anthony Radspieler. 1989. Census Bureau state-by-state foreign trade data: Historical perspectives. Paper presented to the *National Governor's Association, Committee on International Trade and Foreign Relations.* 25 May.

Fieleke, Norman S. 1986. New England manufacturing and international trade. *New England Economic Review,* Federal Reserve Bank of New England (September/October):22-28.

Financial Times. 4-16-91. Mitterand says EBRD is step to united Europe. 1.

_____ 4-17-91. Anti-dumping policy under scrutiny. 6.

_____ 6-20-91a. France to suspend Thomsen support. 1.

_____ 6-20-91b. EFTA and EC progress on cash and cod. 2.

_____ 6-20-91c. Malta seeks to join Community. 2.

_____ 6-25-91. Downturn strikes european textiles. 6.

_____ 6-26-91. EBRD lends $50m to Poland. 18.

_____ 6-27-91a. EC ministers close deal on frontiers. 1.

_____ 6-27-91b. Carmakers in EC aid plea. 1.

_____ 6-27-91c. Brussels tables draft on HDTV standard. 2.

_____ 6-29-91. Comecon put out of misery after 42 years. 3.

_____ 7-19-91a. A multi-purpose deal 'for Europe'. 2.

Fothergill, Stephen and Graham Gudgin. 1979. In defence of shift-share. *Urban Studies* 16:309-319.

_____ 1982. *Unequal growth, urban and regional employment change in the UK.* London: Heinemann Educational Books.

Gardner, David. 1991a. Southern discomfort. *Financial Times,* 18 June, 16.

_____ 1991b. The EC's social divide. *Financial Times,* 27 June, 18.

Gardner, David and Tomkins, Richard. 1991. Patchwork could become a network. *Financial Times,* 24 June, 15.

Gillespie, Robert W. 1982. The Midwest and the international economy. In *The Midwest economy: Issues and policy,* ed. R. W. Resek and R. F. Kosubud. Urbana, IL: University of Illinois.

Ginsberg, Roy H. 1989. *The political and economic implications of the European Community's 1992 plan for United States--European Community relations.* Testimony before the Committee on Science, Space and Technology, U.S. House of Representatives, 101st. Congress, 5-16-89. Washington, DC: U.S. Government Printing Office.

Giovannini, Alberto. 1989. Comments and discussion: Symposium on Europe 1992. *Brookings Papers on Economic Activity* 2:363-368.

Goldstein, Harvey A. and Michael I. Luger. 1990. Science/technology parks and regional development theory. *Economic Development Quarterly* 4(1):64-78.

Griffin, Adrian H. 1989. *California exports: their contribution to the economy.* Sacramento, CA: California Department of Commerce.

Haaland, Jan I. and Norman, Victor D. 1992. Global production effects of European integration. In Winters, L. Alan. (ed.) *Trade Flows and Trade Policy After '1992'.* Cambridge: Cambridge University Press.

Hanink, Dean M. 1987. A comparative analysis of the competitive geographical trade performances of the USA, FRG, and Japan: the markets and marketers hypothesis. *Geographical Analysis* 63(4):293-305.

Harrison, Glennon J. 1988. *The European Community's 1992 plan: An overview of the proposed 'single market'.* Washington, DC: The Congressional Research Service.

Hayward, David J. 1992. *The Impacts of the European Community 1992 on U.S. State Economies.* Unpublished PhD thesis, The Pennsylvania State University, University Park, PA.

_____ and Erickson, Rodney A. (forthcomoing). The Potential Impacts of NAFTA on U.S. State Industrial Economies.

Heitger, Bernhard and Jürgen Stehn. 1990. Japanese direct investments in the EC--response to the internal market 1993? *Journal of Common Market Studies,* 29(2):1-15.

Hellman, D. A. 1976. Shift-share models as predictive tools. *Growth and Change* 7:3-8.

Hirsch, Seev. 1971. *The export performance of six manufacturing industries.* New York, NY: Praeger.

Hoffman, Stanley. 1989. The European Community and 1992. *Foreign Affairs* 68:27-47.

Hufbauer, Gary C. 1990. An overview. In *Europe 1992: An American perspective,* ed. Gary C. Hufbauer, 1-50. Washington, DC: The Brookings Institution.

Jacquemin, Alexis, and André Sapir. 1988. European integration or world integration ? *Weltwirtschaftliches Archiv* 124:127-139.

Kennedy, John F. 1962. *Public papers of the presidents: John F. Kennedy, 1962.* Washington, DC: U.S. Government Printing Office.

Kennedy, Paul M. 1987. *The rise and fall of the great powers.* New York, NY: Random House.

Koekkoek, Ad, Arie Kuyvenhoven, and Willem Molle. 1990. Europe 1992 and the developing countries: An overview. *Journal of Common Market Studies* 29(2):111-131.

Krauss, Melvyn. 1972. Recent developments in customs union theory: An interpretative survey. *Journal of Economic Literature* 10:413-436.

Kreinen, Mordechai E. 1972. Effects of the EEC on imports of manufactures. *Economic Journal* 82:897-920.

Krugman, Paul. 1979. Increasing returns, monopolistic competition, and international trade. In *International trade: Selected readings*, ed. Jagdish N. Bagwati, 88-99. Cambridge, MA: MIT Press.

_____ 1980. Scale economies, product differentiation, and the pattern of trade. *American Economic Review* 70(5):950--959.

Kudrle, Robert T and Cynthia M Kite. 1989. The Evaluation of State Programs for International Business Development. *Economic Development Quarterly* 3(4):288-300.

Langhammer, Rolf J. 1990. Fuelling a new engine of growth or separating Europe from non-Europe? *Journal of Common Market Studies* 29(2):133-155.

Linder, Staffan Burenstram. 1961. *An essay on trade and transformation*. New York, NY: John Wiley.

Ludlow, Peter (ed). 1991. *The Annual Review of European Community Affairs 1990*. Brussels: Center for European Policy Studies.

Markusen, Ann R., Helzi Noponen and Karl Driesen. 1991. International trade, productivity and regional job growth: A shift-share interpretation. *International Regional Science Review* 14(1):15-39.

Mayes, David G., 1978. The effects of economic integration on trade. *Journal of Common Market Studies* 17(1): 1-25.

McConnell, James E. 1979. The export decision: An empirical study of firm behavior. *Economic Geography* 55(3):171-183.

_____ 1987. Employment gains from U.S. exports: Winning and losing sectors and states in 1983 and 1990. Paper presented at the annual meetings of the Association of American Geographers, Portland, OR, April 22-26, 1987.

Milner, Christopher and Allen, David. 1992 The external implications of 1992. In Swann, Dennis. (ed.) *The Single European Market and Beyond*. London: Routledge.

Namiki, Nobuaki. 1988. Export strategy for small business. *Journal of Small Business Management* 26(2):32-37.

Nerb, Gernot. 1988. The completion of the internal market: A survey of european industry's perception of the likely effects. *Volume 3, Research on the cost of non-Europe*. Luxembourg: Office for Official Publications of the European Communities.

Nevin, Edward. 1990. *The Economics of Europe*. New York: St. Martin's Press.

New York Times. 9-22-88. Taking a stand for Europe, Thatcher says. A5.

_____ 10-23-88. The growing fear of fortress Europe. 1.

_____ 1-30-91. Canada is expected to join U.S.-Mexico trade talks. D1.

_____ 8-12-91. At the end of a twisted tail, piggy bank for a favored few. A1.

_____ 10-23-91. Europeans in accord to create vastly expanded trading bloc. A1.

_____ 12-10-91. Europeans accept a single currency and bank by 1999. A1.

_____ 6-4-92. Denmark's signal. A14.

Norcliffe, Glen B. 1977. *Inferential statistics for geographers*. London: Hutchinson and Company.

North, Douglass C. 1955. Location theory and regional economic growth. *Journal of Political Economy* 63(3):243-258.

_____ 1956. A reply. *Journal of Political Economy* 64(2):165-168.

Ó'Cléireacáin, Séamus. 1990. Europe 1992 and gaps in the EC's Common Commercial Policy. *Journal of Common Market Studies* 28(3):201-217.

Peck, Merton J. 1989. Industrial organization and the gains from Europe 1992. *Brookings papers on Economic Activity* 2:277-299.

Radspieler, Anthony and George Mehl. 1991. *The Myth of State Trade Balances.* Unpublished manuscript, U.S. Department of Commerce.

Richardson, Harry W. 1978a. *Regional and urban economics.* Harmondsworth, England: Penguin.

_____ 1978b. The state of regional economics: A survey article. *International Regional Science Review* 3(1):1-48.

Risha, Michael. 1991. A Comparison of the "Origin of Movement" Series and the "Exports from Manufacturing Establishments" Series. Unpublished report, U.S Bureau of the Census, Foreign Trade Division.

Sallnow, John. 1991. The uniting states of Europe. *Geographical Magazine* (February):40-43.

SAS Institute Inc. 1988. *SAS/STAT user's guide, release 6.03 edition.* SAS Institute, Cary, NC.

Stevens, Benjamin H. and Craig L. Moore. 1980. A critical review of the literature on shift-share as a forecasting technique. *Journal of Regional Science* 20(4):419-437.

Stilwell, F. J. B. 1970. Further thoughts on the shift and share approach. *Regional Studies* 4:451-458.

Science et Vie Economie. 1991. BERD: Des golden boys et des grands experts, 72 (May). 14.

Tiebout, Charles M. 1956. Exports and regional economic growth. *Journal of Political Economy* 64(2):160-164.

_____ 1956. Rejoinder. *Journal of Political Economy* 64(2):169.

Truman, Edwin M. 1975. The effects of European economic integration on the production and trade of manufactured products. In *European Economic Integration,* ed. Bela Balassa, 3-40. Amsterdam, The Netherlands: North-Holland.

United States Bureau of the Census. 1991. *Exports from manufacturing establishments: 1987.* Washington, DC: U.S. Government Printing Office.

United States Bureau of Economic Analysis. 1989, 1991. *Survey of current business,* July. Washington, DC: U.S. Government Printing Office.

_____ Bureau of Economic Analysis. 1990. *Statistical abstract of the United States: 1990.* Washington, DC: U.S. Government Printing Office.

United States Congress, Congressional Budget Office. 1990. *How the economic transformations in Europe will affect the United States.* Washington, DC: U.S. Government Printing Office.

_____ Congress, House Committee on Foreign Affairs. 1989. *European Community: Issues raised by 1992 integration.* Washington, DC: U.S. Government Printing Office.

United States International Trade Administration. 1990. U.S. small and medium-size firms should benefit from EC 1992 program. *Europe Now* (Summer). Washington, DC: U.S. Government Printing Office.

United States Representative to the European Communities. 1990. *Letter from Brussels* 3(5), 31 December.

United States Trade Representative. 1991. *1991 national trade estimate on foreign trade barriers*. Washington, DC: U.S. Government Printing Office.

Verdoorn, P. J. and C. A. Van Bochove. 1972. Measuring integration effects: A survey. *European Economic Review* 3:337-349.

Viner, J. 1950. The customs union issue. New York, NY: Carnegie Endowment for International Peace.

Webster, Elaine, Edward J. Mathis, and Charles E. Zech. 1990. The case for state-level export promotion assistance: A comparison of foreign and domestic export employment multipliers. *Economic Development Quarterly* 4(3):203-210.

Wise, Mark and Gibb, Richard. 1993. *Single market to social Europe: The European Community in the 1990s*. Harlow: Longman.

Wolf, Martin. 1992. No need to block the path to convergence. *Financial Times*, 4 June, 5.

Woodward, Douglas P. 1990. The European Export Stimulus and Regional Development in the United States. Paper presented at the University of Pennsylvania and Rutgers University Colloquium, *The European Regional Economic Integration of 1992*. Philadelphia, PA, 16 November.

Yannopoulos, G. N. 1988. *Customs unions and trade conflicts*. London: Routledge.

Zimmerman, Rae. 1975. A Variant of the Shift and Share Projection Formulation. *Journal of Regional Science* 15(1):29-38.

Index

About the Book and Author

As economic integration among nations emerges as the dominant mechanism affecting trade patterns, the global economy is rapidly evolving into a patchwork of regional blocs. International trade is no longer the exclusive domain of sovereign states; its sources are increasingly found at the supernational level, while its impacts are more and more felt in subnational regions. In addition, the increase in freer economic policies all over the globe has so undermined national authority that regional economies are inevitably opened up to international trade.

In this volume, David Hayward considers the issue of regional exposure to external economic events, exploring the role of trade in the performance of American states and regions. Using a shift-share model to evaluate the contribution of exports and imports in the growth of U.S. manufacturing industries, Hayward focuses specifically on the case of trade with the European Community, analyzing the potential impacts of its deepening integration on trade with individual states. He concludes by assessing the distinct variations in states' trade experiences with the EC.

David J. Hayward is lecturer in geography at the University of Auckland.